The Happiest Man in the World

Alec Wilkinson

THE HAPPIEST MAN

IN THE WORLD

An Account of the Life

of Poppa Neutrino

 RANDOM HOUSE | NEW YORK

Published in the United States by Random House,
an imprint of The Random House Publishing Group,
a division of Random House, Inc., New York.

RANDOM HOUSE and colophon are registered
trademarks of Random House, Inc.

Portions of this book originally appeared in
The New Yorker in slightly different form.

ISBN 978-1-4000-6543-1

LIBRARY OF CONGRESS CATALOGING-IN-PUBLICATION DATA
Wilkinson, Alec
    The happiest man in the world: an account of the life of Poppa Neutrino /
Alec Wilkinson.
        p. cm.
    ISBN 978-1-4000-6543-1
        1. Neutrino, Poppa, 1933–   2. Eccentrics and eccentricities–
United States–Biography.   3. Adventure and adventurers–
United States–Biography.   I. Title.   II. Title: Account
of the life of Poppa Neutrino.
    CT9991.N48W54 2007
    910′.92–dc22   2006048643

Printed in the United States of America on acid-free paper

www.atrandom.com

9 8 7 6 5 4 3 2 1

FIRST EDITION

Book design by Barbara M. Bachman

For my wife and son,
and our friend
Alexandra Truitt

The port we sail from is far astern and, though far out of sight of
land, for ages and ages we continue to sail with sealed orders and
our last destination remains a secret to ourselves and our officers.
And yet our final haven was predestined ere we stepped from the
stocks of creation. Let us not give ear to the superstitious gun-deck
gossip about whither we may be gliding for, as yet, not a soul on
board of us knows—not even the commodore himself—assuredly not
the chaplain—even our professors' scientific surmisings are in vain.
On that point, the smallest cabin boy is as wise as the captain.

—HERMAN MELVILLE, *WHITE JACKET*

They went to sea in a sieve, they did.
In a sieve they went to sea:
In spite of all their friends could say,
On a winter's morn, on a stormy day,
In a sieve they went to sea!
And when the sieve turned round and round,
And everyone cried, "You'll all be drowned!"
They called aloud, "Our sieve ain't big,
But we don't care a button! we don't care a fig!
In a sieve we'll go to sea."

—EDWARD LEAR, "THE JUMBLIES"

PART ONE

David pearlman was sitting under a pine tree in Flagstaff, Arizona, when he thought of the play, in July of 2004. He was living, with his dog, in a white minivan that was nine years old. The van had been a gift, a few months earlier, from a woman and her husband who'd befriended him in Key West, Florida. They had also given him the dog. Shortly before he met them, Pearlman had undergone a reversal of fortune—a favorable arrangement he believed he had struck had dissolved instead, leaving him destitute. He was seventy-one years old.

Pearlman was fifty when he was bit on the hand by a dog, in Mexico. For two years he was so sick that he assumed he would die. When he recovered, he felt so different from who he had been that he thought he should have a new name. He began calling himself by the first one that came to him: Poppa Neutrino. A neutrino is an itinerant particle so small that it can hardly be detected. Pearlman incorrectly believed that its existence was theoretical. The name appealed to him, because, being suppositional, the particle represented the elements of the hidden life that exert their influence discreetly. Also, because of the particle's capacity for unremitting movement. Mr. Neutrino is nomadic. I once unfolded a map of the country and asked him to trace the routes he had traveled, and before he had completed the first twenty years of his life the pen had worn through the paper.

The van's backseats Neutrino replaced with a platform on

which he laid three squares of foam for a bed. All the windows except the front ones he covered with duct tape, and behind the driver's and passenger's seats he strung a curtain, so that anyone who looked in the van while he slept would think that it was empty. At the end of June, he and his dog, a female Boston terrier, left Key West for California. Attached to the van was a trailer on which sat a crudely made raft that Neutrino had built from plywood. Some of the wood he had bought, and some he had scavenged from construction sites. The raft was twelve feet long and four feet wide, and it had a small cabin. People who saw it did not usually conclude that it was a raft. It looked like a tree house, or possibly a shed for poultry. It did not look like anything that would float.

On the passenger's side of the van, in letters about a foot high made with rubbery, black tape, Neutrino had written KEY WEST TO CUBA. He planned to sail to Cuba from California, through the Panama Canal. Crossing the country, though, he had thought that he might prefer sailing west, across the Pacific by himself, something that had been accomplished on a raft only once, by William Willis, in 1964, when Willis was seventy years old. In 1947, Thor Heyerdahl, the first modern man to sail some ways across the Pacific on a raft, sailed, with five companions, aboard the raft *Kon-Tiki*, from Peru to Polynesia. Neutrino regarded Willis and Heyerdahl as heroes.

Neutrino drove to Los Angeles and left the raft at a friend's house. His wife, Betsy Terrell, who had for several months been visiting her family in Maine, called his cell phone and said that she wanted to drive out west and see him before he left. They met in Phoenix then retrieved the raft, then drove to the mountains outside Flagstaff to escape the desert heat. Neutrino now felt that if he could make it across the Pacific he could continue around the world and return to Key West. No one has ever sailed around the world on a raft.

The play came to Neutrino intact and all at once, as a species of epiphany. He had begun by thinking what would happen if all the players but the quarterback ran to the same part of the field, and the ball was lobbed to them. Would the barrier of players enclosing the receiver be sufficiently thick that none of the defenders could prevent his catching the ball? And would their approach to the goal line be slow but inexorable? Over the years Neutrino had occasionally amused himself by trying to invent a football play that couldn't be stopped. None of the ones he had concocted, however, had held up when he looked at them closely. When the play occurred to him, he saw exactly how it would unfold, and no means by which it could be prevented.

On the back of an envelope, Neutrino wrote the names of the teams he wanted to have use the play, then he went to the library in Flagstaff and looked up their phone numbers. The woman who answered the phone at Notre Dame said that the coach would call him, but he didn't. Neutrino then called the Arizona Cardinals of the NFL, the University of Illinois, Washington State University, Boston College, the University of Kentucky, Columbia University, and California State University, Fresno. At one of the colleges he reached an assistant coach. He said that his name was Poppa Neutrino and that he had a play that would take the team to the Rose Bowl. He said, "Please don't hang up on me," and the man hung up.

Eventually, Neutrino called the University of Arizona, in Tucson. The year before, their team, the Wildcats, had won two games and lost nine. All eleven coaches had been fired. A receptionist told Neutrino that someone would call him back. The next afternoon someone did—Mike Canales, the new quarterback coach. The season before, Canales had been a coach on the staff of the New York Jets. Neutrino explained the play to Canales, and Canales invited him to meet the next morning at the student center. For fear that Canales might withdraw the invitation, Neutrino did not tell him he was calling from Flagstaff, 250 miles away.

Neutrino drove through the night to reach Tucson. He walked around the campus until it was time to meet Canales. After they had talked for a while and Neutrino had drawn the play for Canales on a napkin, Canales asked Neutrino if he was free to attend the University of Arizona's training camp, in August. In terms of innovation, Canales said, the play struck him as being equal to the forward pass.

Neutrino drove back to Flagstaff. He told Terrell that he was going into football, and she said, "I'm sure you'll do well at it." In a few days, she returned to Maine to study for a master's degree in education.

Neutrino felt that Tucson in August would be too hot for the dog to live in the car. To raise money for a hotel room, he decided to sing for change on the street, in Los Angeles.

Chapter 2

BEFORE SAYING MORE about the play and the raft and what became of them, I feel I should describe Neutrino and his past, and some of the influences that have worked their effects on his character and thinking. I feel I should also say that despite my hopes and plans I have no confidence that I can accomplish this succinctly. My own affection for detail is not the only obstacle. Neutrino's past is lavish and prodigal, and it does not easily compress. When I close my eyes and think of him, I don't see his face so much as entertain a torrent of impressions— his essence, that is, broken up into a series of planes, as in a cubist painting.

Most of us go forward presuming that the future will resemble the present. We have an address. We follow a profession or a trade. On nearly all the nights of our lives, we go to bed knowing what we will do the following day, absent the intercession of good or bad luck. None of these observations typifies Neutrino. He is profoundly responsive to impulse. He does not always appear to have a reason for what he does, and sometimes he goes about things so awkwardly, even ineptly, that he brings on himself and the people around him difficulties that might not otherwise have arisen, but he has ardently imagined who he might be, and he has fearlessly embodied what he imagined. His past is one long poem to the random life. I wouldn't have wished to enact it myself, nor would I care to have taken part, but I respect the achievement.

The novelist William Maxwell said, "I can never get enough of other people's lives." Referring in *The Outermost Dream* to the pleasure he took in published diaries and letters and memoirs, he wrote, "They tell what happened—what people said and did and wore and ate and hoped for and were afraid of, and in detail after often unimaginable detail they refresh our idea of existence and hold oblivion at arm's length. Looked at broadly, what happened always has meaning, pattern, form, and authenticity. One can classify, analyze, arrange in the order of importance, and judge any or all of these things, or one can simply stand back and view the whole with wonder."

Astonishment is what I sometimes feel when I view the shape

of Neutrino's life. He is an old man, and his past has included a great deal of hardship and suffering, much of it his own fault. He chose badly so often that at times I want to rebuke him, even though it would serve no purpose. The past is not recoverable, and it cannot be corrected, and I'm not sure he would change much of it anyway; by his own lights, it has all been logical, albeit not orderly. On the other hand, no setback cast him so far down that he failed to recover. In even the most unfavorable circumstances, he willed himself to prevail. He showed unstinting courage. In the minds of some people, his largest accomplishments place him among the notable, if exotic, figures of the twentieth century, at least I have read stories in newspapers and seen television shows that describe them that way. His failures, his misadventures, his lapses of judgment, his careering assaults against the order of things leave one wishing to avert one's eyes from the impact and the wreckage. Picaresque feebly describes his exploits. For companions in literature I think of Tom Jones, Don Quixote, and a few of the figures who wander the desert in the Old Testament. I am aware that some readers will feel superior to him, or look down occasionally on how he has behaved; surely that is easy to do, but I do not believe that someone is a proper subject, or a laudable figure, only if he has made a lot of money or been a politician, an actor, a freakish public figure, or a criminal. The eccentrics, the odds beaters, the benign connivers, the showmen, the pilgrims, and the raffish self-glorifiers also have their place in the pageant. Nor is it along the periphery. I am reminded of Joseph Mitchell's responding, in 1943, to his subjects being described as the little people. "I regard this phrase as patronizing and repulsive," Mitchell wrote in a preface to *McSorley's Wonderful Saloon*. "There are no little people in this book. They are as big as you are, whoever you are."

Characters who put us in mind of ourselves, or suggest the selves we would like to be, especially if they are handsome and winning and mildly heroic or at least attractively forbearing, and especially if they are amusing and in love and consistent in their behaviors to the point of being undeviating, such characters are usually welcomed and taken to heart. None of the feelings they provoke is complicated, they are lightly and easily borne, and I wish that I had such a figure here, it would make matters so much simpler—the kindly old man with a modest past and a few pearls to share—but Neutrino is not a stock figure, nor is he likely to remind many readers comfortably of themselves, let alone any sentimental or ideal version. Neutrino is an unvarnished apparition from the psyche. The raucous, rambunctious, disorderly, and exuberant interior life raised up and given feet. He flamboyantly represents a version of the Other, and such people, while often having substantial glamour (the misanthropic cowboys Clint Eastwood has played, various poets and artists—Billie Holiday, Bob Dylan, John Coltrane, or Jackson Pollock, for example), such individuals even in their most favorable forms often carry for us an element of unease, of being necessarily regarded as sufficiently different from ourselves that we feel protected against the temptation they present—the resolve, that is, to live passionately and without restraint. From its least sympathetic forms—the bums, the vagrants, the sordid night figures—many of us all but recoil. Neutrino cultivates, exemplifies, and brandishes parts of our inner beings that most of us work assiduously to stifle in the interest of having orderly social lives, not to mention the regard and approval of our peers. Few of us embrace the role of the other, who always risks being shunned, but Neutrino has, and quite avidly. He has never made even the most perfunctory effort to stay between the lines. Such an intention would strike him as

pointless. His openness, his novelty of character, his lack of concern for convention are attributes he prides himself on and has
suffered to protect.

In an introduction to *The Intimate Journals of Charles
Baudelaire*, the novelist Christopher Isherwood writes—and the
italics are his—

> What makes a man a hero, i.e. an individual; or conversely,
> what makes him a churl, i.e. a mere unit in human society
> without any real individual significance of his own?
>
> The term "individual" has two senses. . . . In the realm
> of nature, "individual" means *to be something that others
> are not, to have uniqueness:* in the realm of spirit, it means
> *to become what one wills, to have a self-determined history.*

I wouldn't suggest that anyone regard Neutrino as a model.
It wouldn't be sensible. I don't even myself regard him entirely
as one. Any life of extravagant dimensions always includes peril
and turmoil, and people who emphatically embrace such an existence are generally a trial at close hand. G. K. Chesterton wrote
of St. Francis of Assisi that he "did in a definite sense make the
very act of living an art, though it was an unpremeditated art.
Many of his acts seem grotesque and puzzling to a rationalistic
taste. But they were always acts and not explanations; and they
always meant what he meant them to mean." Neutrino is by no
one's reckoning a saint, but by Isherwood's definition he is at
least an individual. He is "something that others are not," and
the course of his life has been self-determined. He would agree
with Chekhov, who wrote in a letter, "My holy of holies is the
human body, health, intelligence, talent, inspiration, love and absolute freedom."

The bulk of us settle down sooner or later. The past figures more in our thinking. We have fewer adventures. This hasn't happened to Neutrino. Nowhere in him have I observed the fatigue that overtakes so many of us as we age. The sheer force of life running through him is so pronounced that sometimes being with him is thrilling. I do not feel inclined to judge him, any more than I would care for other people to judge me. Nevertheless, after trying more than once, he has sustained a long and loving marriage, and not everyone has. Some of his children have prospered, and some have not, roughly in accord with the natural order. That an old man concocts a novel football play while preparing to cross an ocean on a homemade raft are circumstances I find cheering, inspiring even. ("Innocently to amuse the imagination in this dream of life is wisdom," the novelist Oliver Goldsmith wrote, in the eighteenth century.) My own ambitions, however simple or narrow, I hope will be as undiminished, if I ever arrive at his age. Anyway, I have been broadened by knowing him. What wisdom he possesses he has won from the flames.

In the roomy account of Neutrino's past that follows, laced with colorful characters, parallel narratives, and startling turns of fortune (you be the judge), Neutrino was necessarily the principal source. Whenever he raised someone's name, I tried to find that person. Since Neutrino is elderly, many of the people he mentioned are dead. Sometimes I would find people who were surprised to hear that Neutrino was still alive. These tended to be people who knew him thirty and forty years ago and who regarded him as someone whose optimism, passion, immoderation, and adherence to severe philosophical practices could only conclude before long in his extinction. In other words, they dismissed him as a nut bound shortly for glory. Sometimes they sounded a little disappointed that he had survived. While they regarded themselves as adventurous people, they had lived far more cautiously than he had, and his demise would have affirmed their decisions. Knowing that this reckless and joy-obsessed figure still thrived seemed to make them wonder whether they had lived as fully as they might have. Furthermore, whenever I found someone, what struck me was that his or her recollection was always more extravagant than Neutrino's. Most of us grow larger in our own imaginations as we age. Neutrino had become enlarged in the minds of other people but had remained the same size in his own. I regarded this as a sign of stability and character, of psychic well-being, even while I also regarded his judgment as frequently questionable and occasionally simply unsound. Nonetheless, in all cases of conflicting accounts, I took the version that was less dramatic—that is to say, his. There is nothing in Neutrino of the fabulist or the self-inflater; episodes of zealous self-deception (to which all of us are occasionally subject) I view as being different from mythomania.

To begin with then, Neutrino is about five foot nine, with broad, sloping shoulders. His forearms and hands are so thick that they look like tools. He has a square face, widely set eyes, and a flawless nose. From each of its wings a curved line descends to enclose his lips, like parentheses. His eyes are a chalky blue, like a glaze on pottery. His regard is direct and measuring. He is extremely vigilant. He has a short white beard, and short white hair, which he cuts by gathering strands between his first and second fingers and clipping the parts that stick out. He began losing teeth years ago, and he has only two of them left, one on each jaw. When he started singing, in his fifties, he still had many of his teeth. Not having teeth interrupt the flow of air from his chest has made his singing voice better, he says.

The first teeth that Neutrino lost were the front ones. He was fifteen and had just joined the army, having said he was eighteen. He lost them in a fight with another soldier. The soldier hit him first. Neutrino found the teeth on the ground. It was a very cold night, and he pressed them back into place, and pinched the gums, and perhaps because of the cold, when he took his hands away they stayed where they were, and they were fine for fifteen years. He looked funny, though, because he had reversed them. In the center of his forehead is a scar he received one night as a young man when he came out of a bar in San Francisco playing a trumpet. A kid on the sidewalk asked to see the trumpet, and when Neutrino handed it to him he hit Neutrino with the bell of it right between the eyes.

By nature Neutrino is implacably restless. He has never occupied a house or an apartment for more than a year. When I first met him, through a friend, he was in Los Angeles, singing on the street to collect money to go to Tucson. He had found a place that he liked among the trinket sellers and jugglers and buskers on Venice Beach, and he told me when I left to go home to New York that he was planning to stay there until he went to Arizona for the football camp. The next day, when I called his cell phone from my apartment, it sounded as if he was in a car that was moving and had the window open. I asked where he was, and he said about twenty miles outside San Diego. "I needed to get some motion under me," he said. He has three grown children, a son and two daughters. A third daughter died from an illness in her thirties. (He also has two adopted children and a stepchild.) When I asked the older of the daughters why she thought that her father moved so often, she said, "I don't think he can help himself." I asked him once, "What keeps you moving?" and he said, "I wish I knew that." He thought for a moment. "What it comes down to is, I don't want to ride the same horse in the same race tomorrow," he said. "I want to ride a different horse, or be in a different race."

The solitary apprehension he has been unable to shed, and that has only deepened with the years, is that something significant might have happened for him somewhere if only he had stayed a little longer.

Chapter 3

When neutrino went broke in Key West, it was not the first time. Usually when he has had money, he has disposed of it quickly. He finds possessions oppressive. He has acquired then given away, among other things, a farmhouse with an orchard, a few boats, and a store. "The greatest feelings that I have in my life are when I have nothing," he says. "When I'm absolutely broke, I feel liberated. As a kid, eight and nine years old, I felt that way."

Neutrino is an idealist. His poverty is the consequence of having tirelessly pursued an existence in which he would be free from all burdens—his quest, that is, for the philosopher's stone, the chief means of life, the end of all ends. He has a seeker's belief that deprivation can bring about a state of receptivity, an awareness, in which a person obtains access to territory that lies at the outermost boundaries of what we are familiar with, with what we accept as our selves. He shares to a degree the spiritualist's idea that life is something more than we believe it to be, that there are passageways leading from ordinary experience to an intensified one that has the power to make us feel different about everything that happens to us after.

"When I was a child, I had an intuitive knowledge that human life was ninety-nine percent defeat," he told me shortly after we'd met, "and that you had to do something extraordinary to turn it into victory. I didn't know what that extraordinary thing was. I knew that you could not be common and expect any kind of success. I didn't think of success as worldly, as the accumulation of things, as accomplishments in the realm of commercial life. No matter how attractive a life such as that might occasionally look, you're still going to be facing illness, old age, and death—all the things that Buddhism discusses, the human anxieties and apprehensions—and if you have devoted yourself only to worldly things you probably won't have the ability or the interior resources to grapple with them.

"As a child I was going to save the world. From what and how, I didn't know. I hadn't the slightest idea. Different scientists had saved the world—Jonas Salk had saved the world from polio. Different military men had saved the world. Churchill had saved the world. The world was in a constant state of being saved, and I wanted to take part. Even then I understood that the average man or woman was going to wind up in Flanders Field—no good would likely come to him or her. Once in a while, perhaps maybe, you might remember them for a little while after they were gone. But mostly I was thinking, how am I going to get out of this mess? I had zero ideas. I knew I wasn't afraid. My mother was a gambler. We were always having funny money, or being broke. I wasn't scared of being hungry. If you don't have food tonight, you'll have it tomorrow. I knew that it was important to be extreme. People are always attracted to the extreme. If you're eye-catching enough, somebody's going to want to stop and talk to you. But if you try to blend in, nobody's going to stop and talk to you. Why should they? When you cease to be extreme, you become part of the mass. That's when you need to have a steady income. I have lived my life in such a way that day in and out I meet people who have remembered me for years."

While Neutrino talked, we were sitting on a bench in Santa Monica, a few blocks from the ocean. Neutrino had his dog in his lap. He went on to say that he believes that a person must ruthlessly attack any impediment to his well-being. Passivity is abhorrent to him. For twenty years, he led a group of people who traveled around the country. Nomads in school buses and pickup trucks and sometimes on boats is what they were. He called it the Salvation Navy. They painted signs to raise money and taught derelicts and drunkards to paint them, then they left for another town, where they looked for a shop or a café or a garage that needed a sign. "First we had small attacks on the problem of living an independent and elevated life then we withdrew and assessed our progress and made larger attacks then we gave everything away so that we could go back and attack again," Neutrino said. "Mind you, nobody's interested in repeating it—not my children, not anyone else who was with me—but it defined their lives. It made them self-reliant. It gave them the power to know that no material obstacle could defeat them."

From being a young man with zero ideas, Neutrino became an old man with an ardent belief in a philosophical system that came to him suddenly, although after much reflection, much as the play did, and that he calls triads. He arrived at it after reading a book called *Meetings with Remarkable Men,* by G. I. Gurdjieff. Neutrino was impressed by Gurdjieff's description of crossing the desert on stilts to elevate himself above the sandstorms. Gurdjieff also wrote that a man's or woman's most important task in life is to identify the one thing he or she wants to accomplish before dying.

"For years I've been thinking, How can I be the happiest person in the world?" Neutrino said. "I've had a lot of time to think. How can I have it all? Time is the most important thing, in my estimation. I want to have time to figure things out and get hold of information that's going to help me figure out even more things. The problem with having only one desire, a monad, is that it's limiting. The pioneers were monadic, they had a one-point vision, one thing that they wanted, and nothing could stop them— Indians, sickness, bad crops, strife with each other, and bandits. Then there was a breakthrough into the dyad, represented by the cowboy who would shift jobs, gamble, gunfight, shoot buffalo, bounty hunt, drink, and fight. The example of the cowboy roaming around the country is no longer practical, really. Space is controlled, movement is controlled, and the dyad is not going to solve the problem, anyway. It's only going to create the inverse of the monad. A person trapped in a dyad can only be the opposite of the monad in order to establish an independent identity. Rather than advancement what you have are reaction and rebellion. A teenager who disfigures his body with tattoos and earrings and studs and wears his pants without a belt so they fall down. There's no resolving force. The triad creates the resolving force between the thesis and antithesis."

A woman stopped and spoke to the dog. People in Los Angeles treat dogs as if they were human beings. "How are *you*?" the woman said. She asked if she could pet the dog, and Neutrino let her.

"There are two parts to triads," he said when she left. "The first is that all relationships, all endeavors in life, all situations and circumstances can be categorized by triads. Friend, enemy, stranger. Boss, partner, servant. Give, take, share. Block, assist, remain neutral. Linear, existential, circular time. It's the way our minds think, the way we organize ourselves and our experience, only we aren't aware of it. Triads govern us; no one is outside them yet people aren't cognizant of them. The first triad, which is taken from us as soon as we go to school, is participate, redirect, or leave. Take part—that is, engage—or try to influence what's happening into a more favorable direction, or get up and leave. Anyone who can observe that triad is free to shape his present and his future.

"The second element of triads is a person's three deepest desires. If you can define your three deepest desires, and you can live in accordance with them, you will be happy. Gurdjieff said one wish, but a single desire is too constricting. A monad keeps you riveted. A dyad splits you, so it's unbearable. The triad opens you up. My three tasks have changed over the years, but right now they are to be free—freedom from poverty, freedom from hunger and want, freedom from insult, freedom to travel. The second is joy and all its ramifications, and the third is art through writing, through videos, ideas, through music, through crossing the ocean in a handmade raft, and maybe now also briefly through football. When a person is motivated by the three-sided attack, they become vigilant, judgmental—that is, they assess the things they are engaged in and whether they further or impede their desires—and aggressive in protecting themselves. They're not wandering around hoping God touches them or the universe gives them a break. All I'm interested in is naming and protecting my three deepest desires. They give me the solidity to strengthen my being. By the way, how about we continue this conversation in Costa Rica? It's cheaper."

Neutrino agreed to walk over to the ocean instead. "I'm not fit for society, really," he said. "When we get on the road, in an old rattletrap car, and there's no money, though, I am a start master. I create ways to get food, to get tire changes, to move from one town to the next. I don't consider myself a superior person, but I do consider myself in superior movement. I know how to move and engage with people. I know how to make the fire of life. I don't know the *truth* of life, but I know how to make the fire. People have always been drawn to me because of it. I would say, 'Do you want to live as you're living, with no fire, or a fire that's gone out, or with half a fire, or a fire that only works sometimes, or do you want to live like me, in the fire all the time?' And they would point to the car's flat tire, and say, 'What about that?' and I would shrug and say, 'Don't worry, it's just a problem, we'll solve it.'"

At a corner we waited for the light to change. Neutrino looked at his dog. "Come here, sweetheart," he said. "Are you doing okay? We need to get you some water." We crossed the street. Neutrino gave a beggar a dollar. Two policemen approached. Neutrino stopped them. "I'll go where they don't have doctors," he said, "but I won't go where they don't have cops." The policemen nodded and walked on. "That's in case they see me later playing music on the beach," he said. We sat down on a bench by the Santa Monica Pier and watched the ocean.

"The way you open a certain seer's capacity is you look at something and you make a guess at it," Neutrino said. "You take a guess at it, then you find you're wrong—you couldn't have been more wrong—but you don't stop there. You keep making guesses, and eventually you hit one, and the capacity opens up. You're through the door to the other side. I've done that, and I know it's true."

He leaned over and picked up his dog and settled her in his lap. "The next thing for me is I'm going to hit it big," he said. "I know it. I can feel its approach." He petted the dog so that she seemed to be nodding. He shrugged. "It's just a matter of whether I hit before the heart attack or after," he said.

CHRONOLOGY: NEUTRINO WAS BORN in San Francisco, in 1933. His bloodlines are motley. His father, Louis Pearlman, was in the navy. He left on a ship shortly after Neutrino was conceived and then disappeared. His mother, Vilma McDaniel, married a man named James Maloney, whom Neutrino believed was his father. He was raised as David Maloney. In 1966 Neutrino went to Vietnam as a war correspondent for a small newspaper in San Francisco. The security clearance he was required to obtain turned up his real name.

Vilma McDaniel was an incorrigible gambler. She liked dice games and lowball poker. In lowball poker, five cards are dealt, there is a draw, and the lowest hand wins; the most desirable hand is a straight, of no particular suit, from ace to five. Vilma was descended from a family named Farlow. The Farlows were from Lander, Wyoming. Neutrino's cousin Albert Farlow, who had short legs and was called Stubby, is the cowboy riding the bucking bronco on the Wyoming license plate. According to the Lander Historical Society, the first Farlow to settle in Lander, somewhere between 1876 and 1879, was Edward, who had come from Iowa. He wrote home that a man could make a good living in Wyoming and was joined by his brother Nels, Neutrino's great-grandfather. Edward worked on the movie *The Covered Wagon*, one of the first western films. Stubby, his son, moved to Los Angeles and became a cowboy actor.

Neutrino's impressions of Nels, received from his mother and grandmother, are romantic. They begin with Nels's cutting cordwood in Lander, when he was eighteen. He was said to have worked five hundred days in a row, for a dollar a day, and to have saved nearly all the money he made. Then he apprenticed himself to a saddle maker. At the end of a year he bought the saddle maker's shop. A year after that he built a house in town. He and his wife were married in the house, then shortly after he bought a ranch.

Neutrino's grandmother Eleanor, Vilma's mother, was raised on the ranch. When she was nineteen, she met an Englishman who lived on money from home, a remittance man. His name was Jack Whitehead, and he and Eleanor were married, around 1910. Not long after the wedding, Nels Farlow sold his ranch to the government, which wanted to build a dam on it, and he moved his family to San Francisco, where he put up apartment houses. The Whiteheads went with him. In 1914, Eleanor had an affair with a waiter named Roscoe McDaniel and became pregnant, with Vilma. Eleanor already had three small children with Whitehead. She was seven months pregnant when Whitehead learned that the child was not his. He responded by taking their children to New York, leaving Eleanor penniless. Whenever Neutrino asked his mother what became of them, she told him what her mother had told her, that Whitehead and the children were dead. Whitehead had bought passage to Liverpool on the RMS *Lusitania,* she said, which left New York on May 1, 1915, and six days later was sunk by a German U-boat—an explanation, it turned out, that Eleanor had invented, presumably to suppress any further discussion. I say invented because I managed to find a facsimile of the passenger list for the ship's final voyage, and the only Whitehead on it, in second class, is a Miss Florence.

Shortly after Vilma was born, Eleanor married Roscoe McDaniel, the waiter. McDaniel was from Bolivar, Tennessee. Neutrino remembers him as a charming man who held simple opinions and refused to listen to anyone who tried to broaden him. McDaniel had been followed to San Francisco by a sister named Lucille. According to Neutrino, Lucille, his aunt, was "as stringent about money as it's possible for a woman to be." Roscoe and Lucille's father, William McDaniel, was a newspaperman. Traveling in the South, he had met a woman named Texas Hornsby, in Hornsby, Tennessee; they were married and had Roscoe and Lucille. Neutrino says that William McDaniel felt confined in a small town where he thought that he was smarter than everyone else, and one day he left without warning. Eventually the family tracked him to Denver, where he worked for *The Denver Post*. When Lucille was seventeen, she went to find him. In place of the loving father she imagined herself reunited with, she found a man who liked to drink and who was loud and abrasive and spent more money than he earned. Before long he disappeared again. Lucille paid his debts by washing dishes. When she had saved a hundred dollars she joined Roscoe in San Francisco.

Roscoe had hoped to be a baseball player, but leaping over a fence to retrieve a woman's hat, he injured his leg, and it never healed properly. He made part of his living as a scout for the Cleveland Indians. He and Eleanor divorced after two years. "Roscoe was wonderful sometimes," Neutrino says, "but like his father he was a bit of a redneck and a Tennessee know-it-all, and the trademarks of his southern upbringing were too much for my independent, rancher-raised grandmother." After the divorce, Eleanor supported herself and Vilma by playing the piano in nickel movie houses in Sacramento, Reno, and San Francisco. Vilma sometimes went with her and sometimes stayed in San Francisco with Lucille or with Roscoe. She grew up in the shadow of her mother's remorse at having taken up with an appealing man who proved self-absorbed and unreliable and who cost her, she said, the lives of her children.

Roscoe McDaniel died the day after Thanksgiving, in 1947. On Thanksgiving Day, he, Vilma, her husband, James, Maloney, and Neutrino went to a football game at Kezar Stadium, in Golden Gate Park. McDaniel got drunk and left the game early. The police found him lying in the street and sent him to jail to dry out. Sometime after his heart had quit beating, he was discovered to have been run down by a car that hadn't stopped.

When Lucille arrived in San Francisco, she began buying rooming houses, full of heavy, varnished furniture and dusty carpets. "She grew up in poverty," Neutrino says. "She paid off her father's debts, and now she pinched pennies." The halls and rooms were gloomy, because she wouldn't let the gas mantles be lighted, and the bread in her kitchen was stale. After the boarders took their baths, she washed her clothes in the bathwater, and what comes back to Neutrino through all the years is that they always smelled sour.

Chapter 5

I IMAGINE NEUTRINO'S MIND as a thicket. Here and there are paths that were made by creatures in the dark. Or I see it as a jumble of wires. Some of them are sparking. The chamber that contains them is dimly lit, and there is a smell of smoke and a low hum that sometimes pulses and throbs. Whatever neurological byways through this territory make him able to tolerate excessively anxious experiences were laid, I imagine, by his mother's genes and reinforced by her behavior.

When Neutrino was two, Vilma was introduced to a woman

at a whist game who insisted that she meet her son, James Maloney. "He was pale and not homely, but he wasn't good-looking," Neutrino says. "He was a thin Irishman." Maloney was employed as a fish and poultry man in a market in San Francisco. He had a reputation for applying himself, his character was steadfast, and he was devoted to Vilma. "He adored going places with my mother, because she always dressed sharp. She had style, and carried herself well, and everyone lit up when they saw her," Neutrino says. "You could see how proud he was of her."

Monday mornings, Maloney drew money against his wages and paid a week's rent on a room in a cheap hotel. What was left he gave Vilma to gamble with. Vilma would spend most of her day in bed, "reading and concocting schemes," Neutrino says. If she left the hotel before evening, it was usually to play pinochle or gin rummy.

At night Vilma gambled in card rooms run by gamblers with names such as Sivonian Johnny, the Detroit Kid, and Bones Remmer. Neutrino went with her, and the gamblers gave him nickels and dimes. He was known as Vilma's kid.

Vilma liked taking chances, and her luck was typical—that is to say, she lost more often than she won. With her winnings, the family got a better hotel room. When they were broke, they would move in with Lucille, while Vilma and Maloney raised money for Vilma's gambling. They tended to arrive at Lucille's every two or three months. Sometimes Vilma would leave Neutrino with Lucille for weeks. Lucille was a hard-shell Baptist. She would take Neutrino to church on Sunday, and to prayer meetings and revivals when they came to town. "Tent revivals," Neutrino says. "Shouting and praying and falling on your knees. Jesus speaking in tongues through many different people. They tore you down psychologically, then the breath of fresh air came into your life, and they said that was Christ."

Neutrino's attendance at school was sporadic. Vilma would sometimes appear in his classroom and say, "David, come on, we're going," and Maloney would be waiting in a car at the curb to take them to Reno. "I was always being shifted around," Neutrino says. "And for some reason I loved this. If I ever wanted a more stable life as a child, I've repressed it. My grandfather would take me to the ball field to work with the players, and I would be the batboy, or my mother would take me to the card halls, and I would sleep under the card tables. Anybody else would have become a sociopath, I guess, but for me it was the perfect atmosphere. The feminine trinity of my grandmother with her incredible dark guilt and restriction at having given up her husband and children for a redneck egoist, my aunt with her penny-pinching, and my mother squandering money—the far reaches of Catholic guilt and Baptist encroachment—all of it was so lavish and vivid, and it really tempered my nervous system. The sudden appearance of change taught me immediately to engage, if I saw something desirable. I *had* to engage, because whatever I saw wouldn't be there the next day, maybe even not the next moment. Very rarely and usually never was there ever a second chance."

Now and then in the stream of conversation that passed above his head, Neutrino heard the adults deploring the vagrant life he was subject to, and he would wonder what they could possibly mean. "It may have been a strange childhood," he says, "I suppose it was a strange childhood—obviously it wasn't like anyone else's childhood—but it was the best childhood for me."

It is a flat truism that what happens to us when we are young, especially what affects us deeply, stays with us the rest of our lives. Neutrino's most unshakable ideology was formed abruptly and by chance. It occurred when he was twelve. Vilma had been hired to manage the Bristol Hotel, where a lot of gamblers lived. One evening Neutrino went to the movies at a theater around the corner from the hotel. The feature happened to be a documentary about aborigines. The camera had been held by hand, the footage was shaky, and there were scratches all over it.

"It started with all the aborigines lying naked in a circle, just as the sun came up," Neutrino says. "They're huddled together keeping warm—women, men, children—and they got up and immediately started walking in a long line. As the sun rose, and they warmed up, they arrived at a river, and some went upriver to drink, and some went downriver to wash. Towards noon the entire tribe, except one man, went out in a huge circle to flush a deer to a place under a tree, where the strongest man was waiting. They had started a fire using flint in a pit, and put leaves and coals in it, and they flushed the deer, and the young man jumped on it, and they blessed the deer, and cooked it and ate it. Then everybody took off again. The cameraman, who was also the narrator, stayed with them for weeks. Now and then they'd go to a cave where they had hidden maps about where the wells were. And every four years they would stop and make a village—houses, shacks, make clothes—for thirty days all they did was work. And there was this entire village built. At the end of this festival period they took off their clothes, set fire to the village, and walked away naked. The narrator said they were the happiest people he had ever seen, and the pictures of faces full of light and pleasure showed it.

"I was only twelve, but when I left that movie theater I said, 'That's the way I want to live, I never want anything more.' I was transformed into an aborigine. Having the background of my mother and father—all the movement, the adventure, the thrills amidst the rhythms of feast and famine—it was easy for me to get rid of everything, to shed suitcases of clothes and possessions and go out unencumbered in the shirt and pants I had on. I was never really afraid of things—my mother took the fear out of me years ago—but after seeing that movie, whose title I no longer even remember, the idea of freedom became paramount to me. Remaining free to move, free to plan or not plan, free to have an adventure, free to explore an idea or an intuition, free to make my own choices and determine my future drove my life from that day forward. Nothing else mattered."

Chapter 7

VILMA HAD NO SPECIAL feelings for education—"She thought she was well read because she had made it through *Gone with the Wind*, and regarded Margaret Mitchell as the end of all writers," Neutrino says. Nevertheless, she felt that something was lacking in Neutrino's life, perhaps discipline. It seems never to have occurred to her that she might have provided an example of it herself. When Neutrino was thirteen, she sent him to a private school called the Montezuma Christian School, in Watsonville, outside Santa Cruz. She borrowed a car to deliver him.

Neutrino made friends with a boy from San Francisco named Arthur Schultz, who slept in the bunk below him. Revival meetings came through Watsonville, set up on the campus, and sometimes stayed for a week. After one of them, Neutrino and Schultz found that they couldn't sleep. Schultz had a book and a flashlight, and Neutrino got into bed with him, and they read. Brother Merrill, who discovered them, beat them in their bunk with a rubber hose. "He put a dent in my right shinbone that is still there today," Neutrino says.

When Brother Merrill left, Neutrino and Schultz decided to run away to San Francisco. A cop found them hitchhiking and took them to jail. Brother Merrill collected them. Neutrino ran away again and this time made it home, and Vilma removed him from the school.

How Neutrino joined the army at fifteen is that one night Schultz called and said he had the keys to his father's garage; his father was a mechanic. In the garage was a 1939 Plymouth that Schultz's father had just restored. Schultz and Neutrino took the car and picked up a girl they knew and rode out to the beach.

"Arthur had a pellet gun, and he started leaning out the window and shooting at things from the car, lampposts and lights and stop signs," Neutrino says, "then he sat back and started shooting from inside the car, and of course it wasn't long before the car hit a bump while he was aiming the gun, and he shot out one of the windows." After Schultz recovered from the surprise, he shot out the rest of the windows.

"We took the car back, and it looked just like it had when we got it," Neutrino says, "except all the windows were gone." They left the car for Schultz's father to find, hoping his conclusion would be that someone had broken into the garage.

The next afternoon when Neutrino came home from school, Schultz and his father were sitting in the living room with Vilma and Maloney. Maloney asked Neutrino if he had any idea what might have happened to the car in Mr. Schultz's garage. Neutrino said he didn't.

"After they left, my father was really angry," Neutrino says. "He said, 'You did that. I know you were in that car.'" He came at Neutrino, and Neutrino held him off—"I was fifteen," he says, "almost a man"—but when they were finished Neutrino left the house and went to a recruiting office across the bay, in Oakland, and signed up for the army.

"My father would have taken me back," Neutrino says, "but I just decided it was time to leave San Francisco. Kids I knew were starting to smoke reefers and go to prison. There was a murder in a gang fight in our neighborhood, and the boy who was murdered was someone I knew, and I thought if I didn't get out I was going to end up in jail, if I didn't wind up dead."

Chapter 8

To the soldier behind the desk at the recruiting office, Neutrino presented a counterfeit license, which said he was eighteen. He left Oakland on a troop train on New Year's Eve of 1948. Around nine the next night the train pulled into Wichita Falls, Texas. "They took us to the mess hall, and I saw all this wonderful food—spaghetti and meatballs and salad and dessert, all you want—and I thought, This is incredible," Neutrino says. "Then they took us to supply and gave us blankets and sheets, and I made my bed, and got in, and I looked at the ceiling, and it was the loneliest feeling in the world. I realized I was totally out of my element."

Neutrino lay in bed and thought, What have I done? The boy in the bunk next to his was named Casey, and he was only sixteen. "I could tell he was underage, too," Neutrino says, "and right away we started talking."

Neutrino finally fell asleep. The lights came on at four in the morning. "They took us to breakfast then to the barber and cut off our hair, so we all looked the same," he says. "I couldn't believe that hair was such a big influence on how you look. After that it seemed like forever we stood in line and waited for things."

Basic training struck Neutrino as resembling nothing so much as hazing. By the time two months had gone by, he was despondent. One morning he was awakened in the darkness and sent to guard duty. Casey's bunk was empty, and Neutrino asked where he was.

"'Casey's down in the bathroom,'" they said. "'He's just hung himself.' I went to see, and there he was on the bathroom floor, they'd just cut him down, and he was dead as a doornail. I went out on guard duty, and I'm walking in the snow, back and forth, with my rifle, cold as can be, in the dark, and in my mind there are feelings of absolute loss and loneliness, despair, and I thought, No way am I staying."

Neutrino told his commanding officer that he was only fifteen, and the officer removed him from duty. The officer wrote to Vilma. About two weeks later, Neutrino was called into an office and told that his mother had submitted an affidavit saying that he was lying about his age, and that he was actually eighteen. The problem, Vilma had said, was simply that her son never wanted to finish anything.

"The irony is that my mother and my aunt and my grandmother all supported ideas they didn't believe in," Neutrino says. "Here was my mother talking about the value of staying with a situation until it resolved itself, of being steady and dependable, of finishing what you started, when she would leave anywhere she was at the drop of a hat."

Neutrino insisted he was telling the truth. The matter went back and forth until the captain of Neutrino's unit took him aside and said, in effect, This isn't going to be settled for some time, why not finish your training and get on with your life? It meant, however, that he had to start training all over again.

"When I was done, after twenty-six weeks, I was tough," he says. "I was supertough, because I'd done it twice. I marched in the military parade on graduation day, and I thought, I finally completed something."

Chapter 9

THE ARMY SENT NEUTRINO to a base in Fort Worth, Texas. "Never in my imagination did I conceive of it," he says. "Fort Worth was the last remaining crazy, wild, cow town in America. Wide open, Dodge City. Main Street was filled with bars and whorehouses and hamburger stands, and the bar girls were twelve and thirteen—all the runaways went to Fort Worth—and there's fighting and carousing and wild bouts of drinking, and I'm still fifteen. The army gave me an adaptability test, to assign me a task, and my scores were so low that I wasn't even on the chart. I had flunked every grade I had ever attended and had only one year of high school and no contact with office

work or farming, I just had gambling and fighting and total audacity. I was really unprepared. So they put me in the laundry
room, sorting laundry. In peacetime, when you get out of basic,
the military is more like a job. You have to be there for your
work, and then you're free to leave the base and don't have to be
back until the morning. In a bar I met a girl named Dolly. She
told me she was fifteen, but really she was twelve. Since I was fifteen, we were right for each other. I'd get off work in the laundry and pick up Dolly, and we'd go to different bars. I wasn't a
drinker—I'd drink a Coke, she'd drink a Coke."

One night in 1949, Dolly and Neutrino were in the Long-
horn Bar and Grill when a young man named Frank Turpin
walked in with three friends. "His gang," Neutrino says. "They
were hoodlums—earrings in their ears, long hair in the back.
They sat at a table across the dance floor from us, and Frank sent
the waitress to our table with a note on a napkin asking if he can
dance with my girlfriend. I wrote back and said no. His gang
came over, took me outside, and hung me from a telephone pole.
Some people helped me down, and when I got back in, Frank's
dancing with Dolly. After the dance I collected her, and we left. I
didn't want anything more to do with him. Little did I know he
was going to be with me the rest of my life."

That night Turpin and his gang robbed a man at a club on the
Dallas Highway and were arrested. Turpin called Dolly from
jail. According to Turpin, Dolly began visiting him, without
telling Neutrino, who found out anyway. Turpin was released a
few weeks later. Neutrino insisted that Dolly choose between
them. The three of them would take long walks. "One time she'd
decide me, and Frank would say, 'I guess you won, Dave, you're
the better man,' and the next night he'd be with her."

Dolly played each against the other for about two weeks, and
then she disappeared. A few days later Neutrino met a man he

knew who said, "I found Dolly. Frank's got her in a whorehouse in El Paso. If we borrow a car, we can go get her." Neutrino borrowed a car, but before he left he ran into Turpin. Neutrino said, "Where's Dolly?" and Turpin said he didn't know. "We went to Corpus Christi," he said, "and I was working as a fry cook, and she'd come home every night with her lipstick smeared, and finally she ran off with somebody else." The other guy had invented the story as a means of getting to El Paso. Neutrino and Turpin went to a place on Main Street called The Little Club and talked. "It was like Damon and Pythias," Neutrino says. "We became friends. I couldn't believe that two people could be pulled together that strongly."

Turpin had joined the army at fourteen and was sixteen when he was discharged, a few months before he met Neutrino. With his friends in jail, he was at loose ends. Neutrino obtained some uniforms for him, then moved him into the bed beside his own in the barracks.

Chapter 10

Turpin had grown up poor in Texas. He liked to dress sharp. One night he and Neutrino went to a club in new clothes and shoes. They drank whiskey, and Turpin put red birds and Benzedrine in it. They left the club and went to a park and fell deeply asleep, and when they woke up they were naked.

Neutrino began dating a girl named Dorcus Cantrell, whose father was a policeman. Every time Neutrino left her off at home, he was arrested by a cop who had followed them. One night he and Turpin were arrested for robbing a candy store. At the time, Neutrino, Turpin, and a friend of Turpin's named Worm, who had hung Neutrino from the telephone pole, had been boxing at the National Guard armory. Nevertheless, the police drove the three of them to the candy store. The people who owned the store were blind. The police had Neutrino, Turpin, and Worm say a few sentences, and the owners said, "That's them." Neutrino's commanding officer collected him from the jailhouse. The charges were dropped, but the officer decided it was time to send Neutrino away, and he selected as a destination Okinawa.

Neutrino went to San Francisco for the Christmas of 1949 and took Turpin with him then he shipped to Okinawa. He became friendly with a man from West Virginia whose nickname was Oats. Oats had been playing cards one evening when one of the other cardplayers pulled a gun on him. Neutrino knocked the man out. Oats was grateful. He taught Neutrino to cheat at cards—to use signals, mark cards, deal from the bottom of the deck, and let your hand be seen as if by accident so that the betting was affected in your favor—and they went partners as gamblers.

The soldiers were paid at the beginning of the month. They played cards and typically lost, and by the end of the month their money had been delivered into the hands of the cardplayers who knew what they were doing. Oats and Neutrino prospered. For a while Neutrino carried a thousand dollars in each of his six pockets, and he drove a new Chevy. Oats was owed several thousand dollars by a gambler who wouldn't pay him. He asked Neutrino to stand by the table the next time they played and grab the man's money and throw it in the air. At Oats's signal, Neutrino threw the money, and Oats recovered most of it. The next evening, when Neutrino returned to his barracks, the man was waiting for him.

"His name was Goss, and he was huge," Neutrino says. "I

had been shopping for Easter with my uncle, who was on a base nearby, and I walked through the door with my arms full of packages. Goss ran toward me and launched himself like he was Superman. Soon as he's in the air, I knew what to do. I just lowered my head, as if I were bowing to him, and he hit the top of my head, and his nose split open, lights out. By then I was known as the toughest guy in the barracks. Everybody used to challenge me. One guy, a psychopath, a Mexican, came at me one night with a knife. He put it to my shoulder and dug a line down my arm, and he said, 'You're not so tough, are you?' I grabbed him by the arm that held the knife and began swinging him in a circle. The centrifugal force was so great that he couldn't raise his other arm to resist me. After several revolutions I let go, and he hit the wall, and fell to the floor unconscious. I was so creative in my fighting. I was beyond form. Beyond tactics. I was sixteen, and I had no fear of anything."

Chapter 11

WHEN THE KOREAN WAR began, Neutrino was assigned to drive a bomb truck, loading bombs onto planes. "After months of playing cards and visiting bars, war breaks out—the whole reason for the army in the first place—and now I really have something important to do," Neutrino says. "I'm representing my country."

Vilma, however, felt disinclined to let her only child die at the front. She contacted the army and told them that Neutrino was sixteen years old. Neutrino's commanding officer called him into his office. Neutrino insisted that he was eighteen. The army believed Vilma. Within weeks, Neutrino was in San Francisco dressed in civilian clothes. "I'm back on the street," he says. "Two years in the army, all kinds of adventures on both sides of the world, and I haven't even reached seventeen."

For a while he occupied chairs at tables in various card rooms. A few times he won substantial amounts of money, but mostly he lost, and before long he was weary of gambling.

"Out of boredom, I would make moves no sane gambler would," he says. "I'd had my fill of gambling in Okinawa, where I was cheating, and I didn't want any more of it. My mother never cheated. I never wanted to follow that pathway anyhow. I knew life had other things in store for me."

Chapter 12

BEING STILL A CHILD but having no real home to return to, Neutrino began leading the footloose and romantic American life that Jack Kerouac later glamorized in *On the Road.* The years from when he was sixteen to when he reached twenty-one were episodic, aimless, and furiously transient. Nearly all of them Neutrino spent hitchhiking back and forth on Route 66, as a citizen of what he calls "the Catholic Christian road world. You're on the road or you're trying to get something to eat or you're at mass or a tent revival," he says. "I did whatever was necessary to stay alive—work in a mattress factory, work in a mine, nothing for longer than it took to get the money to get back on the road. The distances across the western states are so enormous, and the cars drove so much more slowly than now, that when someone picked you up you were in this capsule with them for two or three days. We would reveal to each other our dreams and ideals. In the forties and fifties you found people on the road who had some elegance. They were there because they couldn't fit in as farmers or miners or mechanics or sailors, they had no job opportunities. The lives they were having, they were inventing themselves. They had to apply their morality to each situation. You had to be very upright to survive, even when you were hungry or exhausted, because otherwise you were simply a criminal, and sooner or later you were caught and went to jail. You lost your freedom. Out on the road, though, no convention, no organization, no alliance gave any protection. You had to be extremely quick thinking and inventive. It was my whole education."

Late in 1950, Neutrino left San Francisco and hitchhiked to Fort Worth, where he thought he would find Frank Turpin at his mother's house. Instead, she told Neutrino she hadn't seen her son for some time and didn't know where he was. Neutrino hitchhiked back to San Francisco, where a letter from Turpin was waiting. He was in Helena, Montana, in jail for six months for stealing hubcaps. He wrote that he had persuaded a girl to smuggle a hacksaw blade to him and had sawed through the bars in the window of his cell. The rest of the prisoners followed him out the window. Turpin and a friend made their way to a cabin outside town, in a place called Hungry Horse Canyon. The friend had broken his ankle jumping from the window. Turpin walked toward town one morning to get bandages and liniment for him. On a ridge he saw state troopers on horseback. He ran toward them, waving his arms. "Thank God you found me," he said. "They made me escape." For turning himself in, he was appointed a trusty. He was allowed to roam the jail, he delivered mail to the other prisoners, he fetched coffee for the sheriff, and eventually he was assigned to drive the sheriff's wife around Helena. Through her he met the sheriff's daughter, and now they were engaged. In a week or so, when he got out of jail, he was moving into the sheriff's house. All that he lacked to complete his happiness was Neutrino's company.

Neutrino hitchhiked to Helena. He and Turpin walked into a café one afternoon and saw three girls sitting at a table. On Neutrino's behalf, Turpin sent the waitress to them with a note. Neutrino began seeing one of them, Josephine Bonner, the daughter of John Bonner, Montana's governor. After several weeks, she introduced Neutrino to her father.

"I was eighteen, and pure nothing," Neutrino says. "I hadn't heard yet about Stendhal and Molière or Tolstoy or Chekhov. I knew Bones Remmer and Dino Lucci, and gamblers and card games and dice games, and when the governor met me, he definitely didn't want me for his daughter, who was going to go to college. He's too smart to mess with passion, though, so he asked me would I like a job. In Billings, 250 miles away. Working for the highway department, assaying gravel pits—they would bring me gravel samples, and all I would have to do is sift through them, say, This one's good, this one isn't. Very easy and you make good money, he said. I agreed, and he sent me away with a letter of recommendation, 'Please offer the bearer any assistance you can, he's on his way to work for the Montana Highway Department.'"

Turpin, who is no longer alive, told me that he accompanied Neutrino to Billings. Neutrino was shown to an office, where he waited for someone to arrive with samples of gravel. Toward the end of the morning, he looked out the window and saw Turpin sitting under a tree. Neutrino threw open the window and asked Turpin what he was doing, and Turpin said he was simply waiting for Neutrino to quit. He said he knew that Neutrino wouldn't be able to last the day. Neutrino agreed. He piled the desk and his office chair in front of the door, then he went out the window and joined Turpin, and they went on a tour of Yellowstone Park.

After a few days, Turpin returned to Helena. Neutrino began hitchhiking back to San Francisco. North of Reno, in a town called Gerlach, he stopped at some hot pools, where he met a young man about the same age as he, named Danny Elkins. Elkins was wearing cutoff jeans. His socks and shoes and the rest of his clothes were on the freight train he'd been thrown off shortly before by the railroad police. Elkins said that he was an accomplished diver, and he persuaded Neutrino that if they went to Winnemucca, where there was a big pool, he could put on an exhibition, and they could pass the hat. The two of them rode a freight train north and east to Winnemucca and arrived on a triple payday—the miners, the cowboys, and the farmhands. Winnemucca was overrun with gamblers. Elkins was drawn to gambling even more avidly than Neutrino was. They spent the weekend playing cards and throwing dice, begging for change, and fighting. Monday morning the town was empty, and it stayed empty for two weeks, until the next payday. Elkins gave his exhibition at the pool, but hardly anyone saw it.

Chapter 13

FOR A TEENAGER AS IMPULSIVE as Neutrino was, each day unfolded differently. He left Elkins in Winnemucca and made his desultory way back to San Francisco. He was staying with his grandmother when Turpin called.

Nearly a year had passed. Turpin had married a woman named Delores. "Beautiful and petite," Neutrino says, "very sweet, but a hooker and a thief—a pickpocket and a booster," a shoplifter, that is. "She once shot a guy in a whorehouse with a derringer," Neutrino says. "He came at her, and he didn't have permission, and she broke out the derringer. Hit him right between the eyes, but he didn't die—the bullet skipped over his skull."

Neutrino's grandmother lived at the top of a steep hill. Turpin was calling from the bottom of the hill. So many people were in his car that it wouldn't climb the grade, he said. Neutrino packed a bag and walked down to meet them. In the car, a 1949 Chevy two-door coupe, were Turpin and Delores, Turpin's sister and father, who had a broken hip in a cast, a man named Duke, his wife and child, and a man named Jim. Duke and Jim had recently escaped from the Walla Walla State Penitentiary, in Washington. Turpin told me he had met them shortly after the escape, and they had begun traveling together. Jim had a bullet in his head and sometimes had headaches.

The group went south, then east across the desert into Arizona and New Mexico, siphoning gas from trucks at construction sites. Duke and Jim talked about their pasts and jobs they had pulled. Sometimes, on back roads between small towns, Duke and Neutrino would ride on the fender, because the car was so crowded. Sometimes they'd separate themselves from the group and hitchhike to the next town, where they'd meet up again. Turpin and Neutrino found work in a mine but were fired on the second day for racing the rail cars. Duke and Jim couldn't work, because they were wanted. Occasionally the car would pull to the side of the road and someone would run out and steal corn or beans or tomatoes from a garden. Mostly the group ate rabbits they shot with a double-barreled shotgun that belonged to Turpin's father. The gun broke open when the trigger was pulled and ejected the shells, which struck the shooter in the face. It also left powder burns on the shooter's cheeks. No one wanted to fire the gun. Being gamblers, they preferred each evening to draw lots, rather than take turns, to see who would hunt.

Neutrino traveled with Turpin and his family and Duke and Jim for several weeks; then he made a pact with Turpin to meet on Christmas, five months later, in Cherry Grove, Illinois, where Delores's mother lived, and then he hitchhiked back to San Francisco.

Chapter 14

A FEW WEEKS LATER, in the balcony of the Golden Gate Theater watching *The Treasure of the Sierra Madre,* a movie he had seen many times, Neutrino heard someone call his name. It was Danny Elkins, the diver. Inspired by the movie, they decided to go to Mexico. After several months, they arrived in Mexico City, where Elkins obtained a thousand postcards of naked women, possibly he stole them. Each postcard was worth a dollar in trade. A hotel room cost five postcards. Using the cards, they reached Acapulco. Christmas was approaching, and Neutrino decided that it was time to leave to meet Turpin in Illinois. He and Elkins split the postcards they had left, and Neutrino carried his in a pillowcase. He met a man with a stable of greyhounds who needed help getting the dogs across the border. Neutrino rode in the truck with the dogs, and fed them and watered them and ran them for exercise. When he separated from the dog owner, in Louisiana, he was still wearing the sandals and pants and thin jacket he had worn in Mexico. In Mississippi he became so cold that he went into a police station and said he was wanted for escaping from jail, but they didn't believe him. Finally, by panhandling, he raised enough money to ride a bus to Memphis. He arrived late at night and phoned Turpin's mother. She said that Turpin and Delores had written a string of bad checks and were now serving time in Athens, Texas. Neutrino found Athens on a map and figured that, with luck, he could reach it in a day.

Chapter 15

NEUTRINO ARRIVED IN Athens on the Christmas Eve of 1952. It was one in the afternoon. At the jail he asked to see Turpin and was told to come back during visiting hours, which began at two. He went across the street to a café. Bells were tolling in the tower of a church. He had no money. He asked the man who owned the café if he would give him a meal. The owner said, "Get out of here, you tramp." Neutrino started to leave. As he reached the door, the owner said, "All right, come on, kid. I'll give you a meal." Neutrino, exhausted, cursed him, and the man picked up a ketchup bottle and broke it over Neutrino's head.

By the time the police arrived, Neutrino had got the better of the owner, whose wife had watched, smiling, as her husband received a beating. They led Neutrino in handcuffs across the street and threw him in a cell with Turpin, who said, "I can't believe you're here."

The next morning, the judge read Neutrino's name from a scrap of an envelope and asked Neutrino how he wanted to plead. Neutrino asked what the charge was. "Disturbing the peace," the judge said. "Ten dollars or ten days." Neutrino took the jail time because he had no cash for the fine.

Ten days passed, but no one said anything about his being released. Then eleven days and twelve. He was beyond twenty when he heard that they were holding him until the café owner was out of the hospital. A little more than three weeks had gone by when one morning the jailer unlocked his cell and walked him to the front door. They gave him his pillowcase, but the postcards were gone.

Across the street, the owner of the café was waiting for Neutrino with a shotgun. Snow was falling. Turpin and Delores waved to Neutrino from the windows of their cells. Neutrino strode toward the café owner, as if unconcerned. When the distance between them was only a few yards, he ran toward an alley between the café and the building next door. He didn't stop running until he came to the highway, where he hid behind some trees until a car approached in the storm. He flagged it down and told the driver that a man was trying to kill him.

The driver left Neutrino in Fort Worth. On a corner he met two earnest young men named Howard and Robert, who were preaching. Howard and Robert were students at the J. Frank Norris Seminary, and they invited Neutrino to stay with them. J. Frank Norris was a Baptist in Fort Worth who believed that the Bible was to be read as if everything in it had actually happened. For a time he led the largest congregation in the country. He also stood trial for killing a man who had threatened him in his office and was acquitted. Over the following days, Neutrino had long conversations with Howard and Robert, with the result that he enrolled in the seminary.

"It was like home," Neutrino says. "There was companionship, hot biscuits for breakfast, camp meetings, and all the things they talked about I'd heard from my Baptist aunt. I was twenty years old, and after living for so long on the road, I felt like I'd found my place and, if not strictly my vocation, at least my calling." He became an assistant pastor, then he was ordained and began preaching at the Hazel Baptist Church, in Hazel, Texas. One night, after he'd been at the seminary for about six months, he was reading his Bible and consulting a concordance when he came across a reference to Hell.

"I discovered the original word was Gehenna," he says. "Then I looked in the concordance, which said that Gehenna was a garbage dump outside Jerusalem. And I had a breakthrough. I said, 'Christ was saying that for having sinned you go to the garbage dump, where the fires burned day and night.' Which leads me to conclude that Hell isn't literal, it's a metaphor. Which, of course, is great news, glad tidings—there is no everlasting fire, there is no eternal damnation. We've been wrong all these years in our understanding. Christianity is not a fire-breathing, vehement, and violent religion. It's not thuggish and punishing and judgmental. It's compassionate. This is enormous, I can hardly contain my excitement. I'd had my own Enlightenment. I practically had chills. It was late, but I went straight to the head of the seminary and knocked on his door, and when he said come in, I told him I had wonderful news, a great message, hallelujah. He kindly put aside the book he was reading and laid his glasses on it, and asked what I wanted to talk to him about. I said, 'There's no eternal damnation! It says it right here'—and I waved the concordance. 'If you're bad, if you sin, if you stray, you just go to a garbage dump, where you're burned up in garbage!'

"He didn't say anything, he just looked at me, maybe he tilted his head slightly. 'Don't you understand what this means?' I said. 'We've completely misinterpreted the Bible! We can begin again, with a sympathetic point of view! We can be the faith of compassion and forgiveness. We can make amends. Think of the harm and the prejudice and the backward thinking we can undo, the suffering and the misery. Not to mention the peace and the joy and consolation we can bring to the world with this new awareness. We can build a kingdom of hope and well-being and love.' I was really working myself into a fervor. I was brimming with the spirit of rebirth.

"I finished, and he still didn't say anything. He stared at me fixedly. I assumed he was as thrilled as I was and was taking his time to absorb it fully and ponder the possibilities before framing a response. Surely we would ring the bells of freedom and hope together. From his desk, finally, he slowly picked up his glasses, and then he looked at me with the strangest look— maybe it was just that he could think of nothing to say—and in no time at all I was out of the seminary and back on the road again. Highway Sixty-six."

Chapter 16

BRIEFLY, I WOULD LIKE to leave Neutrino where he is, a hopeful young man on the shoulder of the road, an aborigine in training, comfortable in familiar precincts, and describe his hero, Thor Heyerdahl, who sailed partway across the Pacific on a raft, in 1947. Neutrino is years from arriving at his mature phase, but one of the texts that would help him enact it was *Kon-Tiki*, Heyerdahl's account of his voyage. *Kon-Tiki* appealed deeply to Neutrino's notions of romance and endeavor, it enlarged his imagination, and it caused him to think differently about his course in life. As Heyerdahl had, he would nurture a plan that struck no one else as achievable. Also, like Heyerdahl, he would become a figure of ridicule, someone believed to have impulsively undertaken a foolhardy and deadly adventure far beyond his capacities. Finally, like Heyerdahl, he would prove everyone who doubted him wrong.

Heyerdahl was not strictly an adventurer. He was trained in Oslo, Norway, as a zoologist. In 1937 he spent a year with his wife on an island in Polynesia to collect samples of animals and to fashion an explanation for how the animals had found their ways to the islands. Instead he reached a conclusion about how man had arrived. Scholars believed that the islands had been settled by men and women who sailed or paddled boats from Asia, but sitting on the beach one night with his wife, Heyerdahl realized that the currents and the wind all came from the other direction. Furthermore, two periods of migration were responsible for the islands' culture and racial characteristics. The first migration had occurred around 500, and the second around 1100. The second wave of people had unquestionably been a Stone Age people, and no territory was then further from the Stone Age than Asia.

The straightest route to Polynesia was from South America. To Heyerdahl, the enormous stone carvings in Polynesia, the stone heads on Easter Island, for example, resembled sculptures made by ancient South American people. The community of archaeologists whose attention he was trying to engage all had an interest in dismissing his supposition. They pointed out that the South Americans couldn't have made it to Polynesia, because they had no boats, they had only rafts. Rafts couldn't be navigated, the scholars said, and they weren't sturdy enough to sail on the deep ocean anyway. Heyerdahl found drawings of the South Americans' rafts made by the first Europeans to see them.

Each had a large, square sail, a centerboard, and a steering oar, and each was made from balsa logs lashed together. Heyerdahl thought that if he built such a raft and sailed it to Polynesia his theory would be much more difficult to dismiss.

Heyerdahl recruited four Norwegians and a Swede to sail with him. In Ecuador to build their raft, they discovered that balsa trees no longer grew close to the water, where the original raft builders had found them. The trees now grew only in the jungle, and since it was the rainy season, they were inaccessible from the coast. Heyerdahl noticed on a map that the jungle extended to the foothills of the Andes. He engaged a plane to fly him and his crewmates over the jungle to the hills, so that they could come at the trees more easily. Even so, entering the forest was dangerous. The tribesmen who lived there shrank heads, and a year earlier ten American oil engineers had been shot dead by poison arrows. Heyerdahl and his party were going to travel in a Jeep, and if they broke down or became mired in the rains, they might get attacked. In the end, the army gave them an escort. The trees they cut they dragged with horses and tractors to the river then floated them to Peru.

Heyerdahl called his raft *Kon-Tiki,* after a Polynesian god. He and his crew built it in Peru, in the navy's harbor at Callao. They put their logs in the water to see which way they floated most naturally, then they placed the longest, which was forty-five feet, in the center. They had nine logs altogether, and they arranged them symmetrically around the center log. The outside logs were thirty feet long. They were advised to lash them with wires or chains, because rope would fray and split, but they felt that they wouldn't be safe unless they adhered to the ancients' example. They built a deck of bamboo and made a cabin of bamboo canes, and laid banana leaves like shingles on the roof. Where the gaps between the logs were wide, they dropped fir planks five feet deep, two feet wide, and an inch thick, then secured them by ropes and pulleys as daggerboards.

Observers generally had two opinions of the raft. Either it was too small to survive the deep ocean or exactly the right length to be lifted stern and bow by two waves and collapse in the middle. The largest exporter of balsa wood logs told Heyerdahl and his crew the logs would absorb so much water that the raft would sink before they had crossed a quarter of the way. A naval attaché scornfully promised them all the whiskey they could drink for the rest of their lives if they reached the South Sea Islands alive. A man whom Heyerdahl describes in *Kon-Tiki* as "an ambassador of one of the great powers" asked him to his office. "Your mother and father will be very grieved when they hear of your death," the ambassador said. The day before leaving, they drove into the mountains and absorbed, as a palliative, as much of the sight of rock and stone as they could.

They departed Callao on April 18, 1947. They had calculated that the trip would take ninety-seven days. They brought a parrot with them. A boat towed them fifty miles from shore, beyond the coast-wise shipping lanes. Before long they noticed that the raft sat lower in the water. Heyerdahl broke a piece off one of the logs, dropped it in the water, and watched it sink. Later he noticed two or three of the others doing the same thing and staring thoughtfully into the dark water.

The heaving of the raft made them feel as they slept that they were lying on the back of a big animal and feeling it breathe. All night the ropes creaked, like a chorus of complaint in which there were many voices. To examine the ropes underneath the raft, two men would hold the ankles of a third and lower him into the water.

After a week the sea turned from green to blue, and they realized they had left one current for another. When a flying fish landed onboard, they baited a hook with it and used it to catch dolphin. If they left a paraffin lamp out at night, the flying fish were drawn to the flame. They leapt over the raft, and if they hit the cabin or the sail, they fell to the deck. Sometimes in the darkness, they struck the sailors in the face. The cook would fry the fish for breakfast. One morning he found twenty-six of them, but half a dozen was the rule. Another morning one of the crew found a sardine on his pillow. One night a rare fish from the deep came aboard and got into one of their sleeping bags. The fish was three feet long and had a body like a snake. It had sharp teeth that withdrew into its jaw so that it could swallow its prey. Heyerdahl and his crew were the first to see it alive. Previously, only its skeletons had been found. At night, huge squid rose from the depths and appeared as "two round shining eyes" staring at them without blinking, as if trying to hypnotize them, Heyerdahl wrote, and the sight spooked all of them.

Some of the entities they saw they couldn't identify. Occasionally "balls of light three feet and more in diameter would be visible down in the water, flashing at irregular intervals like electric lights." Around two one morning they saw a faint illumination beneath them. It seemed slowly to take on the shape of a large creature. Whether the glow was accounted for by phosphorescence or the creature's body, they couldn't tell. It seemed to be round, then oval, then triangular, then it split into two parts, and then a third part emerged. The creature swam beneath them for hours. Mostly it stayed on the side of the raft where the light was. They judged it to be about the size of an elephant, but they doubted it was a whale because it never came to the surface to breathe. Shortly before daybreak it sank from sight.

They worried about an octopus reaching aboard at night and attacking them, so they slept with knives. If no shark fins were in sight at breakfast, they went swimming. They fed sharks that followed them. One of the sharks behaved almost like a dog, coming up to the raft and opening its mouth.

They had no sense of how far they had traveled, because the horizon was always at a fixed remove. By degrees they grew accustomed to the appearance of the sky at night and learned to sail by the stars.

They were weeks into the trip before the wind fell suddenly and the horizon darkened. When they slid into the troughs between waves, the waves were as high as their mast, about twenty-five feet. After the storm passed, the water became full of fish feeding on one another, leaving trails of blood. Following the second storm, they inspected the ropes and realized that if they had used chains or wires, the lashings would have cut the logs and the raft would have come apart.

On July 16 they hauled aboard a shark that vomited a starfish—a creature, that is, from the coast. The next day they saw birds, and in the days after that even more of them. One evening they noticed that the birds were all flying to the west, as if obeying a signal, and assuming the birds were heading for land, they followed them. They saw land one morning, then concluded that the current was against their reaching it. From the charts they identified the island as Pukapuka. Black smoke rose above it, which they took to be from fires the natives had set to make breakfast. It turned out that the natives were sending smoke signals inviting them to stop. Four days later another island appeared, this one in their path. As they got closer, they heard breakers making a sound against a reef like a waterfall. They looked for an opening in the reef. The black spots on the beach turned out to be people. Before long, some outrigger canoes appeared heading toward them. Two men came aboard the raft. One held out his hand and said, "Good night." Heyerdahl asked if the man spoke English. The man grinned and nodded and said,

"Good night." The crew gave the natives cigarettes. Heyerdahl made them understand that they wanted to go ashore. One of the natives bent down and made a cranking motion with his hand and said, "Brrrrr." Heyerdahl realized that he wanted them to start the engine. When he made the natives aware that there wasn't any engine, their eyes widened, and they threw down their cigarettes and left.

As night fell, four canoes appeared beside the raft. The men asked for cigarettes. Heyerdahl and the crew then gave each of them a line attached to the raft, and the men fanned out in the canoes and began paddling against the wind. One of the crew, in the raft's dinghy, paddled, too. The rest paddled aboard the raft. On the shore, the natives built a fire by the opening of the reef. Night fell. The wind rose. The natives sang while they paddled. The fire got no closer. The singing died out. They paddled for three hours, then the fire began to grow smaller. They tried to persuade the natives to get more people, but it turned out that while there were plenty more people on the beach, there were no more canoes. One of Heyerdahl's crew suggested that he row the dinghy to the shore and bring back more men. Heyerdahl thought finding a passage through the reef at night would be too dangerous. The man said he could take the leader from the canoes as a guide. Heyerdahl said he should collect him and bring him instead to the raft so that they could discuss the plan, but the man misunderstood him and picked up the leader and headed for shore.

Heyerdahl and the crew sent Morse code signals to get him to return. With fewer people paddling, the raft drifted farther from the shore. In the troughs between waves, they couldn't see the fire at all anymore. They became aware that one of the canoes had dropped its rope and left. The others dropped their ropes. One of the canoes came alongside. Heyerdahl gave the rowers a note for the man onshore, telling him to return immediately with two natives who could help him paddle and find the break in the reef. The natives left. In the darkness he heard one of them call, "Good night."

Heyerdahl left a signal lamp burning on top of the mast. The fire onshore was visible only now and then, as if merely an ember. Around ten-thirty they heard voices, and then the dinghy appeared, escorted by three canoes. The crew gave the natives presents, and they paddled home. The leader wept as he left them and gave Heyerdahl a kiss.

They drifted for three days, then set their course for the next island that came into view. It was also surrounded by a reef, but they determined to be thrown up against it and take their chances. The reef held them fast for some moments. The waves that broke over them were twenty-five feet tall. They held on to the raft with all the strength they could summon. The sea nearly crushed them, but they were able finally to jump onto the reef. The water they crossed in the lagoon beyond it was filled with creatures of nearly every color. In the deeper channels, sharks about four feet long crept up on them but turned tail when the crew slapped the water with the palms of their hands. They had sailed for 101 days.

Over their radio they reached a man in Colorado, who asked their names and where they were. When they said that they were stranded on an island in the Pacific, he stopped talking to them. A few days passed, and they saw a sail on the water, then several more. One of the natives who arrived spoke some French, and they learned that the people on the island across the lagoon had seen their fire. The elders among the natives said that because the island was uninhabited the fire must belong to a spirit, which made no one want to visit the island. Then some of Heyerdahl's canned goods washed up on their shore. The natives carried Heyerdahl and the crew to their island. Their chief had been to school in Tahiti and also had some French. When Heyerdahl told him that he was from Norway, the chief replied that Christiana was the capital of Norway. Then he asked Heyerdahl if he knew Bing Crosby.

THE PERIOD OF SETTLED calm in the seminary did not pacify Neutrino's restlessness. From Fort Worth he went to Oklahoma City, then San Francisco, then Kansas City, then back to Fort Worth. He and his mother met in Reno, and the two of them gambled.

Returning to San Francisco, Neutrino got a ride from a man who ran drugs for a chicken farm. When the farm got a big order, the hands had to chase down the birds. It took several days and required amphetamines. Three times a month the driver ran Benzedrine tablets from L.A. to Arkansas. Somewhere in the desert, Neutrino became aware that he had allowed the man to talk more than he should have, "meaning that I had information that was dangerous to him and eventually he was going to realize it," he says. Neutrino felt it was important to offer confessions of his own. Using elements of bank robberies and bad check sprees he had heard Duke and Jim describe, he made up stories about his past. He tried to make the details fascinating but not so elaborate that they were unconvincing. He told crime stories all night. In the morning they parted in Bakersfield.

Neutrino's vagabond years on Route 66 ended one evening in

San Francisco, in 1954, when he was twenty-one and he and a friend named Paul Scoletti walked into a bar in North Beach called the Vesuvio Café, where neither had been before. Three men at the bar—Dave Devine, Indian Jimmy, and Joe Henry—invited Neutrino to sit with them. Indian Jimmy was a Cherokee. He was very handsome, and he said that he was an artist. Neutrino had never met an artist, and he told Indian Jimmy that he didn't believe that he was one. On the bar were tubes of paint. Indian Jimmy began smearing paint on the wall, and Neutrino was persuaded.

Other highlights from the period: Neutrino meets Jack Kerouac and Neil Cassady, the model for Kerouac's character Dean Moriarty in *On the Road.* Cassady talks tirelessly. On occasion Neutrino occupies a booth in the Vesuvio for hours listening to him. In the Vesuvio, Neutrino also meets Allen Ginsberg, who talks passionately and at length about Zen Buddhism. Neutrino hadn't ever heard of Zen. He hadn't heard of Buddhism. Over the years, though, waiting by the road for rides, he had experienced a monotony that sometimes resolved itself into a kind of exalted blankness, an acuity that was at once tranquil and thrilling, and this sounded similar to Ginsberg's description of enlightenment.

With the determination of the self-improver, Neutrino begins to read seriously, especially Molière, Stendhal, Voltaire, and Tolstoy, the writers he heard mentioned most often in the bar.

Sitting one night in the Vesuvio with Indian Jimmy, Joe Henry, and Dave Devine, Neutrino sees two young women walk through the door. One is tall and big-boned, with red hair, pale skin, and freckles, and the other is a dwarf, "about two feet tall, with a hump on her back," Neutrino says. The tall woman's name is Eileen Cahill, and Terry is the name of the dwarf—her last name Neutrino is no longer sure of. The men invite them to their table. The women buy a pitcher of beer. They have driven from New

York for a vacation. Neutrino has a premonition that Eileen is the woman he is going to marry. It is 1956, and he is twenty-three. "I shuddered," he says. "Actually shuddered. She had finally come to collect me."

Eileen and Neutrino begin seeing each other. Terry finds work at a titty bar stripping to "Oh, You Beautiful Doll." The patrons would "hoot and laugh, but after a few minutes they stopped," Neutrino says, "because it was fascinating." In 1957, Eileen and Neutrino have a daughter, Mandy, and are married. Terry, pregnant by the owner of the bar, delivers a baby girl of normal proportions. She lives in an apartment with a Murphy bed. Each night as a kindness Neutrino arrives and lowers the bed. She is afraid of having it fall on her.

Neutrino and Eileen's marriage quickly becomes problematic. "I want to live in a tent or on a truck or a boat," Neutrino says. "She doesn't want to live on a boat, in a tent, or on a truck. Not on bicycles, either. She's a middle-class straight person who has fallen in love with a guy who wants to be a modern-day aborigine. No one's to blame, it just happens. It's easy to say now that we should have known better, but we didn't."

Determined to provide for his family without resorting to regular work, Neutrino grinds knives, unsuccessfully. With money he makes playing cards, he buys an old milk truck. He and a friend fish wood from the bay, cut it up, and sell it door to door from the truck, as firewood.

Meanwhile, Eileen withdraws from the marriage. "She's suffering," Neutrino says. "She won't take part in the party time, she doesn't care about the poets coming over for poetry readings, the artists showing their paintings, and all the talk about books. She's realized she's married into a psychotic situation that the psychopath loves. Adores it. Is totally dedicated to it. Over the moon. I realize that such an attitude must have been abhorrent to someone from a middle-class life, and I don't disagree, but I wasn't middle class. I never pretended to be, or said that I hoped to be. I was raised that way by my mother, and I enjoyed it. My life was crammed with incidents of desperation, release, and joy. Eileen wasn't creative in that way. She lacked the talent, or maybe just the inclination, for taking a whole bunch of loose puzzle parts and putting them on the ground, and making a synthesis of them. My attitude is, They might not fit, but if we file them and color them and turn them upside down and backwards and force them a little, maybe they'll fit."

Chapter 18

ANY TOUR OF TERRITORY as lush and labyrinthine as Neutrino's past, especially if it aims to be, if not definitive, at least satisfactorily accurate regarding the landscape and climate, the manners, habits, and customs of the citizens, is in peril of appearing to meander as much as the past itself. For the sake of economy then, here are the facts involving the following years in their simplest form: a second child arrives, Cahill, a boy, in 1959. Three years pass, and Eileen takes the children to New York, a trial separation. Meanwhile, Neutrino has virulent headaches and is prescribed ergotamine, a stimulant. He believes that the ergotamine endows him with special powers. He can see while asleep, he says, and while awake with his eyes closed. He begins writing a memoir, "Autobiography of a Young Man." He and Eileen and the children reunite in New York, where he becomes super of an apartment house in the Bronx. It is December. From the owner of a junkyard, Neutrino buys a bus, which doesn't run. He replaces the seats with chairs, beds, tables, rugs, and a wood-burning stove. He hangs curtains. He rigs the interior with lights. He welds a tow bar to the bumper. From a breeder in the Bronx, he buys a hunting dog. He plans to tow the bus to Louisiana, park it somewhere for free, hunt the dog in the bayous, and never go hungry again.

On the evening of the first snowfall, Neutrino loads Eileen and the children onto the bus. He settles the children in bed, lights a fire in the woodstove, then leaves them to join the car to the towing hitch. With the bus attached, the car won't move. Never crossed his mind to try moving the bus with the car. Eileen sinks into a deep depression. Snow is falling heavily. Neutrino feels it is imperative to get his family to warm weather. He uncouples the bus, loads their suitcases in the car, and leaves their furniture and the rest of what they own on the bus. In New Jersey, the car's heater gives out. Later, the dog vomits. Finally, in Mississippi, by a field, Neutrino pulls to the side of the road and looses the dog. "Now watch this," he says proudly. The dog cuts back and forth, seeking a track. "We'll never have to work again," Neutrino says. "Dog's going to do all the work for us." Across the field, a car appears, driven slowly by an old black man. The dog runs toward it.

After the death of the dog, Neutrino, Eileen, Mandy, and Cahill drive to New Orleans and rent a shotgun house on Bourbon Street. Eileen soon decides to take Mandy to New York, to visit her family. Neutrino takes Cahill to San Francisco. At a friend's house, shortly before he leaves, he meets a man named Henry Beliveau, who has just been released from the prison at Angola. In Angola, Beliveau had written a book that was 340 pages long, and was composed of only one sentence.

Chapter 19

NEUTRINO AND EILEEN meet up in New York, in 1963, and move into her mother's apartment. The mother falls ill, and her condition turns grave. Her doctor, in his office, shows Neutrino a bottle of pills. "Make sure she doesn't take more than the proper dose," he says. Neutrino nods and reaches for the pills. The doctor withdraws them. He regards Neutrino closely. "Do you understand what I'm saying?" he asks. Neutrino says, "Of course, make sure she's careful with the pills." Speaking slowly, as if to a child, the doctor says, "Mrs. Cahill is very sick. If she should happen somehow by accident to take too many pills, she would slip peacefully away, and no longer suffer." He gives Neutrino a searching look.

To spare Eileen from living with feelings of guilt, Neutrino says nothing about his conversation with the doctor. A few nights later, having gathered himself, he places his mother-in-law's head in his lap—she is unable to sit up. "Here's some pills, Mother," he says. She asks why there are so many. "The doctor says you're very sick, and you need them," he says. She swallows the pills, then closes her eyes. He strokes her hair and rocks her gently. She sighs. He weeps. Her eyelids flutter and her body shivers, as if at death, but instead of dying, she vomits, spraying pills all over the bed, "like a shower," Neutrino says, "and I think, Thank God, I'm not a murderer. I'm picking up the pills, and really crying now from the relief—God saved me from an unpardonable act—but I still have the problem of the mother-in-law."

Mrs. Cahill is dying of loneliness and needs company, Neutrino decides. "I go to the Village and get poets and ne'er-do-wells and has-beens and never-would-bes—everyone I can think of—and move them into the apartment," he says. "There's a guy named Angel, who sits by the mother-in-law's couch and holds her hand all night long. He's just a panhandler. A guy in stagnation, wanting to get by, but he comforts her. And all the people around the house keep her alive, the excitement, the talk and the chess games and the readings, and she starts getting better and better, the miracle is on. One day, though, the in-laws come over. 'Everybody's got to get out of here,' they say. I say, 'If you do that, she'll die.'"

Eileen feels unable to witness the final stages of her mother's decline. Neutrino takes a job as the super of an apartment house on the Upper West Side, and they move. He has friendships with poets and painters and fabulous talkers, from ear benders and incoherent mumblers to bashful, unassuming men who have thought for years about arcane subjects and once coaxed into describing them can hold a listener's attention for hours. Above him in the apartment house lives a Russian chess master. "He comes down to play me one night in the winter, and I still feel I have psychic powers from the ergotamine—I feel like I can see around corners, and I could predict eight moves ahead—and I had him shaking in his boots," Neutrino says. The master finally wins. He suggests they play the following night. Neutrino asks if he minds if Neutrino invites some friends. "I had had the same situation a few months earlier in Washington Square," Neutrino says. "This chess master came, and all these great chess players were there, and they all refused to play him, so I said, 'I'll play you.' I sat down, and I pushed him a pawn, a rook, a bishop, I kept forcing him to sacrifice, then I went, 'Checkmate,' and I thought he was going to have three heart attacks. Of course he wanted to play again. I should have said, 'I thought you knew how to play chess,' and walked away. So this time I went down to the Village, announcing I was playing a Russian chess master."

The next evening the apartment fills with people. While playing, the master reads a Russian newspaper. He wins so quickly that Neutrino hardly has the opportunity to speak. He waits until everyone leaves, then with a chair breaks every window in the apartment. "Snow is coming in," Neutrino says, "the wind is howling, and we're all covered with snow in the super's apartment, and I say, 'That feels better.'

"So that was the kind of thing Eileen was living with. Incredible insight and application of these powers, then the hard times. When they didn't work, I had nothing, no logic, no learning. I could see and make these incredible gestures, but if that ability deserted me, I was a fool, maybe a holy fool, but a fool nonetheless, and even I know that you can't live at such extremes all the time.

"Then I think maybe it got a little bit worse."

Chapter 20

WHAT HAPPENED? In a bar in the Village, in 1965, Neutrino ran into Henry Beliveau, the convict who had written the one-sentence book. As a remnant of his seminary days, Neutrino had been wanting to start a church, the First Church of Fulfillment, "the only church in the history of the world that didn't know the way," he says. He and Beliveau decided to collect as many people as they could "and share enough ideas and experiences that we might generate some third way, a new path. To relate to everybody no matter what his or her position, to empathize with his condition, not as a Christian or as Buddhists or Hindus but simply as researchers. I felt sure you would begin then to see cause and effect, and primal motivation, and who knew where that might lead?"

The First Church of Fulfillment replaced the cross in its iconography with balloons and a party horn. Neutrino became the church's prophet, and Beliveau became its chief priest. Among the members was a man named Morris Gold, who said he wrote speeches for President Kennedy (a claim I have not been able to confirm), and a man from an advertising agency who didn't want anyone to know his name and was called Manhattan Everyman. Neutrino phoned the FBI and said a radical group was forming in the city and perhaps the FBI should investigate them. Then he told the church members that the FBI would be attending their meetings. "I wanted everyone involved," he says, "the police, the FBI, the artists, the con men, the gamblers, the gypsies, and the junkies." Neutrino believed that the church could help junkies shed their habits. Beliveau believed that drugs were a means of salvation.

Beliveau knew a landlord with an empty building, which he persuaded him to let the church occupy. In the basement, Beliveau set up a shooting gallery for amphetamine addicts. One of them set a fire, and it burned down the building. "We gave them the bottom apartment," Neutrino says, "and it was a mistake. We should have given them the top."

The church, minus the addicts, moved into the basement apartment of a town house where Beliveau had been engaged as the super. The addicts he moved to quarters on the Lower East Side. One day Beliveau walked into Macy's and collected an armful of suits and headed for the door, pretending to be a messenger. Manhattan Everyman went to court on his behalf and told the judge that Beliveau was a literary artist—as proof he presented his one-sentence book—and managed to have him released. Christmas was approaching. Beliveau took a seasonal job at Bloomingdale's. He was to carry in a cart, from the sales floor to the mail room, the presents that people had bought and wrap and mail them. Instead, he wheeled them to his apartment. On Christmas Eve, he handed them out.

The church was attracting new members. "Morris Gold was bringing people from Washington, and Manhattan Everyman was bringing people from the advertising world, and there were people in droves from the Village, and lots of parties," Neutrino says, "but I hadn't found the key to complete healing that I had hoped to stumble on, or the solace. Henry's sect believed it was in drugs, but I never thought so. All I found on my own was temporary healing and temporary abatement of suffering."

One morning Beliveau was arrested outside the shooting gallery by two FBI agents. Nearly the entire congregation attended his trial. On the witness stand, he was asked to describe the church and its practices. His testimony was candid. In twos and threes the parishioners began quietly heading for the doors. Within hours most of them had gone to ground.

Chapter 21

Neutrino decided to take Eileen and Mandy and Cahill to San Francisco. In New Jersey he bought a step van that had been used to deliver peanuts. He put a new motor into it, and a rack on the roof to hold bags and furniture, so the family would have room in the truck to sleep. To secure the rack, he drove nails straight into the van's body. A man who was helping him said, "I never would have thought of that."

Neutrino felt that it would be edifying for the family to see the Rockies and the Great Plains in winter. On the first day, entering a tunnel, he knocked the roof off the van. "Now it's a convertible," he says. The interior could no longer be heated. All across the country, when it snowed, the snow fell on them. It was as if they were traveling in a sleigh. Neutrino paid for gas by grinding knives. By the time they reached San Francisco, he and Eileen were barely speaking. He decided that she should be allowed to choose what they did next. She got a job as the assistant editor of a newspaper called the *San Francisco Progressive,* and within a year, she became the editor. Neutrino cared for the children. Meanwhile he finished "Autobiography of a Young Man."

"I showed it to several people and eventually realized that while there were parts of it that were memorable—perhaps even poignant—no one was going to struggle through the rest," he says. "Unless there was something wrong with them, unless they were simply into babble and misarranged words."

Chapter 22

FINALLY THEY SEPARATED. Neutrino said to Eileen, "You're really happy, aren't you?" and she said she was. He said, "I've got to go to the desert, I'm not going to make it otherwise," and she said, "Maybe you should go."

Neutrino went to Gerlach, where years before he had met Danny Elkins, the diver he went to Mexico with. About half a mile outside Gerlach are hot pools where Neutrino spent a month. Then he got a job washing dishes at a café in town. Six months passed, and Eileen came to Gerlach. She and Neutrino discussed getting back together. Neutrino said that he couldn't return to the city, she would have to join him. When her lawyer said, "We'll get him for alimony and child support," she said, "Don't even bother."

Chapter 23

RAFTS: WILLIAM WILLIS, Neutrino's other hero, made two trips on the Pacific in rafts. The first, in 1954, when he was sixty-one, took him from Peru to Samoa, 6,700 miles (Heyerdahl had sailed 4,500 miles), and the second, begun in 1963, when he was seventy, took him from Peru to Australia, 10,000 miles, the longest raft trip ever. The first trip was made on a raft built of balsa logs from a forest in Ecuador lashed together, in imitation of Heyerdahl, and the second trip was made on a raft built of steel pipes and pontoons filled with foam.

Willis was born in Hamburg, Germany, in 1893. He was fifteen when he began working aboard sailing ships. He moved to America when he was seventeen. In addition to being a merchant sailor, he was a longshoreman in California; a logger in Alaska, California, and the Pacific Northwest; a hand in the wheat harvests on the Great Plains; and a wildcatter in the Texas oil fields. In *The Epic Voyage of the Seven Little Sisters*, his book about his first trip, he says that since childhood he had felt "a conviction that by living a vigorous, natural life in accordance with what I considered Nature's laws I could get still closer to her and so partake of her strength. This to me was the path to happiness." Willis wrote six books, among them a book of poems called *Hell, Hail and Hurricanes.*

Willis married a theatrical agent in New York who had an office in Rockefeller Center. To prepare for his first trip, he read charts in the map room of the New York Public Library, on Forty-second Street. He left Peru in June of 1954. His wife made him promise that he wouldn't go all the way to Australia. He took with him a black cat and a parrot. He ate barley flour mixed with water, and a cereal from the Andes. To keep awake, he ate raw sugar and drank instant coffee, usually cold, because his stove took so long to heat water, and then it broke anyway.

As he sat through storms, he wondered how much his raft could take before it would come apart. He described the waves as "a symphony of disaster," and storms as assassins. He worried about falling and breaking an arm or a leg, especially at night, when he often couldn't see and sometimes had to jump without knowing if there was an obstacle between him and the deck.

Fishing for dolphin, he caught a shark, and in retrieving the hook, he fell overboard. The raft sailed away without him. Before his mind focused, he thought how lovely she looked, rising and falling on the waves and with her sail full. Then he realized that the fishing line wrapped around his wrist was attached to the raft. About two hundred feet lay between them. The line was frayed. It had been given to him in Peru by a tuna fisherman who thought it could no longer hold a fish. If it snapped, Willis was lost. On the raft he had line he had bought in New York, but he hadn't got around to installing it. Hand over hand, he began pulling himself toward the raft. His sweater and his pants and his socks and shoes dragged him down. The wind rose. The line cut one of his hands deeply, and the water around him began to fill with blood. He wondered where the sharks were that had been following him for days, particularly one about nine feet long whom he called Long Tom and who for weeks had seemed to be underneath the raft or just behind it. When Willis had finally hauled himself aboard, he found a needle and thread and sewed his hand.

In the middle of July, Willis's stomach began to tighten. It continued to tighten until he felt as if he had been shot. He hoped the pain would increase sufficiently that he would faint. After several hours a voice began telling him to cut out the knot that was causing the pain, and while he stared at a knife in his cabin, he struggled for possession of himself. Sending an SOS he regarded as a gesture of defeat. Even so, he filled the parrot's cage with sufficient food to last several weeks, and he gave the cat extra fish. He wrote a note explaining what had happened, and a letter to his wife, and he tacked them to the cabin door. Setting up his radio took an hour. He sent the SOS; then he took aspirin and lay down in the cabin to see if he could sleep. When he woke he realized that the pain had lessened. He canceled the SOS. No one had responded anyway.

Little by little, Willis recovered his strength. Meanwhile, he felt that he had never been happier. He thought that if he could only sail long enough, "an understanding of all things would come" to him. The dolphins that jumped at night around the raft made sounds like gunshots when they hit the water. The flying fish who landed on the deck tended to find the seams between the logs and fall back into the sea, unless the cat got them first. Willis used the ones he could catch as bait for the dolphins. On nights of the full moon, the entire sea was silver.

Willis was halfway across the Pacific when he discovered that salt had corroded the seams of his water cans. Almost all of his water had leaked out. He allowed himself one cup a day and supplemented it by drinking two cups of seawater, which he regarded as a tonic. He was careful to dip his cup in the water only when he hadn't seen any sharks for a while.

Often, from exhaustion, he had difficulty remembering what he had just been doing. On the first of September, the sun rose with a copper tint that he had never seen. It was there in the evening, too, and he deduced it was an ominous sign. The storm that arrived was dry, meaning he got no water. It lasted two days and filled the ocean around him with sharks. He washed the deck thoroughly each time he fished, so that he didn't slip and fall in among them.

The parrot sometimes reproduced human voices so compellingly that Willis would stop what he was doing to assure himself that he was alone. One evening, when the isolation bore down on him heavily, he began singing and felt better. After that he sang every evening. It took about fifty minutes to sing all the songs he knew. Sometimes he dreamed of New York, where his wife was.

There were so many sharks around the raft one morning that the sea seemed colored with them. A storm arrived, bringing with it, finally, such heavy rain that he was able to collect seven and a half gallons of it. It made him feel rich. He made coffee and sat on the deck and ate raw sugar.

By September, he had sufficient energy for only the simplest work. Trying one afternoon to fix a tear in the sail, he fell to the deck and hit his head. When he woke, it was night. His head hurt terribly, and he wanted to vomit. He passed out again, and the next time he opened his eyes the sun was beating down on him. So far as he could tell, it was the following afternoon. His body was numb. When he remembered what had happened, he felt that his vanity had also been wounded. Nothing short of a fractured skull should have knocked him out, he thought. He drank coffee and took aspirin and gathered himself to work.

In the patterns of light around the raft, he once thought he saw an octopus extending enormous tentacles toward him, and he ran for his ax. Lying one afternoon asleep on the deck, he suddenly woke and in a wave looming above him saw a shark that looked ready to attack him. He jumped up to defend himself. The shark fell, and the raft rose on the wave that had contained it. Occasionally at night, the sparks of phosphorescence thrown up by the bow would seem to merge with the sky, and he would feel as if he were sailing among the stars.

Even though he wore sunglasses, the sun eventually blinded him, and he had to remain for hours at a time in the cabin, bathing his eyes with salt water for the pain. The first island where he might have landed was surrounded by reefs and had no shore. No one answered his radio call for help, so he had to sail past it. During a squall he heard a crash in the cabin but was too busy to address it. The cat had toppled the parrot's cage and killed the parrot. Willis sewed its remains in a piece of sail, put them in the cage, and lowered them overboard. After finding no way to enter a harbor on a second island, he saw an American ship headed toward him, and they towed him to land. He had been at sea for 112 days.

Chapter 24

To illuminate the brighter occasions of the following few years, we return to our former breathless pace: Solitary again, Neutrino begins to feel that the peripatetic life offers the opportunity to address concerns that have been suggested by the bohemians in North Beach and the books he has read. If he walks and broods, he might enlarge himself. Isolation might play a part. It is 1968.

In San Francisco, he buys a motorcycle. Driving down Leavenworth Street, he sees a young woman turning a key in the door of an apartment house. He stops and asks if he might come in for a cup of coffee. She says no. Tea? he asks. No. He asks if she wants a ride on his motorcycle, and she considers and then says yes.

Her name is Maxine Goldstein, she is twenty-two, and a year earlier she had come from New York to study painting in graduate school. After six months it became time to specialize in a style, and she didn't feel ready to, so she dropped out. The morning she meets Neutrino she has decided that she will have to find a job.

Within a few days they have resolved to live in the desert in Mexico. Neutrino concludes that the motorcycle is too dangerous, so he sells it. They ride a bus to San Diego. Carrying two army blankets and a briefcase containing a mosquito net, two plates, knives and forks, and a can opener, they walk across the border. In each cup of her bra, Maxine is carrying a drinking cup, and in a pocket of her skirt that has a zipper she has six twenty-dollar bills.

From Tijuana they walk down Baja. Neutrino sees a man in a small town painting a sign and thinks, I could do that. When they need money, he looks for a place that needs a sign. All that exists of a road through the country is a rutty, two-track path made by the wagons and trucks and the few cars that travel it. Approximately once a day a truck appears, and usually it stops for them. "The towns on the map were always a hundred miles apart," Maxine says, "and when you got to them you saw they were only one house." The people strike her as living in a former time. "Everything they had they'd share," she says, "and they'd never ask for anything in return."

Chapter 25

THEY MAKE THEIR WAY to La Paz, where they board a freighter to the mainland. Hitchhiking, they are picked up by a man who says he shoots pistols for the Mexican Olympic team. He is on his way to pistol practice. All afternoon Maxine and Neutrino watch the man and his teammates load their guns and quickly fire six shots. In the evening he buys them dinner. It turns out that he is a soda manufacturer. After dinner they go to his factory. In his office, there are guns hanging on the wall and guns on the desk. A door in the office opens on a small apartment, where the man says that Maxine and Neutrino can spend the night. It is too late for him to go home, he says. Rather than wake his wife, he will sleep in the office.

From the apartment a window, covered by a shade, looks into the office. Maxine gets into bed, and Neutrino pulls the shade aside discreetly. The man is pacing in his underwear. In each hand he has a pistol. Every few steps he bends over and holds the sides of his head, as if he is in pain. Then he runs out into the street and fires two shots. When he comes back he continues pacing and holding his head. After a while he begins groaning also.

The door between the office and the apartment has no lock.

Neutrino wakes Maxine. In the room is a refrigerator filled with soda bottles. Neutrino quietly builds a pyramid of bottles in front of the door. The bottles left over he spreads on the floor. He moves the mattress to a different corner, then he unscrews the lightbulb, so that if the man opens the door, he will be silhouetted by the light behind him and Neutrino will have a target to aim at with a bottle. Maxine goes back to sleep, and Neutrino sits on the edge of the bed. When the sun rises, he looks through the window and sees the man asleep on a couch. His guns are under his pillow. "So I realized the worst was over," Neutrino says, "and I put the bottles back. We went to his house for breakfast, and just as we finished, he reached over and put a large wad of bills in my hand and said, 'Once you start shooting, it's very hard to stop,' and he took us to the bus station and left us."

Chapter 26

In 1969, MAXINE AND NEUTRINO are in New York, where Neutrino is again the super of an apartment house. In the basement, he begins building a canoe. He tells Maxine that they are going to carry the canoe to the East River, then paddle and drift to Cuba and shake Castro's hand. "He had a thousand plans," Maxine says, "and only some of them ever came into being, and I learned not to object if I disagreed, because I might be objecting to something that might never happen." After six months they go to San Francisco. The canoe, it turns out, is too wide to be carried up the basement stairs. Before Neutrino abandons it, he tries to chip away at the stairs.

Maxine becomes pregnant. "I was so addicted to the road that I wanted to keep moving," she says. Neutrino insists they stay in San Francisco. If they are traveling, he worries that they won't find a hospital when they need to. Ingrid, their daughter, is about a year old when they buy a school bus and travel through Utah, Oregon, Washington, and California, and eventually arrive in San Diego, where Neutrino buys a nineteen-foot motorboat. The boat has no cabin. Maxine suggests they take it to Florida and travel on the Intracoastal Waterway. Neutrino looks at a map and decides to launch it instead in Tulsa, Oklahoma, in the Arkansas River, then travel to the Mississippi and eventually to New Orleans. They leave San Diego towing the boat behind the school bus, which breaks down in New Mexico. For a few hundred dollars, they junk the bus, then stand beside the highway with the boat on its trailer. The man who stops for them has a towing hitch, and he takes them all the way to Tulsa.

Chapter 27

TEMPORARILY, NEUTRINO has tired of solitary wandering. He regards what he has learned about living on the road as valuable and wants to share it. He wants to lead a group of people around the country and have adventures and teach them while they travel how to arrive in a town where they've never been and find work painting signs and a place to live. Someone who can do that can go anywhere and adapt to whatever comes his way and have time left over to read and have conversations and pursue his heart's other desires. Neutrino, now back in California, plans to call his outfit the Salvation Navy.

For the Navy's premises, Neutrino leases a flophouse in San Francisco. Half of it he manages for the owner, and half he rents to members of the Navy, who pay for their rooms with their welfare checks. To learn how to shepherd a flock through spiritual and emotional difficulties, Neutrino adds himself to a group that follows the teachings of G. I. Gurdjieff, the Middle Eastern mystic. The man who runs the Gurdjieff sessions sends the Navy a cook, a black man who has just been released from a mental institution.

"He thought he was an advertising man, but he was really just a guy who was a great cook," Neutrino says. "He would walk around the kitchen describing the campaigns he had waged in the advertising world. Totally delusional." From a butcher Neutrino receives free chicken necks and backs. "There was no meat on them," Neutrino says, "but the supply was endless. They came in frozen containers, and the cook made great-looking meals, using hundreds of chicken backs, and we had people off the streets studying jewelry making and sign painting."

After a year, Neutrino realizes that he has an organization that is collecting clothes and feeding people and teaching them trades, but he doesn't have what he wants, which is a center for interesting, intelligent, and creative people who have ideas to exchange and knowledge to share. He had hoped that people would come and go, as he always had—one person in the door and one person out—but people tend to show up and stay. So he shuts it down.

Rafts redux: william willis made his crossing
to Australia in 1963. He was seventy years old. Searching the
jungle for balsa wood trees was more than he felt capable of. He
built his new raft in a boatyard in New Jersey, on the Passaic
River. He filled three pontoons with foam, placed two of them in
the stern and one in the bow, and welded them together with
pipes. The raft was thirty-four feet long and about twenty feet
wide and had the approximate shape of a sailboat. The deck was
of pine, and he built a cabin on it, and he raised a mast that was
thirty-eight feet tall. In May he floated down the river to
Newark and loaded the raft aboard a freighter that was stopping
in Callao, Peru.

Steel, it turned out, was rigid, whereas balsa wood was flex-
ible. The raft rode heavily. "Its motion was violent and continu-
ous," Willis wrote in *Whom the Sea Has Taken*, his account of
the trip. In a sea of any vigor, he had a lot of trouble standing.
The effort fatigued him. While a boat might hold its course for as
many as three thousand miles without a hand's ever touching the
tiller, Willis wrote, the raft required constant attention. Moreover, steering required so much strength that he could only do it
standing up.

Before Willis left New York, he persuaded his wife that they
could communicate telepathically. He left Callao in July. In August he saw her standing on the deck. He also saw his mother,
who had been dead for years. In September he developed the apprehension that his wife had been killed in a car accident. A few

weeks later he heard a voice telling him that he was doomed and that his only hope for saving himself was to abandon the raft and swim. He arrived in Samoa in November of 1963. In addition to being exhausted, he had a severe hernia. He worried that if he continued it might cause a blockage that would turn septic. His wife insisted he come to New York and be treated. He asked the Samoan government to keep watch over the raft. When the doctors recommended surgery, Willis concluded that, before he could recover, his raft would rust and sink, so he decided to sail with the hernia. His wife wanted to go with him, but he wouldn't let her.

Willis left Samoa in June of 1964. A man and his wife who had been observing his preparations told him that they planned to follow him in a boat and film his crossing. Willis needed whatever money he might raise from his adventure for himself. To get shed of the couple, he arranged to be towed to sea at night. Immediately he had trouble with his hernia. To settle it, he wrapped a rope around his ankles and hung himself upside down, turning from side to side until it fell into place. The effort took several hours. He had to repeat it on a number of occasions.

A month into the trip he tried to go ashore at an island to collect coconuts. He had with him, as a lifeboat, an outrigger canoe, and he boarded it. The sea was calm, and he left the raft unmoored. While he was paddling the canoe, a squall came up and took the raft. Willis turned the canoe to follow it, and the outrigger tore its fittings. It took him an hour to catch the raft.

In August he was pulling a line on the sail one night when the line suddenly gave way, and he fell back hard into an iron boom, with the result that he was paralyzed. When the sun rose, he still couldn't move his legs. The raft drifted. He dragged himself to the cabin and opened a can of beans. It was four days before he could stand. A week later he turned seventy-one.

Willis arrived in Australia in September of 1964. He anchored the raft and waded ashore with his passport. It took him a while to find someone to announce himself to. "I'm Willis from New York," he said.

In 1966, when Willis was seventy-two, he left New York to cross the North Atlantic in a twelve-foot sailboat named *Little One*. He called this adventure "The Oldest Man in the Smallest Boat." He had trouble with another hernia not long after he left and was picked up by a freighter and brought home. He left again the following year. This time he had bad luck with winds and had been at sea for eighty-nine days, when exhausted, he was rescued by a fishing boat. He waited a year for the favorable season and tried again. After eighty days, the boat was found, by a Russian trawler, but Willis never was. He had been seventy-four.

Chapter 29

WE HEAD NOW INTO the Late Period, in which a semblance of coherence finally appears. Still casting about for some way to make what he knows available to people who might wish to use it, Neutrino takes up with The Fellowship of Souls, who follow the teachings of a spirit guide named Michael. It is 1974. The leader of the Fellowship, Sarah Chambers, communicates with Michael through a Ouija board. The Fellowship meets in her house, in the Berkeley hills, and for a while Neutrino and Maxine and Ingrid, their daughter, live in a truck at the bottom of her driveway. Chambers has about a hundred followers, the bulk of them also prosperous. Neutrino spends six months among them and becomes persuaded that they are too comfortable to feel the desperation to act that he does.

"When a man doesn't see his situation as desperate," Neutrino says, "he thinks, This is the way things are, I'll get through it. He doesn't think, This lifetime doesn't come around forever, I have these opportunities to fulfill myself, to discover and learn. They're all very accomplished people, scholars and doctors and lawyers, insulated by money and education and position. They were wonderful, but there was not one person in that group that had any direction. They were like people in the movies—airy people who are so delightful—but they had absolutely no core. I couldn't move them to desperation, and I couldn't work where people weren't desperate."

Neutrino decides to take to the road with Maxine and Ingrid and any members of the Fellowship who want to come with them. Eleven people volunteer. He intends to teach them to take control of their lives by means of imaginative, fearless, and logical thinking—the distillation, that is, of a Gurdjieffian concept called active reasoning. They leave California driving trucks. One truck has been used to move furniture, one to sell hot dogs, one to deliver peanuts, and one to deliver vegetables. There is very little privacy. They are continually stopped by the police.

In Montana a motel owner hires them to paint the background of an old neon sign. Neutrino leaves the group in the parking lot to set up scaffolding. When they try to move the scaffolding, they discover they have forgotten to put the wheels on it. To add the wheels, they tip the scaffolding, which falls over and breaks the sign and the motel's picture window. The police are called. To appease the owner the group has to paint the motel.

"So I realized I am on the road with incompetent people," Neutrino says. "If I had started off with people on a higher level, it would have been fun. But I started with people that had nothing in the way of personal resources. Zero, and minus zero. They are from upper-middle-class whimsy backgrounds, and nothing has ever tested them. They're young. I'm forty-two. I have eleven young people with me that I'm going to lead to the Promised Land. The Promised Land is the ability to actively reason, not to be afraid of the reasoning process. I must have been nuts.

"From that point on I had to find a protected place where we could build up our confidence. Everyone in those days was buying farms, but these people don't have the ability to plow and sow and harvest crops and raise animals. They don't have the competency to labor efficiently. They have the competency to float. For years I've talked about the Salvation Navy, and now I realize I've got to get them to water."

Painting the motel takes a week, then the Navy drives in a caravan to Sioux City, Iowa, the first sizable town on the Missouri River after which there are no dams. In the bayous above New Orleans, Neutrino had seen houses floating on rafts made from barrels. In Sioux City he stands on the riverbank, points toward the town, and like a prophet says, "Our raft is that way." The Navy walks until they come to a factory with a creek behind it. The factory makes barrels. The owner has a number of three-hundred-gallon barrels that have small dents. The customer regarded the dents as flaws and wouldn't accept the barrels. The owner gives Neutrino fourteen of them. In the creek behind the factory, he places the barrels in two rows and lays a floor on them. The raft is thirty-nine feet long and sixteen feet wide. Neutrino calls it the *Miss Leslie.* He rows it down the creek and into the Missouri River. Some of the Navy drive the trucks downriver to Omaha, about a hundred miles, and some travel on the raft with Neutrino. He arrives in Omaha after several days, around eight at night. The next morning, he hears of a house's being torn down. The contractor gives Neutrino wood from the house, and from it he builds cabins on the deck.

The Navy floats down the Missouri and into the Mississippi, putting in to shore to paint signs, and at the end of six months they arrive in New Orleans. They sail into the Gulf of Mexico, and along the Mississippi coast, past Gulfport and Biloxi, and into Alabama. As they enter Mobile Bay, the wind rises, and the surface of the water takes on the appearance of a washboard. The waves grow to five feet, with three feet between them, and shake the raft to pieces.

In New Orleans the Navy builds a raft that has a paddle wheel. For two years they sail along the Gulf Coast, through Texas, Mississippi, Louisiana, Alabama, and Florida, until Neutrino decides that they have become complacent. He gives the raft to a black family of migrant fruit pickers traveling in four cars who stop for them when they are hitchhiking. He decides that the Navy should go to Texas. Two gypsies, Frank and Bob, a father and son, stop for them. The gypsies are transporting three cars to Texas. Until they pick up Neutrino and the Navy, they have been driving two of the cars a few hundred miles ahead then parking one and returning for the other. From Brownsville the Navy enters Mexico.

Chapter 30

By late 1976, the Navy is down to eight people. They paint signs on buildings and trucks, sometimes for pesos, sometimes for oranges, sometimes for tortillas, and they walk and hitchhike and ride trains down the east coast of Mexico, through Tampico and Poza Rica and Veracruz and Campeche, to Mérida, in the Yucatán, two thousand miles. Then they cross over to Puerto Escondido, south of Acapulco, on the Pacific.

Maxine and Neutrino are walking one evening down a road by the ocean. Beside the road is a dog that appears to be dead. His bones stand out prominently, and his head is grotesquely swollen. As they pass, he opens one eye. Neutrino finds a blanket and lifts the dog onto it, then he and Maxine carry the dog to the beach. They place him gently in the shade beneath a palm tree. One of the dog's hindquarters slips off the blanket, and Neutrino restores it. As he does, he has the peculiar feeling that the dog is smiling at him. The dog lifts its head and moves to lick Neutrino's hand. Still seeming to grin, he doesn't lick it, he bites it. His teeth break the skin. Then he dies.

Neutrino tells a Mexican doctor that he's been bitten by a dog with a swollen head that died, and the doctor tells him not to worry. "Nothing's going to happen," he says. "Enjoy being in Mexico."

The Navy hitchhikes to Tucson, then rides bicycles to Sacramento, where they are joined by Cahill, Neutrino and Eileen's son, who is twenty-one. Cahill can throw a baseball with either hand. "He has a pitching motion that was very deceptive," Neutrino says. "The hitters can't read it. Furthermore, the ball has to be halfway to the plate before they could tell how fast it was traveling. All they ever hit is little bloopers."

Neutrino arranges for Cahill a tryout in Mexico with a team that Fernando Valenzuela pitched for. The Navy rides back to Mexico. The heat is relentless. They sleep in the backs of trucks at truck stops or in tents in the bushes of empty lots, waiting until darkness to set up their camp and leaving before dawn, or in someone's backyard if they have permission, or in a motel room, when one can be found that is cheap enough. A newspaper prints an article about the American family riding bicycles to Mexico so that the son can try out for a Mexican baseball team. Neutrino laminates the article. He displays it in restaurants and hotels and asks the managers for a meal or a place to sleep. If his son makes the team, he says, the family will pay him back, and if he doesn't the manager will at least have the story to tell. He is surprised that it works more often at good hotels than at poor ones.

Cahill auditions for more than one team. Neutrino tells him what pitches to throw or how to conduct himself, and Cahill does the opposite, or they argue almost until it is time for Cahill to take the mound. "It's heartbreaking," Neutrino says. "One time they ask him to throw a fastball. He has slow and slower and slower, and another one that went slower, but he has a knuckleball that goes eighty-five miles an hour, and I want him to throw that because it is such an interesting pitch. I figure this would show them a variation they don't expect." The scouts are impressed by the exotic quality of Cahill's abilities, but no one presents him with a paper to sign.

Cahill returns to California. Neutrino, Maxine, Ingrid, Betsy Terrell, and her daughter, Marisa, join a mud circus in Mexico— one that can travel only on back roads, because its vehicles aren't registered. The circus is run by a husband and wife whose children are the performers. The father has taught them to juggle and throw knives, to balance plates and balls on sticks mounted on their chins, to walk a tightrope, use the trapeze, and play clowns. Terrell makes doughnuts and sells them among the crowd during the parade of stars—the walk by the performers around the ring before the show starts. Meanwhile, Marisa, trained by the father, turns somersaults in the aisle. The father also teaches Terrell to walk the tightrope by starting with the rope on the ground, then raising it by degrees. The circus frequently performs by torchlight in towns that have no electricity. The father is a spendthrift. The circus trucks are decrepit. "It takes all day to get the trucks started, then we go two miles down the road and stop and do laundry, and it takes all night to get the trucks started again," Neutrino says. When the father has money, he is more likely to drive a hundred miles to buy popcorn for the circus than to repair the trucks.

Neutrino has the idea that he can establish the family on a solid footing if he can persuade the father to turn over the circus's financial affairs to his oldest son. He draws up a contract, and the father signs it. Neutrino buys a generator, a projector, and several reels of old cartoons. On posters he puts up when the circus arrives in town, he advertises the showing of cartoons before the evening's performance. The first night so many people turn out that there isn't room for them all in the tent. The ones left outside lift the flaps to try to see the cartoons. The circus has to schedule additional performances. With the money, the father wants to buy more seats. Neutrino insists that the trucks be fixed. The son wants the trucks fixed, too. The father refuses to give his son the control he had agreed to, and Neutrino, exasperated, gives up. By the time he and the Navy depart, Terrell is practicing on a tightrope that is five feet above the ground.

As Neutrino leaves Mexico, the arm on which the dog bit him begins to stiffen. The next day it is numb. Over the following few days he falls horribly sick. By the time the Navy reaches Tucson, he can walk only about a hundred feet without needing to rest. Every part of him hurts, and he can't bear being touched. He loses eighty pounds. His face becomes so deeply drawn as to look cadaverous. The sight of him frightens Ingrid to tears. Whenever he sees his reflection, he thinks, I look just like that dog that bit me.

In Tucson the Navy buys a school bus and drives to California. Neutrino quickly feels too sick to continue. He wants to be by himself. He decides to ride his bicycle across the Rockies and into Colorado. He names the town where he will meet the others in two weeks, but he assumes he will die on the way. If he doesn't die, he thinks he might, through the effort of making it over the mountains, recover.

Betsy Terrell is the first to see Neutrino in Colorado, shuffling along the street, and when she does, she weeps. He is in far worse shape than he was when he left them. They return to San Francisco, and Neutrino takes a room at the Bristol Hotel, where he was living as a boy when he saw the movie about aborigines. Maxine and Ingrid, knowing how the hotel figures in his past, assume that he intends to die there. His illness has made him a burden.

"They've had it with me," he says. "They all need a break." Neutrino takes the school bus to Mexico. He has begun to bleed constantly from his backside, so there is always a dark stripe down his pants, from his seat to his cuff. After a few months he goes back to San Francisco. His spirits have been raised, but he still feels terrible. Along the way he checks into a hospital in Texas. The doctors want to operate to discover what is wrong, but Neutrino won't let them. In San Francisco he joins up with Ingrid and Maxine, and Betsy and Marisa, and they return to Mexico, where codeine, the only thing that mitigates his pain, is cheap. Betsy gets hold of a saxophone that has no keypads. It makes no sound, but in a kind of Zen exercise, she fingers the keys according to instructions in a book. She learns the fingerings to one song, "Mexicali Rose." She trades a radio for a saxophone that works and is surprised that she can actually play it. For a year, all of them subsist on what she earns by going into cantinas with Marisa, who dances while her mother plays and passes the hat. They have reached their lowest point.

Having crossed the plains and arrived at the foothills, our caravan slows. The camels are watered, the tents are raised. From here to the market, the sights grow ever more picturesque.

Next, and somewhat inevitably, Maxine and Neutrino separated. Maxine had never cared for the Navy. She liked having adventures in the desert with Neutrino. She moved to Texas. Neutrino eventually took up with Terrell. In 1983, they had a daughter, Jessica. Neutrino was aware of how his illness weighed on his family, and he was intent on finding a means for them to subsist. He decided that they should learn to play instruments and form a band. He called the band the Flying Neutrinos. A woman named Donna Londagin, one of the early members of the Navy, quit her job as a secretary in California and came to play accordion with them. She brought her young son, Todd, who played the trombone. His arms were too short to reach some of the stops. Another friend, Leslie Ronald, played tuba. Marisa played drums. Ingrid danced and sang. Neutrino played guitar, poorly. He was still terribly sick and taking codeine. They slept in doorways and train stations and cheap hotels. "We're homeless and on the street," he says. "At fifty I had to learn a new trade, and we had to start over."

The Flying Neutrinos played in Puerto Escondido, and when it seemed that everyone there had heard them too often to give them any more money, they went to Durango and then to Monterrey. "We were pitiful," Terrell says. "All we did was stumble from

town to town." Americans wouldn't put money in their hat—
"Americans don't like losers," Neutrino once told a reporter—
but Mexicans would. "The Mexicans loved us," Neutrino says.
"We were untutored, we were raw, we were crude and unkempt,
but we were optimistic, and they loved the optimism."

Little by little, the musicians improved. Neutrino took the
band one day to a prosperous beach town. They played "The
Darktown Strutters' Ball," and when they were finished, the
tourists, instead of insulting them as usual, clapped and gave them
money as not usual. Neutrino thought, We're going to New Orleans to learn to do this right. Before they left, he bought everyone black-and-white outfits.

They drove a school bus to Freeport, Texas, on the Gulf
Coast, where they lived for three months in an abandoned boat
shed on a bank of the Brazos River and built a raft. Neutrino
traded the bus for an outboard motor, and they sailed the raft
across the Gulf of Mexico to New Orleans. They landed in the
French Quarter, and the police chased them off. They crossed
the Mississippi to Algiers, where their raft was broken into and
ransacked. They moved, and the raft was broken into again. Finally they moored in a canal beneath an overpass, far enough
away from everyone else that no one bothered them.

Wearing their black-and-white outfits and wheeling their
drums in a shopping cart, they arrived at a square where musicians played. "We looked really sharp," Neutrino says. "We
looked like a bunch of penguins, but it was a knocked-out look."
The black singer occupying the most favorable spot saw them
and stopped singing. To the crowd he had gathered he announced, "We're going to give up our place to this new band just
hit town." He asked Neutrino, "What do you call yourselves?"

Neutrino told him, and he said, "Ladies and gentlemen, the
Flying Latrinos are here."

Neutrino says that he will remember forever the look on the man's face when the band started playing. "He and everyone around us moved away like we were pariahs," he says. The New Orleans *Times-Picayune,* in its issue for December 12, 1985, has an article with the title "Musical Gypsies Park Ark in Industrial Canal." From it Neutrino likes to quote these nicely written sentences: "They are poor, and they look it. . . . As self-taught street musicians, they play tinny show tunes and Mexican ballads with desperate enthusiasm on French Quarter streets while the children dance and smile for the crowd."

None of the musicians they encountered would have anything to do with them. "Nothing," Neutrino says. "I didn't know anything about music, and I was trying to force the issue. If you don't know it, I was thinking, at least force it."

After a few weeks, they met a trumpet player named Joe T. Johnson, who owned a silver trumpet that he called Josephine. "He took mercy on us," Neutrino says. Johnson taught Terrell to sing, and for about two months he worked with all of them on their tonality and phrasing. From his example they drew confidence. For 25 percent of their take, he also played with them. When other musicians saw Johnson performing, they agreed to perform also. Neutrino's plan was to surround himself with good musicians, while Ingrid and Todd, who were talented, improved. Sometimes Neutrino had as many as six other musicians sitting in, each receiving a quarter of the take, so he lost money, but he was consoled by everyone's getting better. To a reporter he said, "We're not winners yet, but we're not the losers we were."

In a bar one night a drummer named Al Jay Schenk explained to Neutrino the principles of the New Orleans rhythm. It was essential, he said, that the guitar play each beat in a four-beat measure, the drums play as if in two-four time—one *two*, one *two,* that is—and against it the bass play the first and third beats. Neutrino went home and woke everyone up, and they practiced until he felt they had absorbed it, and "after that," he says, "we were never without money again."

Early in 1987, Neutrino considered that the Flying Neutrinos were ready for the bigtop, and they went to New York City. Playing in the subways for thirty days, they made ten thousand dollars. They lived in the penthouse of a hotel off Times Square and ate all their meals in delicatessens. Neutrino bought "the biggest panel truck I've ever seen, it looked like a library," he says, and they drove it to a buskers' convention in Halifax, Nova Scotia, where they performed for an amount of money that left them free to travel for several months. When they returned to New York, the subways were full of young men from Peru wearing ponchos and playing guitars and wooden flutes. Neutrino had difficulty finding places for the family to play, so they went to Mexico, where Neutrino met the owner of a small traveling carnival called Circus Hermanos Bells. Neutrino told him that he had a band, and the owner hired them. After they had been with the circus for several weeks, Neutrino suggested to the owner that he should change the format of the parade the circus held to announce its arrival in town. The Flying Neutrinos should play Glenn Miller songs, he said, and the three elephants should sway to the beat. "It turned out to be a complete flop, an embarrassment," Neutrino says, "and the owner was mad at himself for listening to me, so he fired us."

Neutrino persuaded some of the members of Circus Hermanos Bells to start another circus, Circo Teresa. "We had a deaf-mute ninja who had a contortion act," he says. "We had the Flying Neutrino band, we had a clown, and we had a mother and father that sold tacos. Teresa was the mother." It was while traveling with Circo Teresa that Neutrino developed a large sore on his backside. Whatever had sickened him seemed to have bored its way through his body and emerged through the sore, and finally he began to feel better.

Chapter 32

LATE IN 1987 the Flying Neutrinos drove a truck back to New York. The apartments they looked at were too expensive. They slept in the truck. They were parked one night at Sixty-eighth Street and Broadway, near Lincoln Center, when Neutrino was awakened by the sound of glass breaking—some kids had thrown a brick through the window of a jewelry store. Neutrino fell back asleep and dreamed that if the family dressed as Pilgrims they would make a lot of money. He interpreted the dream to mean that they should go to Provincetown, Massachusetts, at the end of Cape Cod, where the Pilgrims first landed.

In Provincetown, Neutrino was given a dilapidated barge. With parts of floating docks that had been thrown away and driftwood he found in the harbor, he and the family built a raft on the barge hull. From scavenged lumber, they built two paddle wheels, one for each side of the bow. The paddle wheels turned by means of a motor that had been part of a generator discarded from the town hall, so Neutrino called the raft *Town Hall.* It was cumbersome and unsightly, but the paddle wheels, painted yellow and blue and red, gave it a rakish appeal. Neutrino kept the raft at a dock near the center of town, and more than once he was asked to move it. The request became a demand, and finally one of the selectmen threatened him with eviction. Neutrino was undaunted. A man named Pidge Carter, whom Neutrino knew from the harbor, asked Neutrino if he would move the raft as a favor, and Neutrino said sure. Carter, Neutrino told a reporter from the *Cape Cod Times,* "was the first person to ask us to move the boat. Until then, everyone had told us to."

Neutrino decided to sail the raft to New York.

In its issue for December 1, 1988, the Provincetown *Advocate* wrote that Lieutenant Robert Hazelton, "a marine inspector for the Marine Safety Office in Providence," said that

the construction grade lumber and nails used to build the boat will not withstand the wind and waves the family will surely encounter.

"I can't see this thing succeeding," said Hazelton. "Partly it's the time of year. The weather is horrendous."

Hazelton said he is concerned the boat's propulsion system will not have enough power to control the boat in anything over 10-knot winds.

"My concern is not that they will come apart and sink," said Hazelton. "But they could lose control and go up on the rocks and into the surf. The paddlewheels have very short blades that can't dig enough water, and they don't go very deep. I can't see it pulling through the tides in the Cape Cod Canal."

Hazelton said the family could do a lot of coast-hugging between Provincetown and New York, but beyond that it is open bay with only one port.

"They think they can duck into a harbor anytime, but they don't realize the storms that can kick up in the

Northeast. They could easily be caught between harbors in a storm. That's how ships have sunk for hundreds of years," he said.

Hazelton said the Coast Guard does not have the authority to interfere with the boat while it is tied to the dock, but it intends to board the vessel as soon as it gets underway.

"If the Coast Guard can make a determination that it's a manifestly unsafe voyage, they could detain the vessel, but not forever," said Hazelton. "I'd like to see people talk them out of it."

The raft made four or five miles an hour. It traveled, as if in slow motion, across Cape Cod Bay, through the Cape Cod Canal, and down the coast. In Newport, Rhode Island, Neutrino ran aground and had to be pushed off the beach by a bulldozer. In Narragansett he was taken to court for refusing to pay mooring fees. On Christmas Eve he ran aground in Connecticut, in front of a house that belonged to the actor Jason Robards. The paddle wheel was damaged, and a huge crew of people helped the family rebuild it. Hundreds more came to see them get under way again.

The following morning, the raft was at anchor, riding out a storm, when Neutrino accepted a tow from the Coast Guard to deeper water. The towline got fouled in the boat's propeller, and the raft ended up on the shore with both paddle wheels broken. A tugboat pulled it off the beach, and the boat's captain towed it to New York.

Neutrino had heard about a nightclub on the Hudson River called the Amazon Village, which occupied a pier not far from the World Trade Center, Pier Twenty-five. He thought the owner might be amused by his raft and let him tie up beside the club. If the owner refused, Neutrino planned to anchor there anyway, since maritime law allows vessels to moor anywhere outside a channel.

The tugboat delivered Neutrino to the pier, more or less the way a tow truck delivers a broken-down car to a garage. Neutrino walked up the gangway. At the top was the actor Jack Nicholson, who shook his hand and said, "You've got a great-looking vessel." The owner, Shimon Bokovas, an Israeli "built like a brick firehouse," Neutrino says, "very strong and very commando," came over. He introduced Neutrino to his security guards, "huge karate guys dressed in black," and said that Neutrino was to have access at all hours to the club and the pier and that no one in his party was required to observe the club's dress code.

Chapter 33

A LOT OF PEOPLE regarded the raft as an eyesore. Kids threw rocks at it. They broke the windows so many times that Neutrino repaired some of them with only Saran Wrap. The Coast Guard told Neutrino that the raft could anchor in the river, but it couldn't leave. "Every time they get under way, we have to rescue them because they either run aground or hit something," Chief Petty Officer Alan Burd told a reporter from *Newsday*. "Their vessel is grossly unsafe," he added. "It's pieced together with scrap."

For several years, Neutrino had thought about building a raft to cross the Atlantic Ocean. If he mentioned the idea to other sailors, they would laugh and say something such as "You have

no idea what the ocean is." When he brought it up among the
fishermen in Provincetown, they stopped talking to him. Enough
of their friends and relations had left the harbor and never returned that they viewed his plan as an insult to their nerve and
seamanship, and him not as the man they had taken him for.

Neutrino began walking around the city looking for materials.
He wanted the raft to be pointed at both ends, like a canoe. The
points would part the water so the raft could make headway in
even the least wind. Floating in the harbor one day were four,
thirty-two-foot-long timbers that had been part of a seawall.
Neutrino decided that they could frame the hull. Shimon Bokovas told him he could build the raft on Pier Twenty-five.

Chapter 34

IN THE SPRING OF 1992, the Flying Neutrinos made
a tour of Europe, beginning in Norway and ending in Belgium,
playing clubs and on the street. From abroad Neutrino sent
drawings to friends who were living on the *Town Hall* describing how he wanted the new raft to be built. By the time he returned, in the summer, they had framed the hull. He and the
other Neutrinos began roaming the city looking for more materials. From a bird sanctuary in Far Rockaway, they retrieved Styrofoam bricks that were floating among the reeds. People brought
them wood.

"When you're homeless, you suffer a lot, then you find a
niche," Neutrino says. Once a week Terrell and Jessica would go

to the terminal for the water taxi that ran between New York and New Jersey, and Terrell would play saxophone and Jessica would dance. In two hours they would make two hundred dollars, which was enough for them all to live for the week while building the raft.

In a trash pile in Tribeca, Neutrino found a parachute, which he laid over a webbing of rope for a sail. His plan was to make the sails not from one piece of material but from many pieces, so that repairing one would mean replacing only the section that had torn. The webbing would prevent the tear from becoming extensive. Layering the material would make the sail stronger.

A heavy sea can batter a vessel to pieces—the wood splinters, the screws and nails are torn from their shafts. Neutrino drilled holes every two feet in the hull and the sides of his raft. He fed rope through each hole, then knotted it, then ran the rope through the next hole, so that when he was finished the raft was woven together like a basket. A structure held together by screws and glue and nails is rigid. A basket is supple. Even if all the carpentry failed, he believed that the raft would remain intact.

"Where did I get this notion? I have no idea," Neutrino says. "From the cornucopia of my mind. Somebody put it in there a long time ago, and it came out in this way."

They launched the raft one evening in the fall. About a hundred people attended. Standing on the pier, they wedged pipes underneath the hull as levers and tipped the raft toward the water. It slid off the pier and dropped ten feet into the river. It landed upside down. Once it had righted itself, it drew seven inches, as Neutrino had planned. With the motor aboard and the family's belongings, including the piano from the Amazon Village, it drew eighteen inches, which was also what he had intended.

Neutrino and terrell decided that, rather than leave for Europe from New York, they would first sail to Provincetown and show their friends their raft. Before they could depart, the Coast Guard boarded them. The officers looked in the cabins and the engine room, they inspected the sails, and then, says Neutrino, they told him, "No way are you going. No way does this vessel even leave the dock." The captain of the port issued an order classifying *Son of Town Hall* as "manifestly unsafe." The phrase denotes the highest category of risk that a vessel can be assigned, and it means that it cannot leave the harbor.

The matter came into the hands of Michael Karr, a Coast Guard commander, who was the chief of the Inspection Department. Karr wanted to examine the raft before affirming the judgment. No regulations or standards apply in the decision of whether or not a raft is seaworthy. "You know it when you see it," Karr says. We spoke on the phone. I asked if he had ever before seen anything resembling *Son of Town Hall*. "Let me think about that. Seen anything like it," he said. He paused. Then he said, "I'd have to say no. It was certainly not like any other homemade craft."

Neutrino recalls that Karr's inspection, made with two other officers, lasted several hours. Karr had heard of *Kon-Tiki*, from which he was aware that a raft is capable of traveling on the deep ocean. *Son of Town Hall* had outriggers, so it wasn't likely to tip over. It had a motor. Careful thought had obviously gone into assuring its buoyancy. Karr asked Neutrino what route he planned to take to Provincetown, and they looked at charts together.

Karr sent his report to harbormasters up the coast. He described *Son of Town Hall* as "a *Kon-Tiki* type raft," and said that, even though it looked strange, the people aboard were competent sailors. He likes to point out that what he gave Neutrino was permission to leave New York harbor and travel to Provincetown. He did not give him permission to "cross the open ocean."

Chapter 36

THE VOYAGE TO PROVINCETOWN was without event, a novel occasion for Neutrino. He and Terrell planned to spend the winter in the harbor working on the raft. Tourists don't visit Provincetown in January. Even so, the harbormaster objected to the Neutrinos' presence. In the spring, Neutrino and Terrell sailed to Gloucester; the harbormaster tried to keep them from dropping anchor. They left for Maine. The harbormaster in Wells also tried to prevent them from mooring. Neutrino insisted—he had repairs to make, he said—and the harbormaster called the police. Neutrino said, "What about maritime law and the Constitution?" The harbormaster said that the Constitution didn't apply. It was a long time ago, he said, and Maine hadn't belonged to the union when it was ratified.

Neutrino decided to find another mooring. The tide was rising. The channel through the breakwater was narrow. Halfway through it, the engine quit. A wave ten feet tall came through the breakwater and hit the raft broadside. The raft flipped over, then righted itself so quickly that Neutrino and Terrell started clapping and shouting. A second wave threw Neutrino into the water.

When he got back aboard, he discovered that the wave had also swamped the motor. The owner of a dock in Kennebunk, across the channel from Wells, saw their distress and invited them to tie up and fix things.

From Kennebunk they left for Europe with four people aboard: Neutrino, Terrell, their daughter, Jessica, who was thirteen, and a friend named Ed Garry. They also had two Rottweilers and a little half-breed mutt they had picked up in Mexico. The first night they were about thirty miles offshore when the wind rose to twenty miles an hour. Instead of steering downwind, the raft turned sideways, and Neutrino couldn't correct it.

"I realized then that I have failed utterly," he says. "No way we're going to make it across the Atlantic sideways." They waited for the storm to pass, then they put in to Portland. They were tied up at the dock, broke and discouraged, when Neutrino, seated on a stool and opening a can of beer, passed out and fell backward into a basin of bilge water. He'd had a heart attack. He says it felt as if someone had punched him in the chest. For nearly two weeks, he lay in intensive care.

While he was recovering, a ship struck a piling in Portland harbor and spilled some oil. Representatives from an insurance company went through the harbor settling claims. They gave the Neutrinos $5,500, because oil had invaded the raft's core of foam and shrunk it. With some of the money, Neutrino bought plywood and made a daggerboard. They took the raft to sea, and when the wind rose they dropped the daggerboard, and the raft sailed downwind.

They put in by the shipyards at Bath. A friend named Rodger Doncaster took Jessica's place. With a wide blue sky above them, they sat on the deck and ate a farewell meal of take-out Chinese food. Their guests left on a rowboat. Then, moving so slowly that the raft left almost no wake, they headed for the ocean. Neutrino was exhausted but also elated to be under way.

"To launch this expedition after all the setbacks and obstacles," he says, "to hold on when the will to say hold on was gone, to go against all the harbormasters that ridiculed this vessel, the police who came to drive it off public property, the near impossibility of financing it on our own, the heart attack, and the failures of design we had to correct—all of it drove me to my deepest, deepest despair. We had taken this wood from the streets of New York and set it in motion, and now either we'd make it, or we wouldn't."

On the third day of the voyage, the sky darkened and the wind picked up. The waves grew to almost twenty feet. Rain fell heavily. Neutrino sat in the stern, in the cockpit, which was raised above the deck, steering. The others, having nothing to do, huddled in the cabin with the dogs, waiting to see how the raft took the beating. The first big wave loomed over them like a wall. They waited for it to collapse on their heads. Instead, the raft rose suddenly. Then the deck tilted toward the vertical, and Neutrino was suspended aloft. "It seemed like I was looking straight down from the top of a building," he says. He thought the raft would pitchpole, then land on him.

"I thought, I'd done all this work, made all these plans, come this far, had the heart attack, only to get out here and kill everybody." It was, he says, "the first and only time I ever remember being scared at sea. There must have been other times, but I can't recall them. This, I recall." Instead of toppling, the raft slid down the wave like a sled down a hill. By the time it had reached the bottom, Neutrino felt sure that it could take the strain. "She would have climbed up fifty-foot waves," he says. "I might not have taken it, but she would."

The storm lasted three hours and fatigued them deeply. On a river, they could have pulled to the shore and rested. On the ocean they kept four-hour watches, and sleep was more difficult than they had thought it would be. Their beds were never still, even a gentle swell rolled them from side to side, and their muscles responded, so that no rest restored them entirely.

The sea changed color according to the sky. The broad black backs of whales broke the surface off the stern. A fishing boat stopped and gave them fuses they needed. In a thick fog they passed close to a fishing boat that crossed their bow hauling a net. Another day a fishing boat came out of a fogbank and the fishermen took pictures of the raft but declined an invitation to board it.

No one had taught them how to read their radar, so eventually they learned on their own that the shapes on the screen were not always other boats—they might also be storms—and that sometimes boats close enough to harm them might not show up at all. They worried most about a fire starting, or falling overboard, or being run down in the shipping lanes by a freighter so big that it might come upon them in a fog without seeing them and never even know it ran over them. It was much colder than they had expected July on the ocean to be. The fog made the air clammy, and the damp cold worked its way under their watch caps and the layers of sweaters and parkas. In the North Atlantic, something called the fifty-fifty-fifty rule applies. If you fall overboard into fifty-degree water, you have a fifty-fifty chance of surviving more than fifty minutes. The water around them was generally sixty degrees.

The anxieties of being aboard a fragile craft at sea preyed most heavily on Doncaster. One morning he sat on top of the cabin weeping and all but unable to move, like a man on a ledge.

"I can't find the willpower to take me through this," he said.

Neutrino asked what he feared.

"I'm afraid of what can happen to the boat," he said, "but I'm mainly afraid about me. About me not having the strength to do this."

Neutrino allowed that it was "scary to cross the ocean in a raft, an untried raft."

"But you three—"

"We're afraid—"

"Don't show it to this level," Doncaster said. "Don't show it at any level, except intellectually. I'm *showing* it. My emotional level is so full of it that it overwhelms the other levels."

"Yeah, but see you've never allowed yourself to feel fear before," Neutrino said. "This is your opportunity. Always before you neutralized it. You're Mr. Neutral. Now you actually feel things."

Doncaster turned and looked over one shoulder at the water, as if he thought he might catch it sneaking up on him. The ocean was calm. He began to sob. "I can't even face this part just off of Maine," he said, "knowing that we're in radio distance of either Nova Scotia or Maine."

"Or Cape Cod," Terrell said.

"Or New York," Neutrino said.

"I know, but seventy-five miles might as well be fifteen hundred," Doncaster said. "I do need to have some level of security."

"Your security is your raft and your friends," Neutrino said.

Terrell, wearing a parka and a life jacket, sat down beside Doncaster and held him, and he was racked with sobs.

"And how do we know you're going to succeed?" she asked finally.

"Because you did?" he said timidly.

"Because you've got no choice," she shouted. "What are you going to do, swim back to shore? You're not going to do that."

After a moment Doncaster rose, spread his feet wide, and stood unsteadily on the roof of the cabin. He stared at the horizon and tried to accommodate himself to the sway of the ocean and the movement of the raft beneath him.

Chapter 37

THEY HAD EXPECTED the Gulf Stream to carry them to Europe, but the stream kept eluding them. At the end of the second week, they stopped a fishing boat, and the fishermen told them that the Gulf Stream was 150 miles from where they were. The fishermen gave them steaks from swordfish they had just caught. That afternoon dolphins swam for hours around the raft, coming so close that they could see their eyes.

On the first morning of their third week, Neutrino woke Terrell and asked for the nitroglycerin tablets the hospital had given him for his heart. He took two of the tablets, and she put her arms around him, and he lost consciousness. "A gentle fadeout" is how he describes it. He came to with her pounding his chest and shouting, "Wake up! Wake up!" About a minute had passed. She put him to bed, and he slept. "We are all very badly shaken," she wrote in the captain's log.

Neutrino woke in the afternoon and got up "acting like nothing had happened," Terrell wrote. They changed the watch schedule to allow him more rest.

The water appeared to be growing warmer, leading them to think that they were approaching the Gulf Stream. Halfway through the third week, according to the charts, they reached it, but their momentum seemed no different from what it had been. A medium-size sea changed abruptly on them one evening and took the tiller with it, and they had to make another. One morning, shortly past midnight, they saw the beacon of a fishing boat dragging a long line—a line, that is, with hundreds of hooks set at intervals. To prevent a collision, they tried to start their motor and couldn't. They dropped their sails and passed close by the fishing boat's line. Neutrino began taking half-hour watches. "All of us are exhausted," Terrell wrote. "All we do is sleep, eat, and take watch."

When a front came through with rain and wind, they would let out the sea anchor, a device like a parachute that floated beneath the surface and helped them hold their course. On watch one day, Neutrino saw a whale by the sea anchor as if he were inspecting it. Some days the current took them back in the direction they'd come from. "We've lost ground, and are farther from France than we were two days ago," Terrell wrote. They began to run low on food and water. At night they turned on a generator and watched movies. One night dolphins played in the dark water around them, leaving trails that glowed faintly from the phosphorescence. The dogs ran back and forth, barking at the dolphins.

After they had been at sea for a month and had spent several days becalmed, Neutrino asked what they all thought about "someone getting on a freighter, going to England and bringing back diesel and fuel; getting on a freighter with the raft; getting a tow from a Portuguese fishing vessel returning to Portugal. We said no to all three," Terrell wrote. "We want to have actually *done* the crossing."

Calculating that the raft had traveled about thirty-eight miles a day over the past seven days, Terrell estimated that they would reach France in fifty-five more days. With what they had got from fishing boats, she thought they had enough food, but there wasn't enough for the dogs. "We seemed to have missed the Gulf Stream entirely," she wrote.

On the night of August 3, they hit a thunderstorm. Rain fell in sheets. The waves were steep and close together. Each knocked the raft off its keel, sometimes as much as forty-five or fifty degrees, "only to come sharply back and be hit again. Slam, slam. Very uncomfortable," Terrell wrote. "Nearly sleepless night." A day later, Neutrino called them together, and they agreed, to go with the wind, rather than fight it, which would take them to Newfoundland, about a hundred miles behind them. If the wind turned around, they would continue to France.

Through a container ship they reached on the radio, Neutrino sent a message to the Coast Guard, saying they would like a tow to St. John's from a fishing boat. No problems, he added, just bad luck with the wind. A day later, just before dawn, a Canadian fisheries patrol boat arrived. They waited for daylight before approaching, then three men came over in an inflatable launch and asked the best way to tow them. Terrell went aboard the fisheries boat, and when she came back, she was laughing almost uncontrollably.

"You could see why people are scared to death to think of taking this boat," she told the others. "There's no way being on it that you get the sensation that you get looking at it from the outside. You're on it, and it feels so peaceful and calm, it's only safe. You look at it from the outside, it looks *scary!*"

The fisheries boat transferred them to a second ship, which towed them to Fermeuse, Newfoundland. They arrived on August 9, after forty days at sea.

For nearly a week a steady stream of people came to the wharf to see the raft. They brought babies and children. Men planted their backsides against the fenders of pickup trucks and folded their arms and shook their heads. When the tide fell, the raft settled below the pier, and they looked at it over the edge as if they were looking into a hole. Neutrino told them that the raft was unsinkable, and that their biggest fear was termites. He asked people how they had learned about the raft, and they said, "I heard about it at work," or "I heard about it from my mother-in-law," or "I come to pick up my husband from fishing," or "My sister told me there was a beautiful yacht, and I couldn't miss seeing it, and I come down, and this is what I saw." One man said, "It's a mortal sin, a mortal sin, and I worked for the Coast Guard in America for twenty years. They ain't never give permission for this. I'm going to find out when I get home."

"Would you rather they spend money on an insane asylum and have the four of us locked up," Neutrino asked him, "or would you rather have us towed in once in a while?"

"I'd rather see you locked up," the man said.

Mostly, though, people were welcoming.

The raft spent nine months in Newfoundland. Leaving Garry aboard, Doncaster went to California, while Neutrino and Terrell spent the winter painting signs in Texas and Arizona. Then Neutrino and Terrell drove to Nova Scotia to take the ferry and left their car in the parking lot. "It's probably still there," Neutrino says.

Chapter 38

WHILE NEUTRINO, TERRELL, and Doncaster were away, Garry lived aboard the raft, in the harbor of Fermeuse. To make money he lettered names on boats. He insulated the raft's back cabin, and he installed a diesel engine and a propeller. Neutrino, Terrell, and Doncaster returned in May of 1998. They had the raft lifted out of the water for repairs. The lift had a scale; the raft weighed seventeen tons. A month later they put it back in the water. The Canadian authorities came to inspect it and were concerned that if they let Neutrino go they might be held responsible if he came to grief, so after taking the raft for a test run, Neutrino and the others slipped out of Fermeuse early on the morning of June 15.

For twenty-four hours an iceberg the size of a gas station traveled alongside them, like an escort. Waves broke against the iceberg, and flocks of birds roosted on it. The danger was not of their hitting it—they could see it, after all—it was that a sufficient portion of the iceberg below the water would melt and the rest would roll suddenly and fall on them.

On their third night at sea, Terrell looked out a window of the cabin and through the fog saw a freighter passing so close that she was alarmed. Doncaster was on watch. He had turned off the radar and was listening to a radio show, so he had not seen the ship. The next morning Terrell called a meeting on the deck. The sea was calm, the raft rose and fell with the rhythm of a slowly walking horse, and the engine made an insistent, banging noise, like a machine in a factory.

Terrell said that Doncaster had refused "to take the safety of this vessel and the people onboard seriously, and that has an effect on me, not allowing me to get my proper rest, which in turn affects everybody else's rest, because if I don't have my rest, I can't make proper decisions.

"Rodger does not feel the fear—the intense fear—that he should have felt when a freighter was about to cut this boat in half," she said. Doncaster looked stolidly out at the water.

"I don't feel I can sleep anymore while he's on watch," Terrell said. "And that means we're going to have to rearrange everything so that we can be on watch."

A few more disparaging remarks were made, then Doncaster, cornered and having had enough, said, "You people are picking on me."

"You're not keeping us safe," Terrell said emphatically.

"I'm doing what I'm supposed to do," he said.

"I want you to keep us *safe*," Terrell said. "You're responsible for the safety of each person on this boat."

"What did I do that wasn't safe?"

"You were listening to the radio," Neutrino said.

"One ear was open," Doncaster said feebly.

"If you cannot wake up, take your clothes off, throw cold water on your face, do something to wake yourself up," Terrell said.

The tone of their remarks became vehement. Doncaster began to shout them down. "What do you want, what do you want, what do you want?" he yelled.

"I don't want you listening to your radio when there are foghorns out there," Terrell shouted back.

Terrell and Neutrino said that Doncaster should have been watching the radar, and he said disingenuously that he had been. Terrell said again that Doncaster wasn't taking the trip seriously, and then she said of Neutrino, "I'm trying my desperate best to keep him from having another heart attack, because I don't want him to die out here at sea."

Neutrino spoke forcefully to Doncaster, saying that he was acting as if he were asleep.

"Because I'm sick, I can't take the sea," Doncaster said. Since Fermeuse he had been overtaken by bouts of seasickness.

"So get off, get off the trip," Terrell said, waving her hand dismissively. "Do me a favor, if you can't do it, don't do it."

"Before, my actions were always good enough," he said.

"No, they weren't," Terrell said.

"Then why do you want me back on this trip?" he asked.

Terrell said bluntly, "I don't."

Doncaster made no reply. He turned and looked out at the sea. His position was difficult. He was among three people who had far more experience on the water than he did. What came easily to them came to him only by means of labor. A raft, however, is too small a territory for four people to occupy and not get along. Doncaster's response was the admirable one. He worked harder, he rose to the occasion.

Chapter 39

A FEW DAYS LATER, on the Grand Banks, Terrell saw the outline of a ship on the radar and began calling it on the radio to determine its course and make sure it saw the raft. She got no answer. The ship's outline grew rapidly larger. What she saw finally on the horizon was not a ship but the front of a storm—dark blue and gray clouds, hung like curtains. Sometimes they were threatened by storms in three of the horizon's four quarters.

The next day the engine would run at no more than idle speed. "It would move the raft just barely," Neutrino says. Garry thought something was wrong with the gearbox. Neutrino thought it was the compression. "Either way, it's beyond our scope to repair it," Neutrino says. They got the attention of a Canadian scalloper. The men aboard were unable to help them, but they gave them some scallops and vegetables, then put them in touch with a fishing boat from St. John's, Newfoundland. Over the radio, their engineer said he would come aboard, then changed his mind. Neutrino offered him three hundred dollars. The engineer came over on a launch and insisted on being given the money. He looked at the engine and said nothing was wrong and went back to his boat.

The engine's breaking down left them with no way to get off the Grand Banks. "Picture the North Atlantic as a big basin," Terrell says. "The winds come across the equator and curve and circle the basin clockwise. The currents follow the winds. The middle is dead calm—the Sargasso Sea. Our plan had been to motor from Newfoundland to the Grand Banks, raise the sails, hook up with the Gulf Stream, and romp across to Europe, but we never on the entire voyage had any considerable current. We never really contacted the Gulf Stream or the North Atlantic Drift, all the currents we knew about from the charts and had expected, but somehow we missed them. On the banks, the winds are confused, because you haven't yet really contacted the major ocean effects. We couldn't get a consistent current or wind, and almost as soon as we encountered the currents, we were blown out of them."

Dolphins swam beside them for days. The dogs whined and barked as the backs of the creatures broke the surface. Garry several times threw a line over the stern to fish, but he never caught anything. One night the sunset covered the entire sky, "three hundred and sixty degrees," Neutrino says, "not a weak point in it anywhere."

Without the help of the wind or the currents, and without an engine, they were traveling about two miles an hour, slower than a person walks. They were, in other words, walking very slowly over the ocean to France. Their biggest challenge was not to be sent backward by the current. They woke one morning to discover that, since they had last taken their position, the day before, the raft had traced a circle.

For days at a time the horizon was shrouded in fog. They were in the middle of shipping lanes. Ships in the North Atlantic are enormous and require great distances to alter their course. Not having an engine meant that the raft couldn't get out of the way of any ship whose course crossed its own, so they had to be especially careful not to overlook or misread any shape on the radar or fail to hear a foghorn. Even a ship two miles away could eventually run them over. Time passed slowly. Day after day the ocean was the color of stones. "At a certain point you begin to feel it's going to go on forever," Neutrino says. "The horizon doesn't change, there's no wind, the current seems stalled, you're hardly moving, and sometimes when you are it's in the wrong direction."

The isolation wore on them. Terrell began to feel unsettled. Having confronted her anxiety one night, she wrote in the log the next morning, "I felt really scared and I thought why, I analyzed it, the first thing that came to me was: I'm out here in the Atlantic Ocean. I am so far from a land mass that everything I see is no longer being influenced by land, the air the light the water, the clouds are all purely water influenced, they're ocean based, there's no land influence going on, and I've never been out this far."

The raft looked like a specter, a ghost ship, as if made from rags and rope and lumber, a vessel from the end of the world, or something medieval, the flagship of nothingness, the Armada of the Kingdom of Oblivion. Being roped together, it seemed broken into segments and to be crawling forlornly over the surface of the water.

They ran low on fuel for the generator, which ran the radar, and decided to use the radar only in poor weather. Everyone felt anxious, weary, and oppressed. One evening Neutrino intercepted

Terrell as she was headed toward the stern. The look in her eyes made him feel that she was no longer in possession of herself. "I want my children," she said, sobbing. "I want my children." He held her and talked to her softly and she wept, and little by little, over the course of the night, she recovered herself.

Chapter 40

GARRY HAD THE IDEA that instead of fighting the current they should sail with it and see what happened. Before long they intersected a crosscurrent traveling the direction they wanted to go, and it carried them off the Grand Banks.

A few days later Terrell was startled by a blast from a horn. She sighted a freighter about a mile away, on a course that was parallel to theirs. The freighter was Russian, and the captain was fascinated by the raft. Over the radio he asked if they needed anything, and they said fresh fruit and vegetables and gas. He circled the raft and brought the freighter alongside, which took an hour. The ship towered above them, and the wash tipped the raft. The captain sent a launch, and Neutrino and Garry went aboard. Neutrino gave the captain CDs of the Flying Neutrinos. The captain gave them fifty pounds of potatoes as well as or-anges and apples and cabbages and beets and fifty gallons of gas. The sailors waved good-bye from the deck. They took photo-graphs. They yelled good luck. Their command of English was imperfect. "Thank you for your show to the world," the captain said. "We'll show the world this floating radish."

The exchange with the Russian freighter took place on July 8.

On the tenth, the seas began to build until they had become the biggest the crew had encountered. Terrell wrote in the log that she felt certain the storm was a full gale. Most of the waves were fifteen feet high, but some were twenty, "truly awesome," Terrell wrote, and instead of following one another in line, like soldiers on their way to the front, they came from all directions, like a mob.

Now and then a wave hit the raft broadside and laid it almost completely over. They worried about a second wave's hitting them before they had recovered and also how many times they could be knocked over and come back.

The storm eventually passed, then another one arrived a week later. This one was less formidable but also had confused seas. They feared that the battering might jar loose the dagger-board, which kept them steering properly. Neutrino called a ship whose outline he saw on the radar and said that they had suffered damage to their hull and needed fuel. The ship asked their nationality and whether they had contacted the Coast Guard. Neutrino said they had been unable to. The ship replied that "it was very difficult," presumably to give them fuel, then didn't answer any other calls.

They were approximately halfway across the ocean, on July 21, when they began to suspect that the radar was no longer working. Throughout the night before, waves had broken over the raft, hitting them so hard that they had felt the raft shudder. One came through cracks in the wall of Neutrino's cabin and soaked him in his bed. Three ships in succession had refused for some reason to pass on messages for them.

They ran nearly out of dog food. Instead of augmenting the dogs' meals with table scraps, they were feeding them mostly from their plates. The dogs would stand in the doorway of the galley and watch Terrell cook.

For a whole day, with nothing in sight but a dark gray sea,

Terrell could smell flowers, horses, "and a certain smell the earth has when it's been tilled and turned and has rain falling on it": the Azores.

On the morning of July 31, a ship appeared "just off port bow coming dead on us, no radio contact," Terrell wrote. The radar had given them no warning of the ship's approach. Finally she raised them on the radio, and they changed their course to avoid the raft. They met a second ship, on its way to New York, which didn't carry the fuel they needed but filled some barrels for them with apples and cabbages and oranges and lettuce and carrots and canned milk and white dinner rolls, and dropped them into the sea for the crew to collect. The only items that stayed dry were the dinner rolls.

On August 3, Neutrino raised on the radio the *Atlantic Companion,* the same ship that had relayed his request a year earlier to be towed into Newfoundland. The captain asked if they wanted the raft to be taken aboard, then he asked why they were making the trip. Neutrino gave him the answer he gave everyone else, "Adventure." The crew dropped two barrels of diesel fuel and a barrel of food into the ocean, and the barrels drifted in different directions at different speeds. It took Neutrino and the others the rest of the day, scanning the horizon with binoculars for the slightest trace of color different from the color around it, to collect them. In the barrel of food were corned beef and fish, twenty loaves of bread, nectarines, plums, grapefruit, apples, oranges, and fruit juice concentrate.

Several days later, from a freighter called the *Dahlia,* they heard that a week and a half earlier a bulletin had been issued, saying that they were overdue and possibly lost.

For weeks they had seen no porpoises or whales. When the wind blew strongly from the south or southwest, Terrell could smell land. They had intended to strike France, but Neutrino had grown uneasy at the thought that, if they pointed toward France, they might enter the Bay of Biscay and, without their motor, meet a circular current that would send them down the coast of Africa to South America. He insisted that they set their course toward Scotland. They hit Ireland instead.

On August 11 a plane appeared. The pilot said that he had been sent by marine rescue, which had received a report of "a suspicious vessel." They were only a few miles from the coast. An Irish government vessel arrived and sent a launch. The men aboard shouted, "Welcome to Ireland," and gave them an Irish flag, which they hoisted, some Rice Krispies, apples, hamburgers, ketchup, spring water, and Irish whiskey. The closest harbor was Castletownbere. Doncaster spoke on the radio with a woman onshore, an official of some kind.

She asked the name of the craft.

"We're the sailing vessel *Son of Town Hall*," Doncaster said. "We have a crew of four. My name is Rodger Doncaster."

There was a pause, then she asked, "Rodger, is this the first time a raft has done this kind of crossing?"

"Yes, it is," he said, "across the North Atlantic."

"And are you all sailors?"

"No, none of us is really a sailor," he said.

During the pause that followed, Neutrino took the microphone from Doncaster and said blithely, "My name is Poppino Neutrino."

Apparently the woman did not hear him clearly. "Okay, Stephen," she said. "What do you do normally?"

"I'm a musician."

"You're a musician," she said thoughtfully. There was quite a long pause.

"Why are you out there on the *Son of Town Hall*?" she asked. Her tone was not combative, but she was clearly confused.

"We're into scrap art," Neutrino said. "We're the parents of the Flying Neutrino jazz band that appeared in Europe last year. They told us about Ireland and France, and we came over to see it. We have one sailor onboard, his name is Ed Garry, he's the captain of the ship. He's an Irishman."

She took a moment to absorb this. Then she said, "Stephen?" Her voice was uncertain.

Neutrino said, "Yes?"

"Three dogs have you?"

By the time they entered the harbor, word of the peculiar craft approaching the coast had spread, and the shore was lined with people. Every room in the town's bed-and-breakfasts had been taken. Neutrino and the others were so exhausted that they had difficulty thinking straight. They accepted a tow. They sat on the deck in lawn chairs and waved to the people. Neutrino turned to Doncaster and said, "Give us a comment."

Doncaster looked off at the water, then he looked back at Neutrino and said, "We have done the impossible."

Neutrino told reporters that they had "broken the scrap barrier." They had been at sea for sixty-two days.

Chapter 41

NEUTRINO WAS NOT the first man to build a raft and sail it across the Atlantic. He was the second. He was the first man to cross the Atlantic on a raft built from garbage. Henri Beadout, a Canadian, crossed on a raft in 1956. From *A Speck on the Sea,* by William H. Longyard, I know that Beadout built his raft from nine cedar logs tied together with hemp. In the center of the deck it had a cabin and a square-shaped sail. Beadout led a group for boys, and he took three boys with him and two cats. He was interested in testing the theory of a man named Alain Bombard, who believed that more people could survive ship-wrecks if they squeezed water from fish and plankton. One of the boys became sick from this diet and was taken aboard a fishing boat. After eighty-nine days, Beadout and the others reached the English Channel.

Bombard, testing his suppositions, had left the Canary Islands, in 1952, aboard an inflatable raft that was fifteen feet long and six feet wide and had a sail. According to Longyard, four days into his trip, his best sail washed overboard. By three weeks he had sores from the salt water. To elevate himself above the seawater that washed aboard the raft he had a cushion. When a wave carried off the cushion, he dove overboard to retrieve it. Before he did, he threw out the sea anchor. The wind caught it and spread it as if it were a sail. Bombard had to swim for an hour to catch the raft. Fifty-three days out, he met the *Arakaka,* a British steamer, and went aboard to send a message to his wife. The meal they offered he declined, in order to preserve the integrity of his research. Then he became aware of aromas emanating from the kitchen. He ate a fried egg, a piece of liver, and some fruit. Back on his raft, he had severe cramps, and until he arrived in Barbados, twelve days later, he thought continually about food. Because he had been alone, he had no means of persuading the world of his results.

Longyard also describes a trip on a raft made in 1953 in the Indian Ocean by Fred Ericsson and Ensio Tiira. Ericsson was from Sweden, and Tiira was from Finland. Impulsively, they had joined the French Foreign Legion, and after being trained in Algeria they were put on a troopship headed for Vietnam. On the way they concluded that they were likely to die there and decided to jump ship. One night near Sumatra they got free from the ship in a four-foot-by-four-foot aluminum tube raft. Almost immediately the raft was noticed missing. The ship swept the ocean with a searchlight, but the raft was so small that the swells concealed it.

When the sun rose, Ericsson and Tiira saw no shore. Because the raft was square, it spun when they paddled. The bread, sausage, cheese, and the wine they had brought with them in a hot water bottle they quickly finished. They ate crabs when they found them floating on strips of seaweed. The current carried them away from Sumatra, so they decided to try to reach India instead. From a shirt they made a sail. The center of the raft consisted of cloth webbing. When sharks attacked them, they beat them off with their paddles, but the sharks tore the webbing. They caught a turtle, killed it with a piece of glass from a broken mirror, and drank its blood. Each promised the other not to abandon his corpse. On the eighteenth day, when Ericsson died, Tiira lashed him to the raft. Sharks assaulted the raft so vigorously that eventually he had to release the corpse. It had kept him company, and the solitude was more imposing without it.

On the thirty-second day, a British freighter passed so close to Tiira that he could see the faces of the men on the deck, but they didn't see him. He banged a flashlight against the metal raft, and someone aboard the ship, listening to sonar, heard it. He weighed only fifty-six pounds.

The fatigue that Terrell endured on the *Son of Town Hall* is not unexampled. Longyard describes how, in 1956, Hans Lindeman crossed the Atlantic, north to south, in a kayak. His boat sat so low in the water that the sea constantly invaded it. Chemicals used in waterproofing the boat made his skin itch. After a few weeks he developed the impression that the waves were questioning him. He saw phantom ships, and he believed at times that he was traveling backward. He refused food from the ships he met, because he thought that he could complete his trip only by remaining independent. When a wave flipped him out of his boat, he discovered that the algae growing on the hull made it almost too slippery to hold on to. He hugged it desperately and fell asleep for nine hours. When he woke, he managed to right the kayak. He had lost all his food except some cans of evaporated milk. His speargun was still aboard, and he managed to shoot some fish. Seventy-two days after he left, he made it to St. Martin.

There is also in Longyard's book an account of a man on the ocean in a small boat who had had bad weather for three weeks. He grew so miserable that he began to cry. He decided that the only way he could make it was to drink all the liquor he had brought with him and pass out. When he came to, the weather had turned. Another man on a sailboat saw lights on the ocean for which there was no explanation, heard dogs barking, and thought a group of children had come to inspect his vessel. Nor could he shake the feeling that aboard his small craft was someone who meant to kill him.

Neutrino recorded the crossing on a video camera. They sailed *Son of Town Hall* through France and into the Mediterranean. Neutrino had intended to continue around the world, but he grew uneasy at the thought of traveling through the Suez Canal. Eventually they tied the raft to a mooring in France and left it with papers giving it to anyone who wanted it. Neutrino sent the tapes of the voyage to National Geographic, which broadcast them on September 12, 1999.

With all the attention, Neutrino began to have a platform for describing his deepest ambition, which was to build a raft that would be an orphanage—the "orphanage raft," he called it. The idea had come to him, he told a reporter, when he heard about an Indian boy—he called him "a carpet slave"—who had fled his job at a carpet factory. "These kids in Brazil and India and Africa are the dregs of the world," Neutrino said. "They're thieves, murderers, some are syphilitic, but I feel as if I've been directed to do something" for them.

Chapter 42

In April of 2000, Neutrino and Terrell and some friends went to Minneapolis to build a raft to sail down the Mississippi to New Orleans. National Geographic sent cameramen. Neutrino and Terrell visited construction sites and asked for wood. By a boat ramp next to a highway, they built two pontoons, sixteen feet long, and put them side by side, with a few feet between them, then laid down a deck. The work took two days, and when they finished, it began to snow.

Their plan was to build the simplest raft and make it bigger and more elaborate as they sailed downriver. In Dows, Iowa, a family gave them wood from a barn they had razed and Neutrino used it to build a second raft, so that he had a platform from which to work on the first raft. Typically, by the time they arrived in a town, the people who lived there had heard of them from a newspaper article or a television broadcast or because someone had looked out the window and seen them or been standing on a dock where they appeared. A lot of people brought them wood and foam. Some people collected material for them in one town, then drove down the river to deliver it to them in the next town they called at. By the end of April, the raft was thirty feet long and had four cabins. They planted a garden on the deck. A woman who managed an RV park told a reporter, "It's the most interesting thing I've ever seen on the river." People began adding themselves to the crew. By July there were thirteen people traveling on the raft.

In August they reached the lower Mississippi, the part of the river that has barges the size of small towns, whirlpools, snags, heavy winds, and a current that can't easily be read—the first thing Terrell saw was a log traveling not up or down the river but sideways across it. In Memphis, Neutrino played piano and sang in a bar on Beale Street. He and Ed Garry, who had joined them, hiked a half mile through the woods one day to get water from a casino. They never stopped enlarging the raft. By the time they reached New Orleans, it was 135 long and 35 feet wide. From New Orleans they sailed to Port Isabel to rebuild the raft so that it could travel on the ocean. National Geographic broadcast their film about them in July of 2001.

Making the raft seaworthy took two years. Meanwhile, Neutrino left Port Isabel to live in New York City. When he arrived, he built a box from sheets of plywood he found on the street. The box was six feet long, four feet tall, and four feet wide, the dimensions of a cabin on the raft. He added wheels from a shopping cart to it. On one side he cut a door that he hung with brass hinges, and on another side he cut a window. He came and went from the box only when no one was around, because he didn't want anybody to know he was living in it. He found a blue plastic tarp of the kind the power company uses on its work sites. Every three or four days he wheeled the box to another location. As a rule he parked the box near a construction site. When he covered it with the blue tarp, people tended to think that it had something to do with the site. In the evenings he would wheel the box to a place where there were a lot of people and sit beside it and play piano and sing for change. He says that his time in the box was nearly the happiest of his life. He woke up feeling that he owed nothing to anyone and was free from any concerns except for how to spend his day.

"Immediate concerns," he says. "It's one of the Christ messages, Think not of tomorrow but only of today." At night people would stand beside the box and reveal themselves to one another with no awareness that someone was listening. In the morning Neutrino would sometimes find on top of the box the ends of the cigarettes they had smoked. He lived in the box for two months. Then, on a ticket bought by a friend, he flew to New Orleans, and from there he went back to Port Isabel.

Neutrino wanted to sail his raft to Cuba. National Geographic told him that if he did, they might assemble another program from the trip. The raft was now sixty feet long and twenty-eight feet wide. Neutrino, Terrell, and several friends sailed it to Mexico. They left for Cuba, in August of 2003, with eleven people aboard. The current they expected to deliver them in three days to the island's south coast took them instead toward the middle of the Gulf of Mexico. The wind died. Then a tropical storm arrived. After it passed, the wind died again. They collected rainwater. A cruise ship gave them food.

After seventeen days they landed on a beach so remote that they sent an SOS. Cuban soldiers responded. It took two days to persuade the soldiers of the group's identity. When the soldiers had been satisfied, Neutrino and the crew sailed to Marina Hemingway, outside Havana. For three weeks they played music and made videotapes of themselves. They left Havana in the evening and raised Key West by the morning. Neutrino gave the raft to Ed Garry. To Neutrino's surprise, Garry said that he wanted it to himself, so Neutrino collected his things and left. Terrell went to Maine to visit her mother.

National Geographic withdrew its interest. Instead of having cash in hand, Neutrino was broke and had nowhere to live. "At seventy-one I'm out on the street and have to start all over again," he says.

Within a week he had begun collecting wood and building a raft.

PART TWO

THE SEA, FOR SOME PEOPLE, is a game field, and the game field, in its turn, is not entirely unlike the sea. Both have their rules and imperatives; both insist on courage; both reward diligence, resourcefulness, and skill; and both appear to require a plan. However, both can also be attacked in a disorderly way, as the inverse of having a plan: I will leave port in my rowboat, for example, and row until I reach the far shore, which I cannot see. Because the catalog of difficulties I will encounter is so broad and unknowable, I can't predict all of them, therefore I will plan for the few I can manage—I will bring food and water, something to keep the sun from burning me, and something to keep me warm in the darkness. The rest I will trust to the guardian angels, and so on. Improvisation on the game field is a weakness or a weapon. Any system designed to respond to given scenarios is always vulnerable to the occasion when those scenarios are absent.

Cunning, surprise, perseverance, planning, audacity, nerve, and responsiveness to impulse characterize Neutrino's approach to manipulating the chaos he has embraced as his context, his ground, of life. The reasoning threaded through all his endeavors is that knowledge can best be acquired by means of experience and engagement. An idea that absorbs him needs its outlet. Years sometimes pass before it emerges completely. Far more ideas are shed than are enacted. Across the plains, he sees his ideal, and sometimes (a few) other people see it, too. Even if eccentrically,

his attempts are toward the aspiration of bringing order to something that is formless to begin with. The older he got, the more
inclined he became to solving a problem in a way that it pleased
him to perform—to place himself in situations, that is, where the
solution would be partly a matter of art. If he had in him a shred
of materialism, I am persuaded that his cleverness, his resourcefulness, and his vitality would have made fortunes, and his story
would be conventional. The background of a prosperous man
whose secrets everyone hoped to acquire. Oddly, and instead,
what appears to be the most random of lives is guided by an all
but unyielding set of rules—the simplest of which is that to act
thoughtfully, to command, is to avoid the harm that is done to
people who face the storm passively. His life has been less a com-
plex of haphazard adventures than the enactment of projects that
presented themselves with varying degrees of urgency, all of them
involving his navigating a passage among them. The play did not
so much briefly replace the raft as it was an adjunct to it—an
amusement, a consort, a parallel pursuit. "Innocently to amuse
the imagination in this dream of life . . ." et cetera and so on.

A football play allowed Neutrino to contemplate idly how to
control a circumstance that appeared to be inflexible—the rules,
textures, philosophies, and manners of the game—while also
brooding on how to subvert them, an intention that always appeals to him. He had for years, more or less, been a quarterback,
a conductor, an artist with a living, seething canvas, and with
football he would adopt his role at a single remove.

Chapter 2

IN JULY OF 2004, when Neutrino, hauling his new raft to the Pacific and stopping in Flagstaff, explained the play on the phone to Mike Canales, the quarterback coach at the University of Arizona, Canales was not at first intrigued.

"We're working with windows," Canales said, meaning that the team intended to exploit the brief opportunities between a passer and his receivers.

"What if the window closes?" Neutrino asked.

"We go to another receiver," Canales said.

"Why not create a new window with the same receiver?" Neutrino said.

Canales said nothing for a moment. Then he asked Neutrino if he could be at the student center at eight the next morning.

Neutrino arrived in Tucson as the sun was rising. When he met Canales, he drew the play on a napkin and said that, once the ball had been snapped, the play allowed the passer to modify the receiver's path. Within the last twenty yards of the field, where ground was severely contested, the play would be most effective, he said. At the goal line, it would be almost impossible to stop.

From Flagstaff, after Terrell had left, Neutrino drove south and parked the raft on its trailer in a storage lot in Buckeye, Arizona, off Interstate 10, near Phoenix, then he drove across the Mojave Desert, to Los Angeles. He ended up singing in Venice Beach, with the dog beside him, among people who sold incense and oils and T-shirts with sayings such as IF I'M NOT HERE, I'M OUT LOOKING FOR MYSELF. At night he parked by the ocean.

Neutrino does not follow football. During his year in high school, he played football and liked it. His mother liked the game. On Saturdays the two of them sometimes listened to football on the radio. If he happens to be somewhere where a football game is on television, he will watch it, but he makes no effort to find one. He says that he doesn't really like to watch football, he likes to think about it. An unstoppable play appeals to his imagination as an artistic and philosophical problem.

Neutrino calls his play the Neutrino Clock Offense. Canales describes it as "more a concept than a play," because it can be employed on any pass play. It is cousin once or twice removed to the sending of signals between a catcher and a pitcher. After Neutrino discarded as impractical having everyone but the quarterback run to the same place on the field, he began thinking, What if a passer and a receiver could communicate with each other while running a pattern?

One day while I was visiting Neutrino in Los Angeles, we sat in a café in Santa Monica, having breakfast. I asked if he would show me the play. He demurred. We had met only a few days before, and I don't think he had made up his mind about me. I said that with all the video shot at sporting events and studied by men in skyboxes wearing headsets that connect them to the coaches on the sidelines, someone would recognize the play the second time it was called.

"It's undetectable," he said.

I said it couldn't be.

"They'll just think the passer and the receiver have a great rapport," he said.

Even so, eventually someone would detect it and concoct a response, I said. He said it couldn't be prevented. I rolled my eyes. Neutrino looked hard at me. A woman stopped by our table, bent over, and petted the dog. Neutrino asked the waiter for another glass of orange juice. I sort of bluffed and said I couldn't write a story about the play if I didn't know what it was. He sighed. He looked at me steadily. Finally he asked to borrow the pencil I was using to write in my notebook.

He moved our dishes aside and unfolded his napkin on the table. On it he drew two *x*'s six inches apart. The *x*'s represented the passer and the receiver, he said. He drew a line to connect them. Around each of them he drew a circle. In the circles he drew the numbers on the face of a clock. Each of the *12*s he drew on the axis of the line between the *x*'s, so that the clock faces bore the same relation to each other.

"Quarterbacks move their hands around all the time," he said. "They hold the ball by their shoulders, by their chest, by their hips. They hold it with one hand, they hold it with two. No one knows what it means. Maybe it means nothing. Maybe it's just where they're comfortable holding the ball." He laid the pencil on the table. He wrapped one hand around the other and held them under his chin. "With the clock play, the quarterback holds the ball by his chin, that's twelve o'clock," he said. He lowered his hands. "Quarterback holds the ball by his waist, it's six o'clock. Left shoulder, nine o'clock; right shoulder, three o'clock."

"And that means?" I said.

"The receiver sees twelve o'clock, he goes deep," Neutrino said. "Six o'clock, he comes back toward the quarterback. Nine o'clock, he goes ninety degrees left, and three o'clock, he breaks ninety degrees right."

He sat back in his chair.

"Those are the first four positions," he said. "Next comes one, four, seven, ten. Then two, five, eight, and eleven. No matter which direction the passer and receiver turn, they are always in the same relation to each other regarding the clock, so they always know what the signals mean. Simple geometry. It's as if they had radios in their helmets and were talking to each other."

I could see that Neutrino was pleased—why shouldn't he be?—and I could see the appeal of his reasoning, but I was also skeptical. Partly this was a matter of protecting myself. I didn't really know him. A few days earlier, to meet for the first time, I called his cell phone, and he gave me directions to where he was. "Look for an old man with a dog sitting on a bench," he said. From the bench, we walked to a café and had something to eat. The psychopaths I had interviewed, usually in prison, depended heavily on charm that was imaginary—they bragged and preened and fussed, they leaned forward and looked earnestly into your eyes with a creepy sincerity. Neutrino's manner was measured and even modest. When I asked about his people, he told me about the Farlows, but he didn't mention that his cousin was the cowboy on the Wyoming license plate; the Pioneer Museum in Lander, whom I later consulted to check the veracity of his stories, told me that. When I called Neutrino after talking to them and said, "Do you know who the cowboy on the Wyoming license plate is?" he said simply, "My cousin Stubby." Any questions I asked he answered thoughtfully. Every once in a while, though, I would say something that seemed obscurely to provoke him, and he would fix on me a look that was unsettling for being so candidly self-interested. I thought that if the play was unsound, I ought to know about it now rather than find out after I had committed myself to following him.

"One problem," I said.

"What's that?"

"It won't take long for someone to figure out the signals."

He didn't say anything.

"Or for a player from a team using the play to be traded to another team and give up the whole thing."

"I've already thought of that," he said.

"You have?"

"Of course."

"How?"

"Rotate the clock."

"Pardon?"

"Turn it sideways, turn it upside down," he said. "It doesn't matter. Make twelve o'clock six o'clock, or make it three. The constant thing is the relation between the quarterback and the receiver. The quarterback holds the ball high on the regular clock face, it means break long. If the clock face is upside down, twelve means six, break toward me. If six is now nine, where he holds the ball means something different, and it can't be predicted."

It took a moment for the elegance of his thinking to be borne in on me. Neutrino had found a vulnerability in the game, a seam. As it is now, the moment a receiver turns his head toward the quarterback, or over his shoulder to look for the ball, the defender knows to guard him more closely. The pattern the receiver was instructed to run, he has run. The fakes he intends to throw, he has thrown. (Of course, a player's first glance might itself be a deception, but the longer the play has been in progress, the less likely this is to be the case.) The receiver has arrived, as it were, at the end of his orders, and the quarterback knows it, and the defender knows it; in fact, the whole stadium knows it.

The pattern of a receiver's path is a text the defender reads, waiting for the resolve—the receiver's gaze at the quarterback or over his shoulder for the ball. Once that occurs, the defender assumes the advantage. He has only to stay close enough to the receiver that the quarterback will regard the pass as fraught with

complication—to close the window, that is—or to worry the receiver sufficiently that he can't catch the ball or knock down the
ball or intercept it or tackle the receiver if the catch is made. The
receiver has to catch the ball while apprehensive about how hard
he will be hit when he collects it. The quarterback, in his turn,
has to keep the pass from the defender's hands and deliver it
safely to his receiver, to a place, that is, where he can catch it
without being compromised by anxiety over his well-being.

With Neutrino's play, the conventional last step of the engagement—the receiver's glance at the quarterback—becomes instead the first step. No longer is there a text for the defender to
read. Or what text there is must be regarded as code rather than
text. The exchange between the passer and the receiver is a secret
intended to work the defender's demise. He no longer knows
when to react, and when he does apprehend it, the awareness
will have come too late for him to enact it. If the receiver, under
instructions from the quarterback, who has been watching the
defender's movements, has traveled in one direction while the
defender's momentum carries him in another, the defender will
have to be twice as fast as the receiver to cover the same ground,
and that isn't possible. The receiver, on instructions from the
quarterback, will bolt in one direction or another, and the defender has no idea when or where, he knows only that it will
happen when he is least prepared to respond, because the quarterback is manipulating him. Once a team has become comfortable with the play, a quarterback could even announce at the line
of scrimmage, "On the clock," and with the clock face inverted,
the defenders would still be at a loss.

The receiver does not commit himself until the passer's arm is
in motion. Then he breaks for the territory indicated by the
clock. By the design of the play and the players' engagement, the
receiver has gained ground on the defender. The defender may

tackle him immediately, but the pass has been completed. If the defending team's response is to put a second defender on the receiver, they become vulnerable somewhere else on the field. If two receivers are running the clock and four defenders are engaged, they become very vulnerable. The play could make defending against the pass so difficult that significant parts of the field might simply be conceded to running the ball.

"You're the defender, I'm the receiver," Neutrino said. "I don't move until you tell me to. It's like ballet; you can bring the receiver and the ball together with the most graceful tactics." He gave me back my pencil.

I congratulated him.

"If I go to Tucson, and they give me a third-string passer and a third-string receiver, and three weeks to work with them," he said, "they can take the first-string defender, and I bet he won't be able to stop the play." He sat back in his chair. He bent over and petted his dog. "It all has to do with advantage," he said, sitting up. "Every area that my mind goes into, I seek advantage. At times I've felt a lot of guilt about this."

Then he asked me if I was going to finish the eggs on my plate. He leaned across the table and scooped them onto the napkin he had drawn the diagram on. "The dog would like them," he said.

Chapter 3

NEUTRINO STAYED IN Venice Beach for about ten days before he left for San Diego. For two weeks he parked beneath a highway overpass, in shade so the dog was comfortable, and in the evenings he sang for tourists on the waterfront. During the first week of August, we met in Los Angeles, to drive to Tucson. Neutrino had taken the tape off the side of the van. Bits of dust and sand had clung to the edges of the adhesive left behind, so you could still read KEY WEST TO CUBA, faintly, as if the trip had already been accomplished.

So that I would be comfortable, Neutrino vacuumed his car. Because he couldn't get all the dog hair off the passenger's seat, he covered it with a coat. Like a Frenchwoman from the past, Neutrino often applies perfume when he isn't able to bathe. He uses the cheapest fragrances, typically ones he buys at a drugstore. We would be crossing the Mojave Desert. Years before, in Mexico, when Terrell was pregnant with Jessica and fatigued by the heat, Neutrino pulled his car to the side of the road and opened the doors. He flagged down a truck and had the driver knock them off. The driver enjoyed it so much that he wouldn't accept any money. Neutrino thought that he could cool the van for us by filling the interior with ice. He bought four plastic laundry baskets and put them behind the front seats, beside his bed. Before he picked me up, he filled the baskets with bags of ice.

We left Santa Monica after breakfast. By the time we reached Palm Springs, the day was hot. The sky was a pale blue. Neutrino said that what he had loved about the bedouin's life he had lived in the desert was that you wake up and start to move. On the dashboard was a paperback copy of the Bhagavad Gita. The dog sat between us, on a blanket. Now and then, Neutrino would pour water on the dog. The water would splash on me, but I don't think he knew it, because he was watching the road. Then he would pat the dog, and water would fly off her. Then the dog would shake. Neutrino fell in behind the slowest moving truck on the road. He figured that any vehicle coming toward us that crossed into our lane would hit the truck. Cars passed us going so fast that it was as if they were fleeing something. Every few minutes, Neutrino would stick one hand through the curtain between the seats. "Yeah, that's working," he'd say. "I can really feel it cooler now. You feel it?" The water leaked onto the floor and made the red dye on the side of my canvas in-flight bag run over everything inside the bag and stain it red, but I didn't know that until later. About once an hour we would stop and empty the water from the plastic bags, and every two hours we would buy more ice.

In the desert the land was puckered like the skin of a raisin. Here and there were so many high-tension wires that they divided the sky like lines on sheet-music paper. We crossed bridges over dry rivers. The riverbed and the land around it were the color of linen and looked more like a beach than a riverbed. A sign said one of them was the Gila River.

We ate lunch at a café off the highway. The café had a picture window looking out on a parking lot and across the desert to hills. Neutrino said that it was the kind of place where he would have stopped and asked the owner if he wanted a sign painted on his window. He said he hadn't spoken to Canales since the day they had met, and he hoped that he hadn't changed his mind about the play.

We paid our bill. Neutrino walked the dog, then we emptied the water from the bags of ice, and Neutrino started the car. "Which task do you think is more difficult?" he asked. "Getting a scrap raft across the North Atlantic, or this play introduced into football?"

I told him I didn't really know, but he wasn't likely, anyway, to die trying to introduce a play into football.

"You're right," he said, and started the car.

THAT AFTERNOON, NEAR PHOENIX, we left the highway and drove through fields and past warehouses and stores
until we came to a dusty lot and a building that was low and
long, with a roof hanging over the front of it shading the door. A
handsome, dark-haired Mexican woman was sweeping the doorway, and when we turned in to the parking lot, she leaned her
broom against the doorframe and went inside. A man with black
hair and a face the color of tobacco came out. Neutrino said,
"Remember me?" The man smiled and said hello. "I just wanted
to show my friend the raft," Neutrino said. "That all right?" We
followed the man into a small, sleepy store that sold toys and
children's clothes and CDs of Mexican singers and drinks, then
into a garage that had tires and tools spread around it, then into
another dusty lot, where there were a few trucks and beat-up
and derelict cars and, on a trailer, like a rare bird among a flock
of sparrows, Neutrino's raft. It was the first time I had seen it.

When I recall the moment, I feel my eyes widen. I expected a
sleek, handmade craft, a stylish vessel, varnished and elegant, a
craft to bear up proudly to the life-and-death task being asked of
it, and it was a scrappy, scuffed-up, bummy-looking, broken-
down wreck of a doghouse on a bed of plywood. It looked like
something a child had made. There was a cabin about four feet
tall at the back of it and in front of the cabin a deck large enough
for Neutrino to sit in a chair. No seam was tight. Where there
were gaps, you could see pieces of Styrofoam drink coolers. Some
of the plywood was new and some was splintered and peeling and

had weathered to a dark gray. The back of the cabin was made from a section of a sign that Neutrino had painted in Key West for Katha Sheehan, a woman he met who was running for mayor. Sheehan and her husband had given him the van and the dog. Dark yellow letters on a yellow ground spelled ATHA FOR AYOR. The boards were held in place by screws driven deep into the wood and at angles, instead of being flush with the surface, and the intervals between them were uneven.

"How long did it take to build?" I asked.

"About four hours," he said.

I nodded.

"I designed her for speed," he said.

I wrote "Speed" in my notebook, then I underlined it, because I couldn't think of anything to say.

"She'll ride high in the water, just plane," he said. He extended his hand slowly, with the palm toward the ground.

"The gaps aren't a problem?"

"Nope."

Neutrino pointed to where on the sides he meant to install outriggers. Then we walked back through the garage and bought some bottled water from the woman at the store. Neutrino told the man he would send money for the next month's rent. We got back in the van and drove toward Phoenix, and when we saw a motel from the highway I said, "That looks okay," and we pulled off and I got a room. We ate dinner in a Mexican restaurant where there were a lot of families and a man who went around the room playing guitar and singing. Neutrino gave him five dollars and spoke to him in Spanish, and they settled on a song for him to sing.

Before I left Neutrino that night, he wrote my name and room number on a sheet of paper and put it on the dashboard, in case the motel checked the cars in its lot, then he walked the dog and went to sleep on his bed in the van.

The next morning the road lay out in front of us like a carpet the color of tin. "I'll look at Canales's face, and I'll know where the play stands," Neutrino said. "He's either into acceptance or rejection. Or maybe bewilderment—you showed up." In the fields by the road were bales of hay. "I think it's going to be a straight thing," he said, "but I'm prepared to be totally disillusioned, without courting disillusion."

The dog came and sat between us. A pickup truck passed us. In the bed were some fence posts, and a Mexican boy who was laughing. "I'm not going to butt my head," Neutrino went on. "If the football world doesn't understand me, that's the end of it. I'll go pick up the raft and head for the Pacific, which is the plan anyway." He petted the dog. "I'm moving toward certain points," he said, "and I see with all my heart and soul that they might not happen today, but they will happen."

In Tucson, I rented a car. I checked into a motel beside the interstate, then we went to look for the football stadium to see if we might run into Canales. It was Saturday, and the camp opened Sunday. Out of shadows beneath the stadium seats a man appeared driving a golf cart and pointed to the low brick building that had letters above the doors saying ARIZONA FOOTBALL. The doors were locked. We peered through the glass at the reception desk. Everything inside was so still that it looked like a diorama. Neutrino decided to walk around the stadium to acclimate himself, he said, then we went to dinner at a Denny's.

"You're watching TV, it's late at night, and an infomercial comes on," Neutrino said, laying down his menu. "'I changed the game of football,' I say. 'How about giving me some money to change children's lives? A floating orphanage.' What do you think?"

I said I wasn't sure.

"Okay," he said. "That's fine. Okay. How about 'I had an idea to change the game of football. It didn't work. How about sending me some money to try something else?'"

We ordered, and the food arrived. "My mind is a very aggressive mind," Neutrino went on. "The way I check it out is I reverse it. I make a bet that the opposite of what I want to happen will happen. It's either-or. Either Canales accepts and allows me to participate, or he rejects. How can we find out which is the truer? Bet on the opposite. If you bet on what you want to happen, you'll be nervous. But if you bet the opposite, you'll know what the odds are."

The waitress brought Neutrino a Diet Coke, and he said, "Thank you, dear." Then, "I'm going to bet my van that Canales doesn't accept me. I bet that when I go down and smile, he rejects me. If he does, I win two thousand dollars and keep the van. If he *accepts* me, I lose the van and the money. I'd need twenty-to-one odds to make this bet. He's just not going to reject me. I know it.

"By the way, you going to finish that bacon? The dog would love it."

Chapter 6

Neutrino slept that night in the van in the parking lot, and the next morning we went to find a cheap motel for him and the dog. He said he wanted to look in the part of town where people were just hanging on. Crossing the city back and forth, as if descending like Orpheus the steps into the underworld, we saw, by an exit ramp, a motel that was a single story, painted green. The parking lot was dirt with gravel laid on it. Neutrino asked to see a room, and we followed the clerk into the parking lot. A man came out of his door and when he saw us he opened it just wide enough to slither like a lizard around the edge of it, then he shut it. From another room a man was carrying boxes to his car, which had a coat hanger for an antenna. His movements had a mechanical quality, as if the task were a ritual. Each room we stepped into was small and dark. Neutrino turned on the air conditioners and sat on the beds, which sagged like hammocks. The clerk made him pay in advance, and when Neutrino asked whether the price could be discounted if he stayed for a week, the clerk shook his head.

That afternoon we drove back to the football offices. Groups of young men were standing around in T-shirts and sandals and shorts. One at a time they bent over a card table by the reception desk and solemnly signed a sheet on a clipboard, then were given a folder with forms to fill out and told where to go for a physical. Neutrino leaned toward the receptionist and said, "Mike Canales here?" The woman said he was, and Neutrino said, "Tell him Poppa Neutrino's here, please."

She spoke into a phone, and we heard Canales, apparently in a room next to the one we were in, say, "Oh, yeah," and she put down the phone and said, "He's coming."

Canales turned out to be tall and broad-shouldered, with a square, handsome face. He was about thirty-five. He was wearing a short-sleeved shirt and shorts and sandals, and he had short, black hair made shiny with a tonic and parted on one side. He shook Neutrino's hand and took us into his office.

We sat down at a table. When the play came up, Canales said that he was interested in any innovation that would help him win. "We're on the same page," he said. "I want to win, and I want to be there for the breakthrough." He said, though, that Neutrino needed to understand how complicated introducing the play would be. "It's not just one-on-one, passer and receiver," he said. "It's the five guys blocking for the guy making the pass, and the pattern and how they know what to do. It's a whole system."

"You give me two players, and I figure it'll take maybe four days, and they'll be ready," Neutrino said. "The receiver doesn't even have to catch the ball or retain it. That's another talent, to have the courage to take a hit. All he has to do is break from the defender and have the ball hit him. If it works, it's an almost zero-interception plan."

"I'm with you, Pops," Canales said. He turned to me and said, "I call this play the Pops Offense." He turned back to Neutrino. "What I have to do, I have to check if that's possible with the NCAA. A lot of times you're not allowed to have outside consultants."

Neutrino opened his mouth to say something but seemed to think better of it. Canales said that no one was allowed on the field but the coaches, and that Neutrino wouldn't be able to attend their meetings either, but he could attend the practices. Neutrino seemed to slump. Canales said that he would try to work the play into the practice, and at the end of practice he and Neutrino could talk about how it was going. "The idea," he said, "is to get it out there and see if it works. If it doesn't work, no one knows anything about it. If it works, you're the man who taught it."

"If this play works, what does it mean?" Neutrino asked.

"It would be like the forward pass," Canales said. "Like the West Coast offense. It would be the next chapter in football. If it goes, we make history, and I'm all for making history."

After the meeting, Neutrino and I drove around Tucson looking for a place to talk. We stopped at a coffeehouse, but it was dark
and hot and full of desert rats and people clearly avoiding whatever they were supposed to be doing. The atmosphere struck
Neutrino as gloomy, so we went back to the Denny's. Neutrino
called Betsy Terrell and had me tell her that we had arrived in
Tucson and that, far from having been turned away, he had been
welcomed. She and Neutrino talked for a while, then Neutrino
hung up and said, "My take is that I was in. He was glad to see
me. I'm sorry that I'm not going to be able to work with the
quarterback directly." He shrugged. "He's the quarterback
coach, and I'm the coach of the quarterback coach, I guess."

A little Latino boy raised his head over the edge of the booth
next to us and Neutrino smiled at him. The boy ducked, then
raised his head again. "What I had to do was reclose," Neutrino
said. "Hi, sweetheart," he said to the boy, who grinned broadly.
Then to me, "I had to establish again the interest and desire. I
just had to reaffirm what our relationship was. I told him that
I'm not going to bother him, I'm not going to interfere, then he
told me that I could be assured that he would come and talk to
me after practice."

He let out his breath slowly. "For the last six weeks I've been
planning every possibility," he went on. "My mind was to guide
him to get to that point, where he talked about the forward pass.
Just to get his opinion, and you heard it. So why wouldn't he try
to implement it if it could be the next chapter?"

Neutrino and the boy played hide-and-seek until the parents
told the boy to sit down and not bother us. Neutrino said that
his next move would be to borrow money from a friend in New
York to pay for a month at the motel. After that the weather
would turn cooler, and he could live in the car again.

We paid our check. "There's only one thing, and I have to

work on it," Neutrino said as we walked toward the car. "When Canales decides to put the play operative, and he really gets two guys that can handle the mentality and imagery, some of these guys may have been raised on digital clocks. We might have to retrain their whole visual system."

Chapter 7

On the way back to the motel, Neutrino talked enthusiastically. "First, we don't confuse these guys," he said. "We get them to where they can do these moves very simply. Twelve, three, six, and nine. After they get those, they work on one, four, seven, and ten. By the end they'll be so perfectly timed, they'll be like ballerinas." He said that he needed to buy a notebook and an umbrella to sit under during practice.

"I've been spending six weeks preparing for this day," he went on. "This was a thing that nobody in his normal mind would do. My talent is being able to say, 'Let's try this,' and that comes from my mother. I think I just had the receptors for it to be passed down easily to me. Plus the Gurdjieff teachings. They really made me aware that there are two kinds of people—ones that can do, and ones that can't."

The field where the Wildcats practiced was a couple of miles from the football office. Canales had told us where it was. "What I want to do now," Neutrino said, "is find that field, then go home and take a nap."

The next morning Neutrino was asleep when I arrived at the motel. He had only just gone to bed. I waited for him to dress, then we walked the dog in the rubbishy lot behind the motel. What had kept him awake was concern over what he would do if the play didn't catch on with Canales. "If I go to practice for the next week, and I feel he's not devoting attention to this, he's not desperate enough, if at the end of the week he and I aren't conspiring together, I'm going to try other teams," he said. "If he doesn't develop a rapport, I go back to Notre Dame, Columbia, I go to teams in all the leagues. I can pick another team and stay loyal to Canales long as I don't pick one he's up against."

Neutrino stopped to let the dog sniff a bottle cap.

"Now I don't feel a victim of someone else's situation," he said. "I feel empowered. I know how to behave from here on out. I sit in the stands, take notes, Canales talks to me, he sees I'm not going to interfere. Everything goes smoothly. The play advances, and if it doesn't, I have other means of attack."

He began walking. The dog trotted ahead of us. "This is the most important thing I know," he said. "A person receives impressions every second. The direction and quality of those impressions are going to form the future, not the present, because the present is being responded to by the past. But if you concentrate, if you really pay attention, if you are alert, you can structure the input of the present, which gives you your feeling for the future."

When we got back to the motel the clerk was holding a hose above a scrawny bush that was planted on a sour little corner of soil by the sidewalk. The man who had been loading boxes the day before had raised his car's hood and was peering into the engine. He wasn't wearing a shirt, and his back was red from the sun. The trunk had so many boxes in it that it was also raised. It looked like a car in a circus act. The passenger's door was open, and in the seat was a woman whose hair was blond and dry as straw, like a doll's hair. She was wearing a red halter top and blue-jean shorts and was bent over, with her hands covering her face, and she was weeping. A man who had been smoking a cigarette and standing in a doorway came over and looked into the engine and said something to the other man, and they shook their heads, deliberately, as if being judicious. The clerk put down his hose and went with Neutrino into the office so that Neutrino could pay for his room. Neutrino came out and said, "How do I look?" I said he looked fine, but that maybe he might want to shave, it would make him look younger. "I don't want to look younger," he said. "I want to look older. I want mine to be the very face of wisdom."

The practice was at six in the evening. We arrived at five-thirty and parked behind the buses carrying the players. The buses were idling, and their drivers stood on the sidewalk with their hands in their pockets, as if mildly embarrassed not to have a purpose any longer. The windows were dark, so we couldn't see the players. Neutrino paced up and down the sideline. Then he asked me to film him making remarks about attending the first practice. When he finished, he nodded and walked out of the frame. The sky had a hazy sheen to it, like nylon, and in several corners, above the hills, there were pitchforks of lightning. The lightning was the reason the players hadn't left the bus. "Probably going to cancel," one of the drivers said. "Go back to the athletic building and run drills indoors." After about forty-five minutes, the drivers, as if taking matters into their own hands, got back on the buses, and they pulled away from the curb.

Neutrino and I went to a Vietnamese restaurant for dinner. The waitress was the owner. Her husband cooked the food. We were the only customers. She asked Neutrino his name, then kept calling him Daddy. She told a long story about her stepfather, an

American soldier, who had died a few weeks earlier, without her having a chance to say good-bye. "You know, Daddy, it make me so sad," she said.

At the motel, Neutrino asked me to wait until he had got his door unlocked. In the frame of a doorway several doors past his, I could see the burning red dot of a cigarette, like a little ruby.

Chapter 8

AT BREAKFAST NEUTRINO SAID, "Last week the important thing was how quick Canales acts on the play. Now, I don't care how quickly he acts. It's how quickly can I act. The goal is not to get the University of Arizona into the Rose Bowl using the play. That was a mistake. The goal is to get the play out and used. I want to go up to Flagstaff, see the Arizona Cardinals, maybe Northern Arizona, then through Colorado and Kansas, then to South Bend and hang around Notre Dame till they listen to me. That's the team I want to see really work this. I won't do it forever, because I have to get back to the raft, but I can leave it in the storage lot for a little longer anyhow."

He hooked his elbows on the back of his seat. "I'm unwinding now," he said. "Tomorrow you'll see a totally different person. I have no consistency."

That evening we drove to the practice field. The sky and the pointed hills in the distance came together like a set of teeth. Neutrino made notes on the back of an envelope. He walked over to where Canales was watching the quarterbacks and receivers and stood close enough that he could see what they were doing but not so close that Canales might think he was hoping to be invited to join him. Canales walked around with a clipboard and seemed vexed much of the time. At one moment, he hunched his shoulders and lowered his head and shouted, "Wake up, this ain't high school." Each time a drill concluded, he joined the other coaches in the middle of the field and Neutrino walked briskly to the sideline, so as not to appear to be in his path. He kept thinking that Canales was setting up the play. "This is it," he'd say, "this is it," then the quarterback would take several steps back from the line of scrimmage and the receivers would race up the field and the ball would fly through the air and he'd say, "That wasn't it." He gave me his video camera and stood beside the field with the players in the background. He rubbed his hands together and said, "It's been a long afternoon, I've got some good impressions, and while I'm on my way to launching the Pacific crossing, I'm going to be spreading this play across the football fields of America." He walked out of the frame, then asked, "Did you get it?"

The shadows on the field grew longer. The sky deepened. Several young women, black and Latino, began arriving, some of them with children, and sat on the sideline. When the players left the field, in groups of three and four, the children ran up to some of them and held out their arms and yelled, "Daddy." Neutrino stood by the gate that led to the buses, to wait for Canales.

He paced. He looked over at Canales, then he looked away. "He's got to stop, or I'm out of here," he said. Canales walked toward us with three of the other coaches. He stopped when he saw Neutrino. Clearly he was tired. He looked at the ground and spread his feet and said that his lower back hurt from standing for so long.

"If I can spend a little time with you, and tell you all I know," Neutrino said, "then it's in your hands."

Canales nodded, shifted his leg, and winced.

"It's a lost opportunity otherwise," Neutrino went on. "It's worth fourteen points a game."

Canales said he would talk with Neutrino, but he didn't know when. He had meetings all the following day. He looked at the ground and shook his head, as if the problem had no solution, then he said, "How about tomorrow morning at seven in my office? We'll talk for half an hour, then I'll go to my meetings."

"Tomorrow morning," Neutrino said. "Thank you very much."

As we drove around looking for somewhere to have dinner, Neutrino said, "Half an hour. That's fine. After that I'm out of here. I'll go to Flagstaff. I can sleep in the car, and I won't pay rent."

We ate at a Mexican restaurant. Afterward I drove Neutrino back to the motel. He said he thought that the important thing to establish in the meeting was the balletic movement involved in bringing the receiver and the ball together. What he hoped to do was persuade Canales to leave his office and go out to the parking lot so that he could show him the movements. "It's like a piece of art," he said.

I said I thought that the last thing that would appeal to Canales would be the elements of art. He was a man who had to win football games, not enact philosophies of style. Neutrino leaned back and looked at me as if he'd never seen me before in his life.

Neutrino drove himself to the meeting. When I arrived, he and Canales were sitting at the table in Canales's office. Neutrino was saying how simple the play could be. He had realized, he said, that the ball didn't need to be moved all around the quarterback's body—to two-thirty, say, and four-fifteen—it had only to go to twelve, three, six, and nine. And it didn't need to cross the body for nine. The quarterback could indicate nine by holding his left hand apart from the ball.

"The secret is getting to the players without having them change anything they already do," he said. "You can say to the quarterback, Can you throw from here?"—he began moving his hands around his torso—"from here, from here, each position a new one. You work with them for two or three weeks, you'll see if they can take it on. If they can, you can gently introduce the movement into the playbook. By the time you're ready for USC, the simplicity of it will be absorbed."

Canales nodded.

"It's a fourteen-point spread, call it the Neutrino spread," he went on. "If a team went from two and ten to five and seven because of the coaching change, it's possible with this play to go another four or five games and a bowl spot."

Canales leaned back in his chair. "Let's say you're going to do this," he said. "First of all, I go to camp and find out if I've got a quarterback who can throw from different positions. Second, I've got to find an end who can read the body language of the quarterback. If he can't do that out of the box—read ball placement and arm movement—I'm struggling. Then I have to figure out how to install the whole thing without affecting the other twenty players."

"Why would it affect them?" Neutrino asked. "You already have a buttonhook play that everyone knows, just run it that way—short sprint, quick pass. The difference is the defender won't know where it's going, you can change the receiver's pattern after it's started."

Canales agreed. "There's one more thing," he said, though. "You're going to have to devise a way by which the receiver knows the play is on. If it's a straight buttonhook play, then does the quarterback hold the ball up above his head, or down at his shoulders so everyone can see it? That's the one thing I haven't figured out. How do you tell everyone it's on?"

Canales rose and stood in front of one of those shiny white boards that restaurants in shopping malls write their specials on and began drawing black circles and x's. "What we call Play Z is the only one in our playbook that has a one-on-one between the end and the defender," he said. He drew a circle around the figure representing the end and from it a line to the defender. "The end reads from the defender's position and turns away from whatever way the defender goes. Where's my red pen? Here it is. I'm a color man. It makes it easier to teach, keep things separate." He began drawing a path for the end in red, then he drew the paths of other players in blue and green.

"What you're saying has a lot of truth to it," he told Neutrino. "It can work and be effective, and I'm looking for another word for truth, but I can't think of it. Anyway, I agree it can work. I'm worried about the time system, but let's dump that for now. It's on Z read, we're running the play on Z read, the end knows it's going to be done, he makes his break when the quarterback moves his arm, not until."

Sitting in his chair, Neutrino cocked his arm. "Nobody moves until the quarterback has his arm in motion," he said.

"We've got to give him some perimeter guidelines to help him, though," Canales said. "These kids are all learning. There's a lot of teaching involved. It has to be simple." He took the cap off one of his pens and wrote KISS on the board. As he wrote he said, "Keep it stupid—sorry." He rubbed out "stupid" with his hand and began writing again. "Keep it simple, stupid," he said.

"Absolutely," Neutrino said. Then, "Last thing, and I'm out of here. Can I borrow a piece of paper?"

Canales handed him a piece of paper from his desk and sat down. Neutrino drew three circles on it and spoke briefly about how understated the movements of the quarterback's hands could be.

"I'm with you a hundred percent, Pops," Canales said.

Neutrino leaned back. "One more thing," he said. "I think the slower the receiver goes, the more advantage he has, because then he makes his break—a sneak play."

"Sure he does," Canales said. "But then there's the time factor. These kids have one-point-seven, two-point-three, or two-point-five seconds to throw the ball."

"How far can a guy go in two-point-five?" Neutrino asked.

"These kids? About twenty yards," Canales said.

"Have him go five."

Canales shook his head. "The receiver can't be slow until he makes his move," he said. "He's got to go as fast as he can and be what I call 'stay friendly.' It means to be in control."

Neutrino said, "Well—"

"Point A to point B, we got to go as fast as he can, then—"

"Have him walk backwards from the line of scrimmage and watch the quarterback the whole time—"

"He's got to move as fast as he can," Canales said, shaking his head again. "Otherwise you don't gain any ground."

I was concerned that Neutrino was going to bring up ballet.

"I've got to have it simple," Canales said. "I've got to be able to put it into jock talk."

"How difficult you think it would be to get it in there?" Neutrino asked.

"I'll take some of the third- or fourth-string guys, we'll try it during the one-on-one time, we have about ten minutes every day for that," Canales said. "If I can get it to work with them, I can move it to the guys up the line."

"It's not a next-year thing then?" Neutrino asked.

Canales shook his head. "While we're in camp here, we can work on it and hope to get it in by the fifth or sixth game," he said. "The best time to do it would be inside the twenty-yard line, when the field's got smaller."

Neutrino said they had disposed of all he had on his mind. Canales nodded and said that it was time for him to go to a coaches' meeting. Neutrino stood up. "It's yours now," he said. "You'll see subtleties I haven't even dreamed up."

Canales and Neutrino shook hands, and Neutrino thanked him and left. I asked Canales how he had heard from Neutrino. He said that Neutrino's message had been passed to the coach, who had sent it to him. It had arrived during the week in the summer that he reserves for talking to people about ideas. He had visited Neutrino's website, which shows him with a full beard, so he hadn't recognized him immediately when they met. "We talked for an hour," he said, "and the more I listened, the more I understood. 'These are the variables to making a pass play,' I said, and I wrote them down for him. 'These are the parameters, these are all the components. If you can convince me after dealing with them, we'll keep talking,' which we did."

I asked if when he had extended the invitation to attend the camp, he had expected Neutrino to appear.

He thought for a moment. "In the back of my mind, I thought he'd show up," he said. "I just didn't expect him the first day."

Chapter 10

A T BREAKFAST NEUTRINO SAID that he had felt discouraged the night before but now he felt better. He thought that he had accomplished his purposes. "He took a point of view, and I took the opposite," he said. "I made him defend his point of view, then I agreed to it." He ordered oatmeal and toast and orange juice.

"I've been so close to the golden ring, and I've hit it a few times," he said. "When I made it to Europe, it was called 'the Sail of the Century' in the New York *Daily News,* up there with Chichester and Slocum and Robert Knox Graham. Now it's a new challenge. Canales is saying that he thinks this can work, and he's going to get it in. There's no more I can achieve here."

That day, for pleasure we drove south on back roads through the high desert, visiting towns Neutrino had been to thirty years earlier. The land was green and rolling, and the sky was clear and pale blue. We asked directions in a grocery store to a road we saw on a map but couldn't find. The girl at the cash register shook her head and said, "You don't want to take that road, it's not paved," but we did and it turned out to be a stony track through steep hills that went nearly to the border. The valley and the cattle we saw here and there and the unspoiled hills stirred Neutrino, and he started singing.

> He always sings raggedy music to his cattle as he swings
> Back and forward in his saddle on a horse,
> A pretty good horse that's syncopated gated
> As he trots a funny meter to the roar of his repeater how
>   they run
> When they hear the mighty bellow of his gun.
> The cows all know he's a high-falutin, rootin'-tootin' son
>   of a gun from Arizona
> Ragtime Cowboy, talk about a cowboy
> Ragtime Cowboy Joe

We ate lunch in Nogales then drove back to Tucson, and the next morning I flew home to New York. In the paper I bought at the airport I read that the University of Arizona Wildcats were having difficulty finding a quarterback. None of the candidates had arrived in camp with the job promised to him, nor had any of them managed to separate himself from the others.

Chapter 11

Neutrino moved out of the motel. He drove slowly north. For a day he felt fine, then his spirits fell, and he wasn't sure why. He came across a car circle of Indians parked around a fire, and they let him add himself to it and talk, and slowly it was borne in on him that he felt downcast at the reception he had received at the University of Arizona. He believed that he had brought the team something that would change their fortunes, something they needed, and they had said that they would try to get to it soon. They hadn't, by his lights, been sufficiently desperate. If they didn't regard his play as tilting the game in their favor, then someone else would. He decided that, before he made the crossing, he would give the play to as many teams as he could.

He left the Indians and the car circle and drove to Flagstaff, where the Arizona Cardinals were holding their training camp. At the field he saw a corridor down which the players and coaches would walk on their way to the locker room, and where fans were permitted, and he took up a position along it. He made himself the last person in line. When the coach arrived, Neutrino asked for his autograph, then he met his eyes and said, "I've been waiting three days to talk to you, may I have ten seconds?" The coach said he could have more than that, and Neutrino explained the play to him. When Neutrino finished, the coach said, "You thought of that?" He asked Neutrino to make drawings of the play and bring them the following morning.

Later that day Neutrino visited Northern Arizona University, a rival of the University of Arizona. The coach liked the play. "You have to understand, though," he said. "Last year, we went nine and three. We won our division. I can't afford to tamper with our system." Neutrino thanked him for his candor.

I called Neutrino. Having decided on a course of action, he felt better. He was determined that the play would succeed. "I'm not going to be in the audience," he said. "I'm going to make the play work. I may fail, but I'll get up and rest and go back again.

I'm seventy-nine percent imagination and eighty percent failure. It doesn't bother me. As long as I put in full effort, I know I'll hit it eventually."

Neutrino gave the drawings to the Cardinals coach, then left Flagstaff to find more teams. He had no notion of where he would find them, he simply felt sure that he would. He made his way slowly northeast, toward South Bend, Indiana. "You're moving as if you were in a dream," he told me. "You're directing the dream, and you're directing yourself in the dream, thinking, This is a place where I can light and maybe settle, or you think, I'll go someplace else in my dream."

In northeast Arizona, in the Navajo Nation, out in the badlands, he saw a football field. The field was empty. Next to it was a school and a settlement, Red Mesa. According to a sign, the field belonged to the Red Mesa Redskins. Neutrino drove a few miles farther, to the trading post at Teec Nos Pos. He walked the dog around the parking lot and let her play with some strays, then drove back to the football field, and this time there were players spread over it.

From a distance the Red Mesa coach, a man named Pita Olomua, saw Neutrino walking toward him. Olomua assumed that Neutrino was lost and would ask directions. Neutrino's unhurried pace and his somber clothes then made Olomua wonder if he owed anyone money. He tossed a football up and down. He watched his players, then turned back and looked at Neutrino growing slowly larger. When Neutrino finally reached him, he said, like a prophet, "I have a football play for you."

Olomua is not a Navajo. He is from Samoa. He is in his forties. He is tall, with black hair, a round face, dark skin, and the big arms, small waist, and broad shoulders of a hero in a comic book. When he was eleven, his family moved to Hawaii. He and his wife wanted to raise their children on the mainland, so in 1995 they moved to Phoenix. A man he knew from Hawaii was superintendent of the school in Red Mesa. The team had a dirt field and was close to giving up on football. They lost so often and the scores were so one-sided that they were having difficulty getting boys to take part. In 1999 the superintendent offered Olomua the position of head of school security and asked if he would help with the football team. The lavish green Astroturf field rolled out like a rug in the badlands was paid for by money Olomua raised from the government.

The Navajo boys tend to be small, slight, and fast. When they play what Olomua calls the cowboy teams and the farmboy teams from the big schools off the reservation, they get manhandled, and sometimes they get hurt. Olomua tries to overcome the Navajo disadvantage in size by using different formations and intricate plays. He hopes to catch the bigger boys flat-footed. "I like to mix it up," he says. As he listened to Neutrino, he tried to imagine the play.

"Mr. Neutrino's talking about the receiver moving real slow and facing the quarterback, not turned away," he says. "It really took me by surprise as far as something new to the football world, because I'm used to all the speed, and the split second where you freeze the defender."

Olomua thought the play was possibly the advantage he sought, and he invited Neutrino to practice on the following day to teach the kids the clock. Neutrino slept that night in the van by the side of the road. The next day Olomua introduced him to his first-string quarterback and receiver, two lanky boys who ran like gazelles. Neutrino told Olomua that the movements of the play would take three or four weeks to absorb, but the boys seemed to take to it quickly. He and Olomua saw the play as a means of methodically advancing down the field, one short pass after another to three o'clock, six o'clock, or nine o'clock. The boys, however, kept throwing the hero pass to twelve o'clock.

Chapter 12

Neutrino decided to stay in Red Mesa for the football season and make a video of the Redskins using the play. For money he thought that he might pick up scrap or burn wire—burn off the rubber coating, that is, to get the pure copper. Most people won't take the time to do it. He slept several nights along the state road, then went looking for a place where he could park. About a mile down a road in back of the trading post he found a little wind-whipped cluster of buildings with a barbed-wire fence around them that were the premises of the Navajo Christian Church. He told the pastor he was working with the football team and asked if he could park in the church's yard, and the pastor gave him the use of a hoedown, an eight-sided room that the church kept for guests. The hoedown had a bed and a pool table. During the day an old man visible from a distance walking slowly along the dusty road would arrive and play pool. Neutrino spent his mornings having breakfast and walking the dog, and his afternoons at the football field.

The Redskins were permitted an hour and a half for practice. For two days, the first- and second-string quarterbacks and their receivers worked on the play. On the third day, Olomua's manner toward Neutrino was unexpectedly remote.

"He wouldn't even look at me," Neutrino told me over the

phone. "He went out on the field and just kept his head down. The receiver I had been working with wasn't there—he had some family problems—so Olomua gave me a new receiver. Something's really happening, though, I can feel it. He's not acting the same toward me. I figured I had to get the new receiver up to speed really quickly.

"I'm working with him carefully, trying not to overload him. Finally, Coach Olomua comes over, and he tries to defend against the receiver, and he can't do it. Then I get the picture. He's thinking, What am I doing taking advice from this seventy-one-year-old white man I don't even know who isn't even a football coach? He called in a few more defenders, and the group of them couldn't stop the play either.

"Then he called over the team. I told the receiver, 'Don't worry about the other players, it's a distraction, just do what you have to do.' They kept adding people—they put the full monty on trying to stop it—and the whole team couldn't do it. It cannot be stopped. I saw then that Olomua must originally have thought, We've got this play and it's an innovation, and it's going to make us win, then it dawned on him, he doesn't know if it works. It works one-on-one, with no distractions and plenty of time to throw the ball, which is how he's been running it, but he doesn't know if it works in the context of the game. After it was proved to him, he turned really positive. He said, 'Tomorrow we're going to get some more receivers, and keep running this play until we have it.'"

Coach Olomua said, "One night, two days after I met Poppa, I couldn't sleep, tossing and turning. I'm trying to figure out how the quarterback can do this with all the defenses coming. Do I need a big line, does it take more time than a regular pass, which is already difficult enough? Can any receiver, any quarterback play it? How can I even put it into my whole system? Is it going to upset everything else? How do I even let everyone know we're running it? I was so happy when I first got the play, and it was so original and no one else has it, but now I have to sit down and think about it. Is it right for me to do this? How does this benefit my kids? I decide I really have to test it. So next day I go to the field and try to defend it, and I can't. Even if you see the signal and know what it means, the receiver moves first, so he has a step on you. All he has to do then is catch the ball. I put two guys on the receiver, and it still works. Three guys, it's working. Then I was very happy."

Olomua devised a signal to send to the quarterback when he wanted the clock play to run. At the line of scrimmage, the quarterback would yell out, "Clock." He also appointed one of his coaches, a Navajo named Sandy Benally, to superintend the quarterback and the receivers while they practiced the play, which they did every afternoon for the bulk of their time.

Every Friday, Neutrino would call the office of the Arizona Cardinals and leave word on the coach's answering machine of how the play was evolving at Red Mesa.

Chapter 13

MOST AFTERNOONS, NEUTRINO would set up a folding chair next to the pay phone at Teec Nos Pos and call me. In the background I could hear trucks on the state road, car doors opening and closing, dogs barking, and the conversation of people walking into the store. Now and then someone would pull up beside Neutrino on a Harley, and we would have to wait until the rider turned off the bike.

"I'm out here in the desert, which is my favorite landscape," Neutrino said one day. "Right by the four corners. I had to take a seventy-eight-year-old Indian to get his tooth fixed the other day, and I was in gorgeous country. Cattle just came up and looked at my dog. They're the same color as she is. She's having a great time running around with the strays. The people are so gracious. And they're kind of stoic. They're not like Mexicans jumping around and whooping it up, which is another form of existence I am fond of, but this is different. They're so polite. Pitiless in a way, but polite."

He said that typically he had to move every day "amidst adversarial tasks to feel expressive. I'm here for nine weeks, I know it will be hard, but I want to do this so the game of football is changed forever. I feel like a warrior doing this. Sometimes I think, What am I doing out here in the desert? I'm out in the desert because I'm doing this adversarial task. I'm out to alter football at this point. And later I'll take the raft. I see the world as having to be altered."

The pastor asked Neutrino if he would teach music at the church. He also asked if he would lead a Sunday school class. A woman in the congregation thought she knew of an empty trailer where Neutrino might live. Meanwhile, the play had progressed. "It's no longer rough-and-tumble," he said. "There's a softness and a sweetness to it, then there's a hard hit after they get the catch. A sweet movement, hands in the air, arms stretched out, then bang, they're hit."

He had thought of refinements. "I'm going to tell them to slow down," he said. "Every time they do the clock, there should be no tension. The easier you are, the easier it is to do. You stop at five yards, then bam, you go hard, an explosive break from still-ness to violence. I'm going to bring one, four, seven, and ten into it, too. These kids are really flying with it. By the time they get this down, they'll be doing one-fifteen, and three-forty-five, combinations I hadn't even thought of."

That night, he said, he was going to a tent revival at a settle-ment called Sweetwater. "All Indians," he said. "I'll play guitar. Maybe sing. I'm not going to take on whether they're intellectu-ally correct, or historically correct, I'm just going to feel the spirit, like I did as a child. Let it sink into me."

The Red Mesa Redskins played their first game on Septem-ber 3, a Friday night against Tohatchi, a Navajo town in New Mexico. The day before the game Olomua had the receivers and the quarterback run the play for the entire practice. "The coach thinks they got a shot at the state title with the clock," Neutrino said one day on the phone. "They have a great team. They have some talent guys, but the rest of the team is trained. They don't leave any space, they're in and out like darts, they cover their assignments."

Olomua allowed Neutrino to make suggestions to the play-ers. "Next thing I'm going to introduce them to is breathing," Neutrino said. "Relaxing. Try to bring it into the huddle. Take three seconds of their valuable time and breathe together. Here's what I explained to them: you have a peak, and there's nowhere to go but down when you reach it. You cannot go beyond it, otherwise you haven't by definition reached a peak. You reach it just once, and you can't get back, so what you do is you stay just below it by breathing. You've just exploded your energy into an outburst in a play, now you have to bring it back into you, you cannot just automatically run back into the huddle and continue without intervening with the conscious thought of breathing. Otherwise you spend yourself and your effort. You decline. Olomua's letting me go through the entire team when they're on the field, and say to them, 'Breathe.'"

Red Mesa beat Tohatchi, 42–18. "It looked like a real battle when they started. Tohatchi had a good-sized team, and they played strong," Neutrino said. "But Red Mesa were like little pros. They ran hard and hit hard on every play. After the first eight or nine minutes, they started to take it away. Coach Olomua was going to use the clock in the fourth quarter, when the outcome was already decided, and I said, 'Don't put it in.' The big game is next week against Shiprock, and there may have been somebody down there scouting, not that it would have done any good. I told him he should get experience with all his old plays, and save the clock for a surprise."

Neutrino called Notre Dame and described the play to the coach's answering machine. No one called back. A few days later he called again and got the coach, who said he had listened to the message. He asked Neutrino to send a tape of Red Mesa using the play. Neutrino's video included his describing the play's mechanics and footage of the players practicing it. He sent the tape with the following remarks, "The Neutrino Clock Offense allows a passer and receiver to exchange information after a play is already under way, thereby gaining an enormous advantage over the defender. Using one of four simple hand signals based on the face of a clock, a passer, having observed a defender's preparations, can send a receiver away from the defender and toward an unoccupied piece of ground. Within the tight confines of the last twenty yards of the field, or in the end zone, the advantage makes the pass play virtually unstoppable."

Neutrino also called Canales, who said he had been practicing the play when he could. His season was going poorly, though, and an innovative play was less important to him than finding players who could block, run, and tackle, pass and catch footballs.

ON THE EVENING OF September 10, a Friday, Red Mesa played Shiprock under the lights at Shiprock's field, about thirty miles from Red Mesa. Nearly everyone in Red Mesa attended. "Shiprock's a big team," Neutrino said. "There's only the trading post in Red Mesa, but Shiprock's a four corners town, and they have all these players, so Red Mesa was nervous. I could tell by the way the quarterback was warming up. I went out on the field to each of the players and said, 'Breathe, all you have to do is breathe,' and that became my mantra. 'Coach told me to tell you to breathe.' I was hiding behind his authority.

"They all started to breathe, and their passes sharpened up, they settled down. At the kickoff, Number Twenty-two caught the ball, and he ran ninety-eight yards for a touchdown. The crowd went wild. He cut through all the players like a jigsaw. Only twelve seconds on the clock. Red Mesa kicked off. Shiprock's first play was a pass. It's intercepted and run back forty or fifty yards for a touchdown. Next was a Shiprock fumble and a Red Mesa recovery and a run into the end zone. Before we got to one minute and fifty seconds, Red Mesa's twenty-six to nothing. They were so pumped up. Four minutes into the game it's thirty-two, nothing. That's a pass. By then Coach Olomua and the team were in a state of total discomposure. They had come apart. I went to Olomua and said, 'Breathe, breathe,' and he went, 'I'm trying.' He's walking up and down the sideline hyperventilating. He's making the mistake of trying to stay on that pace, on that peak. No way it can be done. Before the first quarter's over with, they scored thirty-two points. At that pace, it's a hundred twenty-eight to nothing.

"My feeling was, he should put in the second string, really pull back. Let the team collect themselves. Regroup and recover. He didn't do that. He put the first-string defense in, which is really the first-string offense, or close to it. The first-string defense tried so hard to keep Shiprock from scoring, they exhausted themselves. And from that time on, Shiprock outplayed and outscored Red Mesa, twelve to six. The final score was thirty-eight to twelve.

"By then I was totally exhausted from trying to calm them down. The game was like a battlefield with all the exhaustion on the sideline, the frenzy. Meanwhile, things went so fast that once again we didn't get a chance to use the play. I didn't want to bother Coach Olomua, but in the last few minutes I said, 'Coach, I need some footage.' He said, 'Shiprock will think I'm trying to pour it on them.' I said, 'Just a little short pass, for the camera.' He said, 'Okay,' and they called the play, but it's not a short pass, they went for twelve o'clock, they went for the score. The pass was thrown, I saw the ball go up through the lights, and come down into the fingertips of the receiver who's out in the clear, then he dropped it, he's so exhausted. So the play went in and had its debut, but it's not completed."

Chapter 15

Toward the end of September, Neutrino went to another tent revival. As the preacher talked, Neutrino began to feel, by the preacher's gestures and the tone of his voice, that he was laboring a point, and he further intuited that the point was that the figure of Christ and its representations were the most important element of Christian doctrine. Neutrino stood, interrupting the preacher, and said that love, not the life of Christ, was the church's most important teaching.

The next day the pastor knocked on the door of the hoedown, and he and Neutrino discussed the Bible. The pastor insisted that the Bible represented the literal word of God, and Neutrino said that it didn't. The pastor told Neutrino that he could continue staying at the church but that no one on the reservation cared to hear his views on religion. Neutrino felt that he had been rebuked. Furthermore, he began to feel that people turned away from him when they met.

"Maybe I don't belong here," he said on the phone. "I thought I did, but I guess I was wrong." He sounded tired and disconsolate. "The thing is," he went on, "I have no idea where I do belong." He thought maybe he should leave.

"I sat all night thinking of what to do," he said. "I felt called strongly to go to San Francisco and do a pilgrimage to all my old childhood places, like an old elephant going to the bone ground. I'm not sure I should, but I need somehow to restore myself if I'm going to make it to the Pacific."

I had never heard him so cast down. I asked if anything would change if he found somewhere other than the church to stay.

"I live in the car, so I don't need the room and the pool table and the electricity he's offering," he said. "But my feeling is that everyone here's on their own slow momentum. They don't want to kick it into a higher gear—spiritually or intellectually. Which means that either I have to descend into their emotions and thinking or I have somehow to stir them up, but you can't move people that drastically. You can give them inspiration, you can encourage them, but they have to move themselves. Everyone here has other things on their mind now besides the play and what I have to offer as a missionary, I guess, if that's what I am. It's like you meet a woman, she's really crazy about you, she makes room for you, now she's going back to her life. The novelty's exhausted. They can't keep focused on me, or they'll lose their own lives."

He seemed then to brighten. "The play's in, though, the play's going on," he said. "Even if I have to leave, and I can't stay forever— the raft is waiting—they're going to be using that play. We've gone too far, and they can't stop now."

I thought Neutrino might feel better if he had company, and I wanted to see what the play looked like when it was being used—I had only seen it as a drawing on a napkin—so on the Friday after the Shiprock game, I flew to Tucson and drove west about 120 miles to meet him in Sanders, Arizona, where Red Mesa was playing Valley Sanders High School, whose team is called the Tigers. In Sanders I stopped at a gas station to ask where the football field was. The guy at the cash register walked me outside and pointed past the pumps and the canopy and said go about a mile and turn left, and I'd see the lights. I added my car to the line of cars going down the road. Every one of us made the same turn. I paid five dollars to park at the high school. About two hundred people had driven the 130 miles from Red Mesa. The sun was setting. Above the hills in the distance, the effect was as if the doors of an immense furnace had been thrown open. Neutrino, wearing a dark shirt, dark pants, and a snap-brim hat, was standing in one of the end zones, pointing the lens of his video camera at the field.

The teams were throwing footballs and running quick, snappy plays. The Tigers' uniforms were yellow and blue. Red Mesa's uniforms were red and white. Neutrino said that he had driven slowly south from Red Mesa, and the trip had taken all day. Several times he had pulled to the side of the road in order to read the Bible. "I'm still having a dialogue with the pastor up there," he said. "I told him the Bible has inconsistencies. He said, 'You're not a saved Christian.' I looked at him and said, 'I believe I am.' I've had the spirit in me many times, especially when I was growing up and going with my aunt to tent meetings."

We started walking up the sideline.

"Gurdjieff had this expression called vulgar reading," Neutrino said. "It means you pick up the scripture and begin reading wherever it falls open. So today I stopped under a tree to read the Bible, and as vulgar reading would have it, I turned to the perfect passage, Acts 1:16–19, where Peter talks about Judas feeling so terrible for betraying Jesus that he bought a field with the money he'd made from his treachery and fell down in the field, and his insides burst open. Then I turned by chance to Matthew 27, verse 3 through 5, where Matthew said Judas felt so bad about turning in Christ that he gave back the reward money and hung himself. Surely Peter and Matthew were there at the same time and saw the same thing, but they present completely different explanations you can't rationalize away, so that's proof. I'm going to show it to him tomorrow, see what he says."

We reached the Red Mesa bench as the ball was kicked off by Valley Sanders. The Sanders players ran after it, away from us, then several seconds later, as if in retreat, came running back toward us, following Number 32, Craig Begay, on Red Mesa. "They'll never catch him," Neutrino said. "When he gets started, he's like a racehorse." Begay ran past us and was in the end zone before any of the Sanders players had reached the ten-yard line.

The teams lined up for the extra point. "Here comes the clock," Neutrino said. "The end's on the clock."

"How can you tell?"

"Because instead of looking at the defender, he's looking at the passer."

The ball was snapped, and the receiver ran into the end zone watching the quarterback, who sent him into the clear at three o'clock, but he seemed to have taken his eyes off the ball to look at the players coming toward him. Briefly he held the ball in his fingers then he dropped it.

Before the first quarter ended, Red Mesa led, 32–0. Their followers were whooping and cheering. Every time Valley Sanders had the ball, someone yelled, "Get the quarterback." The sky turned dark above us. A crescent moon appeared from behind some clouds. Red Mesa returned a punt to make the score 38–0. On the following kickoff, the players began clapping and shouting. Neutrino went up and down the sideline yelling, "No, contain yourself, don't waste it. Contain yourself. Explode on the field, not on the sidelines." The kids calmed down, but not immediately, as if to suggest that the idea to quit had been theirs.

At halftime they ran to one end of the field and took off their helmets. They sat in a half circle and leaned back against the helmets as if they were beach chairs and listened to Olomua. He stood beneath the goalposts with the huge night sky above him and told them to pay attention. "You should have your head on a swivel," he said. Then he said, "Everybody okay? Nobody hurt?" They all looked at one another and shook their heads.

Over a loudspeaker an announcer conducted a raffle. "Anybody have seven-zero-eight-zero?" he asked. "Seven-zero-eight-zero?" A man stood up in the stands and produced the number and went onto the field. A football had been lined up for him to kick through the goalposts. He took a run at the ball and it squibbed off to the side. He raised his arms and closed his hands into fists, and the crowd applauded.

"The road's going to get tougher," Olomua said. Then, "Who

hasn't been in yet?" A few boys shyly held up their hands. The crowd sang, "Happy Birthday, Joey," their voices sounding tinny and childlike over the speakers.

Olomua began the second half with the second-string quarterback. He called for the clock play, but the quarterback fumbled the ball. Red Mesa recovered it, though. On the following series, Olomua put the first string back in, and on the first play, a pass, they made it 46–0.

"Ladies and gentlemen," the announcer said, "the mercy rule is invoked. Thank you for coming and see you on the thirtieth. Thank you for supporting Tigers football." The teams lined up to shake hands, and Neutrino walked alongside them, taping them with his camera. Olomua then called the players together. "Behave yourself, and do your homework," he said. "Practice Monday." Neutrino congratulated him. "I wanted to get it over with," Olomua said. "We have a long way to go to get home."

Chapter 16

NEUTRINO AND I WALKED to the parking lot. He got his dog from the car, and we walked back to the field. Everyone else was heading in the other direction, toward the cars and the gym, where there was a dance. Each time the gym door opened, we saw a yellow patch of light and part of the walk that led to the door.

"All week my emotions have been torn," Neutrino said. " 'I want to go to San Francisco, maybe I'll just go to the Pacific. I want to get out of Red Mesa.' And there's been nobody to talk to. Tonight, though, my emotions really became absorbed by this. I have to go back to last week to explain this. Last week these guys come out of the chute, and a minute forty-nine seconds after the opening whistle, they're ahead twenty-six nothing. Before the first half's over it's thirty-two nothing. It was overpowering. The coach overamped. The team started hyperventilating. Everybody fell apart. From that point on, Shiprock beat them twelve to six. Take away that first quarter, Shiprock wins the game. I know this behavior has to stop. They're not going to be able to survive it mentally. They'll be exhausted. All week during the practices I talk to them. I go to the cheerleaders and ask them to create a cheer about breathing—breathe, breathe, breathe. Something like that, I don't know, I'm working on it. Anyway, all week I'm going to them saying, 'Breathe, pay attention. Stand on the sideline, explode on the field.' "

Neutrino waited for me to catch up to him; I had fallen behind while writing down his remarks.

"Just before you got here tonight," he went on, "Coach Olomua had everybody in a circle at the end of the field—he was giving them a pep talk. He talked for a little while, and I thought he was finished, but he was really only pausing, I think, for what do you call it, emphasis. I thought the guys were about to break up, so I said, 'Coach, can I say a word?' And as I'm saying that, he's just beginning again. He thinks I've interrupted him. His eyes grow cold, and he looks at me in disbelief, that I would be so rude. I felt terrible. It was like, uh-oh, here it comes, total rejection. But I didn't give it up, it was too late to, really. I just looked at him, and he said, finally, 'Okay.'

"I told the kids that they had got overstimulated the week before. 'You've got to pay attention and breathe and compose yourself after every play,' I said. They were listening carefully—when I looked into their faces, it was like their eyes were a tunnel connected to mine. After I finished, I looked over at the coach, and he was a little more relaxed, he'd forgiven me my intrusion. Then I apologized."

The dog stopped, and so did Neutrino.

"On the sidelines before the warm-ups I was going along saying, 'Compose yourself,' and Coach O picked it up," Neutrino said. He began walking again. "The two of us were doing it. I could feel the power in the team. They were ready to come out any time they were called upon."

We had arrived in the end zone. The field lights were still on, giving the air a silvery quality. "So this is a night of thinking and going over things," Neutrino said. "My emotions have caught up to the position I'm in."

He looked out over the field. He shook his head slightly. "My goodness," he said. "What a thing we're doing here."

Chapter 17

THAT NIGHT I TOOK a room at a truck stop near the gas station where I had asked directions. Neutrino spent the night in the parking lot. When I met him for breakfast, he was sitting in the van and talking on the phone. A Bible was open on his lap. On the seat beside him was a notebook, and on the page he had written, "Acts I, 16–19."

After breakfast I followed him up a two-lane road that led back to the Navajo Nation. It went initially up and down small hills through scrubby land. Barbed-wire fences penned in sheep. Every few miles a set of stairs, like stepladders, went up one side of the fence, crossed the wire, and went down the other. For months at a time, the ranchers left dogs in the fields to protect the flock. The dogs were meant to catch rabbits for themselves. Neutrino had heard from the pastor in Teec Nos Pos about some dogs near Sanders. The dogs had been in the fields so long that they had become emaciated, he'd said.

When Neutrino pulled to the side of the road, I pulled over, too. He pointed to a field, and eventually I saw a small brown dog, thin as a stick and not much different in color from the ground, as if he had risen up from it. Neutrino got a bowl of dry dog food from a bag he kept in the van and called to the dog. The dog lowered his head and slunk toward us. He stopped about thirty feet from Neutrino. His tail wagged faintly. Neutrino spread the food like a man broadcasting seed in a field, then he went back to the car and got more. The dog came closer. Other dogs began to appear from behind bushes and the tops of the low hills, regarding us with suspicion. In all there were five. Neutrino talked to them for a while before we left.

The land flattened. The road led straight to the horizon, then over low hills, as if it were a track leading up to a ramp we would launch ourselves from. Here and there were houses so remote and desolate that merely to inhabit them seemed an act of courage. At Klagetoh, just past a Mennonite church, I followed Neutrino into a yard where a tractor was parked. Three sullen dogs appeared from under the tractor. One of them put its paws on my window and looked me in the eye. A girl came out the door of a house, and Neutrino spoke to her, then the two of them walked toward a shed on the back of the property, with the dogs following them. The girl went into the shed and came out holding an air hose. Neutrino needed air for his tire and had stopped at the house thinking they would have an air compressor. As he filled the tire, I asked how he knew to stop.

"A feeling," he said. Then, "Actually, feeling is too old world," he said. "You turn it over to the Holy Spirit." He said he was kidding. "I must have seen the tractor and thought they had to have air."

He thanked the girl and gave her the air hose, and she put it back in the shed. An older woman came out of the house and stood on the lawn and watched us leave.

Driving on the long, straight road through the desert, it seemed as if the landscape I saw in the rearview mirror was the same as the one that I saw through the windshield. The sky was so big that I could see rain that would never fall on me. We passed signs for bingo games and tent revivals. A boy swinging a rope drove cattle along the shoulders of the road. In Rock Point there was a sign by a ranch that said HOME OF BENNY BEGAY, 1998 BAREBACK CHAMPION. Wherever Neutrino saw a dog in a field, he pulled over and gave it food.

I took a hotel room in Kayenta, about fifty miles west of Red Mesa. We watched television for a while. I asked Neutrino if he wanted to clean himself up before we went to dinner. He filled the bathtub and got in. Then he started singing so loudly that I decided to take a walk.

Chapter 18

THE NEXT AFTERNOON we drove to Red Mesa in my car. Neutrino insisted that I divide my awareness between the shoulder of the road and the wheels of the cars approaching. He said that before I would notice a car crossing into our lane, I would see the wheels turn. It would be essential then to leave the road, no matter what the terrain. He also insisted that I fall in behind the biggest truck we could follow, and on the occasions when I grew tired of driving so slowly and seeing nothing in front of me but the back of the truck and pulled out to pass, he would say, "I guess you're just determined to get us killed." I thought he was making too much of the dangers of driving on Indian reservations, but then a few days later I was awakened at eight in the morning by a car's driving into the front of a bus and the sirens of the police cars and ambulances arriving. The hotel receptionist told me that the driver, a Navajo, had been "taken to heaven."

The bottoms of the clouds over the badlands, reflecting the ground, were the same tawny color as the land. Neutrino sat quietly. When he finally spoke, he said, "I still don't feel I've accomplished my mission in life."

I asked what his mission was.

"I'm waiting to see," he said.

I wasn't sure how to play that.

He went on to say that he thought it might have something to do with religion. "I've been reading the Bible off and on for sixty years, since even before the seminary, and I'd find contradictions, but someone would always say, 'Well, what if you look at it this way,' and when I did the contradiction would dissolve. These are facts, though. They're—I guess you're just bent on getting us killed."

I didn't say anything.

Neutrino shrugged. "Well, as for my mission, for me the best possible attitude is, I'm going to overcome everything until I can overcome nothing," he said. "I'm going to feint and deflect and sidestep and retreat and approach and attack until I've accomplished my lifetime."

When we reached Red Mesa, we went to the Christian church. Neutrino wanted to pick up some things. The hoedown was locked, so he walked across the yard and climbed several steps and knocked on the door of the church office. The pastor's wife, a Navajo, opened the door. She was wearing a T-shirt and baggy turquoise pants. Neutrino stood below her on the step. Accompanied by dogs, they walked across the yard, where the dirt was packed so tight that their heels made a sound as if they were walking on pavement.

Neutrino spread dry dog food on the ground for the strays that gathered around him. His own dog sat on the driver's seat, making a breathy little yap, like a squeeze toy. When we drove away, one of the dogs followed us along the dusty road. It ran close to the tires on Neutrino's side of the car, and I couldn't see it. "Go slow," he said. "A little to the left, stay in the center, little more, *all right now gun it*!" After a few seconds I could see the dog in a cloud of red dust pull up in the rearview mirror.

At practice the quarterback and the receivers worked with Sandy Benally, whom Olomua had asked to take over the play. The boys would call signals, then the quarterback would step backward and the receivers would race down the field. The quarterback would hold the ball high, then throw a long, arching pass. Benally would step in and say, "Where's the advantage there?" When the boys returned to the line of scrimmage, their heads hung sheepishly.

"You want to use this play when the defender is in tight," Benally told them. "Then it's deadly."

The boys had embellished their movements with fakes to the left and right as if they were being swarmed while trying to throw.

"It happens too fast," Benally yelled at them. "You don't have time for fakes. Throw the ball." Then to the receivers, "You don't break till the ball leaves his arm, that's when you go. Not a second before. That's where the surprise is."

Olomua brought over a player to cover the receiver, and Neutrino and I watched them run the play. It worked each time. Benally wanted the boys to move faster. "You have to start practicing for when you're in there with the big boys, and you're scared," he said. "You're thinking they're coming fast, and you've got to keep it simple." The boys were taking five and six seconds to get rid of the ball. "You have less than three seconds," Benally said. He stood at the line of scrimmage, and when the ball was snapped, he began counting aloud. If the quarterback hadn't got rid of the ball by the time Benally reached three, he threw a football at him from close range, hard.

On the way back to Kayenta, Neutrino said that, like Tolstoy, he wanted to start a new church, a practical one devoted not to Christian mysteries but to the life of Christ and the pursuit of happiness. He was going to call it the Church of the Seven Levels.

Chapter 19

AFTER BREAKFAST THE NEXT MORNING, we drove east, through Mexican Water, Red Mesa, Teec Nos Pos, and Shiprock, about 130 miles, to Farmington, so that Neutrino could buy a video monitor to edit his tapes. A few weeks earlier, he had seen one behind the counter of a pawnshop. After we picked it up, we ate lunch in Farmington, then drove back to Red Mesa and stopped at the mission so that Neutrino could leave the monitor in the hoedown. We watched practice, then talked with Olomua until he begged our pardon and said that he had to take his wife to dinner at the café in Mexican Water. As we drove back to Kayenta, Neutrino said that he had been reading the Bible more often lately than he usually did, mostly because of living at the mission.

"The Church of the Seven Levels is going to be about the three deepest desires," he said. "People have too much of the wrong information or not enough of the right information. It's apparent all over the planet. Without the three deepest desires, too much energy, too much suffering and futility, goes into areas that are not of a deep satisfaction. Triads, the seven chakras, the nine points, and absolute love, these are going to be the philosophical starting points. If you can attack them, the church welcomes that. The church invites any increase of purification and power. You have to be prepared, though, to do extensive dialogue and exchange, because I have been working on these ideas for the last forty years."

The dog climbed into his lap, and he petted her. "I was teaching music the other night at the mission, and this Navajo woman got ready to sing a hymn," he went on. "It's called 'At the Cross,' and it goes, 'At the cross, at the cross, when I first met the cross, it was there that my cares were relieved,' and she sang it with such profound feeling, such fervor and such humility, that I felt that even if her cares were relieved for only that moment, it was a joyous thing. I've experienced that release from despair. At tent meetings, getting the spirit. Hitchhiking across the desert when I was young, going three and four days without eating, you'd break through into this other experience of rapture. I'm an old man now. My existence is wonder and joy. Versus sleepiness, dullness, lethargy, and being torn between not being able to wait until life is over and also being afraid that it will be."

Caught here and there in the barbed-wire fences were plastic shopping bags that billowed in the wind like flags.

"To escape the burdens of life there is a doorway your mind has to go through," Neutrino continued, "and the doorway partly consists of leaving some kind of arrow or set of directions that other people can use. People in North Beach used to say I was the freest person they had ever met—I had nothing else except freedom, no knowledge, no learning, no sophistication, no polish, but I had freedom in spades—and without being destructive, without breaking laws or causing harm, I have been in this state of freedom for years. More than half a century. And I've thought for some time, How can I describe a pathway to this state of freedom that other people can grab on to? Not everyone will want to, of course, maybe almost no one will, but some people will. How do I know? Because if something is deeply interesting to one person, the chances are that it will interest someone else. You can't tell how many other people, but you can assume one at least. So how can I provide it for them, because the things I have learned have taken me a lifetime to accomplish. How can I make it easier for someone else?"

He petted the dog.

"If a skeptic comes into the Church of the Seven Levels, they're free to modify those principles as long as they understand what the principles are," he said next. "I have had arguments with people for decades, and haven't been able to prove even to myself until last week that the Bible had mistakes. Did Jonah go in the belly of a whale? Did Daniel come out of that lion's den? Now with these two descriptions of the way Judas died, I have proof. So the first thing we have to say is, As human beings, do we lean on our own understanding, or do we lean on

God's? Are we heretics if we lean on our own understanding, and the answer is yes, we are heretics, but we have to be. The circumstances demand it. We're going to have to lean on our own understanding and modify it day in and day out. This church will be separate from the Bible. We're going to study Matthew, Mark, Luke, and John, because they were there. Whatever mistakes they make are going to be minimal, compared to the ones that Paul is going to make, that Timothy is going to make. If you want to study the rest of the Bible, you can do it on your own time. You don't do it on church time."

Chapter 20

The next morning in the parking lot of the café in Kayenta where we always ate breakfast a Navajo man walked toward our car. Neutrino began talking to him. I was already sitting at a table when I heard Neutrino in the parking lot shouting. I went back outside. There were pickup trucks between me and Neutrino, and I couldn't see him until I found an aisle among them, and then I saw that he wasn't shouting at the vagrant, he was shouting at the white man who owned the café. The white man had told the vagrant to find a job and get off his property, and Neutrino had yelled at the white man, "He *has* a job! He's a *beggar!*" Neutrino gave the man five dollars—at the time he had seventeen dollars to his name. We went inside and sat down. The owner, a middle-aged man who had drawn his long hair back into a ponytail, came through the door from the kitchen a few minutes later and slightly broke stride when he saw Neutrino, but he didn't say anything.

During the night, lying awake in his van, thinking about the church and football and the raft, Neutrino had decided to leave Red Mesa and return to the crossing. The play belonged to Olomua and his team, he said, and would thrive without him. Having defined the church's principles, he intended to leave its founding to others. A woman he knew in Maine was willing to start the first parish. Red Mesa had a game the following night, and a week later the most important game of the season against a school off the reservation called St. Johns. Neutrino planned to drive to Buckeye and collect the raft, then head for the Pacific. He thought he should see the St. Johns game, which would be played not far from Buckeye, but he didn't think he ought to stay in Red Mesa any longer.

At practice we sat on a metal bench on the sideline and watched Sandy Benally lead the Navajo boys through the play. I went over to observe them more closely. No matter which direction I turned, Benally stood sideways to me, as if observing some obscure formality. He tossed a football up and down, and I had the feeling that to interrupt him with a question would be discourteous, so I went back and sat with Neutrino. The wind was blowing, and it was cool enough that he had his hands in his pockets, and his shoulders hunched. "The way he's training them now is perfect," he said of Benally. "So fluid. He starts slow and works it all together, then he speeds it up." While we watched, Benally took over sending signals and threw passes to the right and left, so that the receivers could practice catching on both sides. "He's taken it two or three steps beyond me," Neutrino said. "I'm the innovator, and they understood the innovation. And now they're making it their own. They're going to be talking sign language on the field like gunfire it'll be so fast."

Benally left the boys to practice and walked over to us. I asked how the play was going.

"You have a big line, you buy these kids three or four seconds, you can kill with this play."

"Do you have a big line?"

"No."

I looked at my shoes.

"Where this would really work is the pros," he said.

"You got it perfect," Neutrino told him. We watched the fleet, skinny boys, like stick figures running up and down the field, the ball rising, then falling into their hands. When one of them made an artful catch, Neutrino would applaud.

Olomua walked over to us. He said that the clock was the perfect play to use against the cowboy teams that overran his own. His players would invite them in, set the trap, and send the ball over their heads. In the next game he planned to put two receivers on the clock. "We'll watch how they use their cornerbacks," he said. "If they play deep, we'll use it. If no one's open, we'll bring one of them in, six o'clock. Twelve o'clock and six o'clock are always going to work, unless the defender grabs the receiver. If you're the defender running full speed downfield to cover the receiver, you can't reverse in time to catch him if he goes to six o'clock." He and Neutrino nodded, then Olomua said, "You're going to see some clocks this weekend."

Benally had gone back onto the field, and I walked over to him. A mile or so in the distance was the mesa that the town is named for. A few miles from it is another mesa, this one white. I pointed at it and said, "What's the name of the big white mesa?" Without looking at me, he said, "White Mesa." I asked if the horses I saw sometimes from the road were wild, and he said they were. He said that people in Red Mesa occasionally round them up. "They get two or three SUVs and run them down," he said. "You look through the herd for the youngest ones, throw a rope around their neck, then leave the SUV and let the horse drag it for a mile or so. It will faint from the rope closing its windpipe, and you have to get to it quickly. They don't want to get caught. If you corner them on a cliff, they'll jump off. They'll do anything to kill themselves rather than be taken. They're bad tempered. Even when you have one, you have to be careful not to be kicked or punched or have them rear up on you."

I walked back and sat in the stands with Neutrino. "The only thing I could do now that would ruin it is open my mouth," he said. Then he stood, and as a means of getting himself into shape for the crossing, he walked the track that circled the field. When he came back around, we left. The boys were still on the field.

"I'm fed up with football," he said. "All I'm thinking about now is raft fittings and wood and procedures. Trying to take what I learned on the North Atlantic and apply it to another ocean." Olomua invited us to come the next evening after practice and have Hawaiian barbecue with him, and we thanked him and said we would.

We ate dinner at a hotel in Kayenta where Neutrino liked the nonalcoholic wine they served—the reservation is dry. On his napkin he drew for me the outriggers he planned to add to his raft so that it would remain upright, at least he imagined that it would, in all but the heaviest seas. How it would all come together—the design of the raft, the finding of materials, the provisions, the launch itself—he wasn't sure, but he felt confident that it would.

When we left, he folded the drawing and put it in his pocket and carried on my napkin what remained on our plates to the dog.

THE NEXT MORNING I WOKE Neutrino by calling his name through an open window of the van, and we drove to breakfast. "I had the feeling this morning that I hadn't a care in the world," he said. "It was the best feeling."

"Were you up walking the dog?"

"No, it was when I was asleep," he said. "I was up all night thinking about details, and I fell asleep around five."

When we got back to Neutrino's van, it had a flat tire, and the battery was dead. We drove around Kayenta looking for a shop that fixed flats and down a dirt road on the edge of town found a shacky little garage guarded by some bony dogs. A man lifted his head from beneath the hood of an old car and said the owner was having lunch. I asked when he might be back, and the man said about an hour. We waited for a while, then another man drove up. I asked if he knew where we might find the owner, and he pointed at a trailer parked broadside to us on a lot next door. A girl answered our knocking. The owner was sitting at a table with some cold cuts and a container of milk. He said he'd be over in a few minutes. Getting the tire fixed and the battery charged took the rest of the day, so we never got to Red Mesa for the practice. Olomua shared the barbecue with the other coaches.

RED MESA PLAYS in the North Canyon Conference, which has seven teams. Their game on the evening of September 24, a Friday, was at home against Many Farms, another member of the conference. The sun was setting behind the gym when Neutrino and I got to the field. The teams were running drills. Behind them was a hand-painted sign, white letters on a rust-colored ground saying REDSKINS. The refs stood on the sideline throwing a football underhanded among themselves, trying to give it the perfect spiral. The Red Mesa placekicker, Delvecchio Sarracino, a small, good-natured boy whom Neutrino had been working with, ran at the ball and sent it in a line drive that struck the crossbar and fell back. "He's tired," Neutrino said. "He's been whacking it awhile already." The Many Farms team was called the Lobos, and they had black pants and gray jerseys with white numbers. Most of their players were bigger than the Red Mesa ones.

The refs called the captains to the center of the field and tossed a coin in the air. The boys solemnly followed its path by moving their chins up and down. A voice over a loudspeaker said, "Remember, they are friendly rivals, not enemies." Neutrino and I stood with the players on the sideline. Red Mesa scored almost immediately. Olomua came over and spoke to Neutrino, who nodded and turned to me as the players lined up for the extra point and said, "It's the clock." The receiver read the signal for three o'clock and doglegged into the clear, but the ball slid past his fingers.

As Red Mesa prepared to kick off, Neutrino said, "See how quiet they are? They're contained." Behind us, cheerleaders faced the crowd. "If you're all for the Redskins, stamp your feet," they yelled. The lights above the field came on. A three-quarter moon rose above the mesa. A Redskin player ran a punt into the end zone, but a penalty was called, and the ball was returned to the field. The Many Farms team yelled, "Who wants the ball? I want the ball." The Red Mesa players began yelling, "Redskins, do you want it?" Neutrino said, "Big mistake, they're blowing their juice now."

After Red Mesa's second touchdown, Olomua yelled from the sideline, "Clock, right," but no one kept the Many Farms linemen from bearing in on the quarterback, and the play fell apart. Even so, the score before long became 48–0 for Red Mesa, and the mercy rule was invoked. Only one of the touchdowns had been scored with the clock play. Olomua had hoped the clock would undermine the rush of the Many Farms linemen, but his kids had trouble getting rid of the ball quickly and catching it. Neutrino shook hands with Olomua and Benally and wished them well. "We're going to keep working on it," Olomua told Neutrino. "We're going to work on it all spring and summer, and by next season you won't believe what you'll see."

On the drive back to Kayenta, Neutrino seemed excited. "We're done with football now," he said. "Everything in my mind is going toward the raft."

Chapter 23

RED MESA LOST its game to its rival, St. Johns. Neutrino didn't attend; he was already in California with the raft.

The Redskins won their next game 52–6, scoring two touchdowns with the play. When I called Olomua from New York in October to ask how things were going, he said that the play was working fine, but the boys were having trouble catching the ball. During the practices, everything went smoothly, but in the games they were worried about being hit. He said that he was going to teach them to catch the ball, then fall down.

PART THREE

Neutrino regards his life as composed of experiences that have expanded one into another. He tends to take an endeavor as far as he can, then he sheds it. Sometimes it's ripe, and sometimes it isn't. Sometimes the parting is abrupt, and sometimes it's fluid. Some experiences—rafting, for example—he has taken further than others; he has built the largest and most complicated rafts and taken them to more places and on more arduous voyages than anyone else in the world. Sometimes a new undertaking is connected to his old one, one raft disposed of and a new one begun, and sometimes it lies outside the context of his typical pursuits, as with football. The eclipse of one experience does not always signify the embrace of a new one. It isn't like having connecting flights.

Like many people who behave capriciously, Neutrino believes he acts only after much reflection. His idea of existence requires constant refreshment and renewal. He is delighted by novelty. If he has ever become so absorbed by a pursuit that he hasn't been willing to discard it for another that seems more appealing, I don't know what it is. I once told him that his behavior was inconsistent. He shrugged. "A series of incidents have created your present reality," he said. "Because of the forces involved in anyone's life, better situations are going to come along than the one you're engaged in. If you can break the alignment without hurting somebody, why not break the alignment? Death is going to break your alignment eventually anyway."

Neutrino is as profane a figure as I have ever encountered, but there is also something sanctified about him—his insistence on remaining uncorrupted by material ambitions, his almost desperate responsiveness to joy, to being footloose and feverish, to moving forward with his arms opened wide, and his eyes on the horizon. A producer who worked with him at National Geographic told me that she regarded him as "a brilliant man who had done everything he could to free himself of the conventions that occupy the rest of us." Her tone conveyed her respect for his having done so but also bewilderment at what repaid all the hardship the accomplishment brought with it.

Neutrino is a wanderer, an exile, an outcast, a bedouin in the wilderness of the republic. The disciplines he practices are so severe that they amount nearly to mortifications. He also has a flinty pioneer side, a prospector-on-a-tear sensibility. There must have been many more like him in earlier times, chasers after stakes and claims, odds players, followers of the reckless and wild hope, especially among the citizens of the western territories, where his ancestors came from. The present landscape allows less room for divergent ethics, and there is less tolerance among us for independence. Neutrino would never escape a modern childhood without a label and a prescription. Anyway, by the time he announced that he was done with football, I had grown accustomed to his desultory habits of mind. Maybe I should say that I had resigned myself. Why it never became an abrasion between us is that I also admired his nerve. Like most people, I have sometimes wondered, What if I simply stepped out of my life? What if I shed all the things I regard myself as being, as simply as one takes off a coat, and assumed a new identity? What if I let nothing restrain me? Who would I be? What parts of myself that

I keep under wraps might emerge? Would I be happier? Actors use stage names, writers use pen names, and become different people from who they were. Their work changes, they feel differently about things, they make different choices; they appear liberated from their pasts.

Most of us adhere to and protect with some vehemence the version of ourselves we are most familiar and comfortable with, the things we have acquired, what reputation or status we possess. Neutrino fearlessly demised nearly everything about himself time after time and began again. His restlessness was not a matter of unease, it was a characteristic of his headlong progress, of his belief that each moment must be attended for what it might offer or reveal, even though such a practice was both formidable and exhausting. Day in and day out, he discarded the parts of his identity that chafed him, picked himself up like a nomad and moved to new ground, presented himself to new people and adapted. Sometimes in new circumstances he was expansive and boastful, sometimes he was brash, sometimes he was charming, and sometimes he was recessive and watchful. Whatever he was, he remained an individual and solid at the core—Carl Jung somewhere remarks that a hallmark of psychic health is the capacity to be oneself in all situations. Neutrino was someone who regarded his interior life as vital and rich and as still emerging, still susceptible to being shaped and still worthy of attention. From my closest friend, William Maxwell, the writer, who died at ninety-one in 2000, I learned that death, especially at the end of a long and happy life, is not something to fear. By Neutrino I was made aware that life is not something to shrink from either.

I shared with him an affection for subversive intentions, and his acceptance of being an outcast. I am of the tribe that never really feels at home anywhere. It is part of my temperament, and I have made peace with it, at least I think I have. When I was a child, I always wanted to be the one in the class who the others never felt they knew. I wasn't any particular brand of misfit, I just mean that the solitary, more than the gregarious, was glamorous to me. "Lone wolf" was the term that I heard the adults use and slightly disparage, which made it seem even more desirable as an epithet. Neutrino deeply embodied such an ethic, and it made me feel that we shared a fundamental agreement, one that didn't need to be discussed or referred to, a bond, even though his version of such an existence was far too extreme for me.

Chapter 2

BEFORE NEUTRINO LEFT the Navajo mission, at the end of September, he gave money to the pastor to feed the small dog that hung around the churchyard and chased cars. "He hates that little dog," Neutrino said, "but I'm going to arrange for someone to call him and say, 'How's the dog doing?' Keep the pressure on."

From Red Mesa, Neutrino drove to Buckeye. He brushed the cobwebs off the raft. The wood had darkened to the color of driftwood. For several days he removed screws and boards and put them back on in other places. He couldn't decide if he wanted the prow to be flat or curved.

Now that he had devoted himself to the crossing, the rigor of it began to prey on his mind. "I'm emotionally prepared," he told me one day on the phone. "I know that everywhere I go it could very well be my last time there. I have no misgivings. For a while I was thinking, Could I put this off, can I delay it? It was very daunting—the last time to see my wife. Maybe never again see my children. The final day in Red Mesa I started to think, I don't want to leave the dogs. I don't want to leave football, and the reservation. The pull was very strong."

In Buckeye, Neutrino added the outriggers he had drawn on the napkin in Kayenta. He also decided to make the bow and stern pointed. "The double ends split the water," he said. "You need that for oceangoing, not for river." He wanted the raft to draw five or six inches, to sit, that is, as high as it could in the water—the higher it sat, the less resistance the hull would create, and the faster it would travel. A vessel with a shallow draft could make shore quickly, if a storm approached. If the engine quit, less effort would be needed to row the raft, or to gain shore using a kedge, a bucket on a rope you throw into the water and retrieve. Also, the higher the raft sat, the less likely it would be to come to harm in the surf. Thor Heyerdahl built *Kon-Tiki* from balsa wood. The wood gradually absorbed water. The raft sat lower and lower, and Heyerdahl was concerned that it might sink before it made land. Plywood doesn't absorb water easily. Moreover, plywood is laid on in strips. It can peel off in layers and still have integrity. Any water Neutrino's raft absorbed would be an advantage. He designed his rafts so that the part below the water was heavier than the part above it. If the raft flipped over, the heavier part would seek to restore itself, and the raft would turn upright again.

"I'm very excited about the design of this raft," he said. "It's different from any other raft in the world. Other crafts have had elements of it. Some of the lifeboats they put on the decks of cruise ships are almost unsinkable and self-righting."

I asked where he'd seen them.

"On the ocean," he said. "When I see a ship at sea, my eyes

are crawling all over it. I'm reading a text. This raft's got to be absolutely friendly to the water, it's got to shift and turn and float upside down and right itself. It won't break apart, because it's so light, and it will float like a cork. I've been lying awake nights thinking all this out—the dimensions, the parts, each little shift. That's what allowed me to come up with the play, this kind of going over and over—what if we did this here and that there, what would happen? I've done this for years with rafts. I've created a part of my mind that can take things apart and put them back together. If I'm interested. If I'm not interested, I'm helpless."

The crucial thing, he said, was to have a core that could be modified as he disposed of problems involved in the design. "My core is a twelve-foot section filled with foam," he said. "It's twelve by four, and ten inches thick, like a big mattress, and I can build on it all kinds of shapes. Last night I came up with a whole different prow shape. It's going to rake, which will make it twice as fast. Instead of taking three months to cross to the first landing in the Pacific, it might take me a month to a month and a half. I'm going to rake the stern, too. The water will pass under it, instead of being obstructed. I think I can build points off the rake, like a false prow, that will skim above the water and lift the raft over the waves. The best rowboat I had was in Bath, Maine. It had both a rake and a prow, and it took the seas beautifully. The important part of this design is, the raft's never cutting through the water. Whatever resistance you have multiplies as you go faster, so if you can get your boat up off the top of the water, you burn less fuel, the wind takes you farther. If you're rowing, the task is diminished. With the Atlantic crossing, I wanted stability— I had a crew, I needed a big boat—but now speed's important."

In Key West he had planned a core that was thirty-two feet long, then realized he wouldn't find a trailer long enough to carry it. Twelve feet was the length of the trailer he had. A small raft could easily be taken aboard deep-ocean fishing boats and freighters if he grew weary of traveling alone. And the benefit of a malleable design was that, if he guessed wrong, he could pull up on a beach and change everything.

"If I have to switch on a beach to a pointed prow, I'll just have some rough times beforehand if the waves get too high," he said. The design he had currently was something "a Green Beret would feel comfortable with," he said. What concerned him most was his stamina. "Things have changed," he said. "I asked myself, at seventy-one, Am I stronger or weaker than I was when I crossed the Atlantic? The answer is, I don't have as much physical strength, but I have more emotional strength. I'm stronger mentally, too. Even so, I should still have enough in me to make it through this chore."

Chapter 3

NEUTRINO WANTED TO LAUNCH the raft from Mexico. He thought that a favorable harbor might be Puerto Penasco, on the Sea of Cortés, where he had been years ago. Leaving the raft in Buckeye, he drove down to see if the town was still as he remembered it. At the marina, he met a man he had once given things to when he was shedding possessions. The man, it turned out, was a cousin of the assistant captain of the port. Neutrino hoped this would give him some influence if the captain wasn't sympathetic to his leaving the harbor in a raft made of boards held together by ropes and screws. He drove back to Buckeye and planned a trip in the first week of October to San Diego.

"There's a lot of things I need to get that aren't expensive, but you can't get them except in a nautical town," he said on the phone. "I need a ship-to-shore radio—a small one you can hold in your hand—and a GPS locator, so I can read my position from the global positioning satellite. Plus I need watertight bags to protect them."

He expected that when he described his plans to the prosperous boaters at the marinas in San Diego, someone would give him the electronic equipment, which was how he had equipped *Son of Town Hall*. Collecting the equipment and finishing the raft would take two months, he thought. By the middle of December, he could leave Mexico.

Chapter 4

Neutrino didn't go to San Diego. He went to Las Vegas. He left the raft in Buckeye. On a map he drew a circle that had Las Vegas at twelve o'clock, Los Angeles at nine, San Diego at seven, Yuma, Arizona, at six, and Phoenix at four. Within that circle he felt that he would find the materials he needed. He had always disliked Las Vegas, he said, but he hadn't been there in years, and he thought perhaps he had judged it unfairly and ought to give it another chance. He was about twenty miles outside the city when he felt oppressed and confused. He parked under a tree and fell asleep.

"When I woke up, it was all so clear," he said.

"What was?"

"I'm going into painting," he said. "I'm going to become a painter of seascapes and landscapes and self-portraits."

"But I thought—"

"Listen, thousands and thousands of tourists are going to be coming into my path," he said, "so I'm going to have the five Ps: paintings, postcards, prints, photographs, and posters."

"But what about—"

"Let me explain something," he said. "What I'm doing now, I'm living in such a way as to condition myself for isolation then superficial engagement then back into isolation. I'm not counting on any other exchanges, except maybe some phone calls. And I'm feeling solid and optimistic. At the same time, I'm trying to create movement within a frame. My life involves random behavior opposed to periods of specific focus. Any minute I have to be ready to pick up anchor and ship my gear or even drop dead. Anyone who's awake is responding to stimuli. Whether you're aware of it or not, you're accepting, rejecting, and denying, you're going through a whole psychic process. And you hope eventually to get where you're intending to go. I'm in this circle now that has one opening, which is down to Baja and launching. The boundaries, by not being either too limited or too expansive, give me movement, novelty, and possibilities. I stopped by Lake Mead, back of the Hoover Dam, and there's boats everywhere. People are gambling, they pawn their motors, it's easy to park a trailer. Right now I'm sitting in an abandoned truck canopy. It's huge, and there's no one around. I can see the freeway."

"So you're feeling better?" I asked.

"Before I took that nap, I was in a total state of confusion and dismay. Should I go to New Orleans and see Ingrid before I leave? What about Maine and see Betsy? What about San Francisco, and my trip to the boneyard? Are there other people I should see, Maxine, make a whole farewell tour? No, I have to stay in this circle. Here I can solicit equipment, I can paint pictures. I can't do this in Oklahoma or Texas or Florida. Forget about Maine or San Francisco or New Orleans. Yesterday I bought the art supplies I need. I'm going to start painting. I was a sign painter and a kind of a draftsman—not a great draftsman by any means, but a draftsman nonetheless, I don't have to be Rembrandt—and I'm going to be able to copy pictures that were taken of the *Son of Town Hall* and me around the world. I'll make half a dozen oil paintings on canvas board, they can pack easily. Plus, I'm playing chess. I'll advertise, 'Play chess with the North Atlantic champion.' When the tourists come, I'll talk about the trip. They can buy something. I also bought sign paint, so I can do boat lettering wherever I put in. All my thoughts are going into the five Ps, though.

"I'll return to Buckeye in a day or two and pick up the raft, come back here, it's a great place for me to make money with paintings, and I'm not on private property so much. In about six weeks, I'll be able to shoot down through the gap to Puerto Penasco, and I won't need anyone's help. When I take off, I have to be prepared to deal with medical problems, separation from the people I know, exile. I have to be able to draw into a foreign port, anchor up, rest, go out and meet some people, protect the raft so that vandals can't break in and steal the motor, get medicine if I need it. I've taken into my system since you left as much of the problem as I can deal with, and I feel very confident. If there's any change in my emotional attitude or will to do this, I'll let you know immediately."

Neutrino stayed in Las Vegas for a week, then he drove to Buckeye. He didn't return to Las Vegas. I don't know why he changed his mind. I was sort of afraid to ask. He remained in Buckeye and worked on the raft in the Mexican storage lot. He slept at a truck stop. He didn't bring up painting or the five Ps again.

I began to suspect that he might not leave for months, but the next time I spoke to him, about a week later, he seemed to have recovered his sense of purpose. "I'm so in love with my raft now," he said. "I woke up the other night, and I thought I was going to have another one of those sessions where I spend hours meditating over details and not sleeping well. I started to unravel the design, attack it and change it, and I thought, Will you never be satisfied? Then I realized I had the perfect model already. It's gone from twelve feet to fourteen feet. The design changed—a few shifts here and there, more foam in the cabin, two little pyramids on the side, and it's unsinkable. I'll be dry, and no matter what happens out on the ocean, this raft will be fleet and float and be self-righting. A hurricane can come along, and I'd say, 'Let's get in the raft and go ride in the hurricane.' It's very freaky to look at, that's true, it can't be denied, just some plywood shaped a certain way and some sticks, and I'm going to cross the Pacific in it. All I have to do now is put it all together."

I asked how he was otherwise.

"I'm trying not to let anything get to me," he said. "If a person doesn't want to hear from me, I just wish them well and go down the road. I'm not emphatic anymore. If I need to relax, I lie down in my car, have some canned vegetables, maybe some canned crab, think about creative things. I feel I'm in the midst of this swirl. It's an idea I took years ago from the Sufi dancers who spin like whirling dervishes. I wanted to be a whirling dervish over the face of the earth, so that I would pick up influences and respond in a whirling dervish way. Expand and enlarge, increase without obstacles. I went about this for twenty years with the Salvation Navy. We gave away property and money and cars and trucks, and we acquired them. So much is happening now in this swirling way, so much activity, and I think, Don't rush it, don't be impatient. Don't demand, just keep it alive. Keep steering and moving and circulating and wonderful things will happen."

I asked how he kept it alive.

"You have to be desperate," he said. "You don't have to be serious, you can have fun—you hope to have fun, to be diverted and amused—but you've got to be desperate. This really matters in one way that I get this adventure right, even if it doesn't matter in another way. We're all of us in the middle of this life-and-death swim, and death's going to win, no question, but we can delay it. I am always asking myself, How can I become more involved, more passionate, and less vulnerable? When I see some of the mistakes I made in my life, I feel I must be a terrible person, and some of the successes make me think I'm a great person, famous to myself. If I'd had a little more information, no doubt I might have done better. Then I invoke the Buddhist concept of emptiness, and that everything's constructed from the void—anything is possible, and we're the pilots. On this raft, as long as I'm in movement, if I'm in some place, and it's not working, I'll move to a place where it will. I'll move from unsavory situations to pleasant ones. Eventually I will move across the ocean and maybe around the world. Where does it end? The grave, of course, but I'm going out of this life as what I have worked and striven my whole life to be, a free man—free of possessions, free of greed, free of worry and strife. Free of anything superfluous."

LATE IN OCTOBER OF 2004, Neutrino attached the trailer to his van and left Buckeye. Feeling that he would know where to stop when he got there, directing himself in the dream, he drove south to Interstate 8, then west, through Gila Bend, Theba, Sentinel, Aztec, Dateland, and Yuma, and into California. At El Centro he left the interstate and drove south. In Calexico, above Mexicali, he saw old signs he could offer to repaint and bars where he could sing. On the outskirts of town he found a storage yard where he could park the raft for a dollar a day. He had decided that instead of Puerto Penasco he would launch the raft from San Felipe, in Baja, about 120 miles south of Calexico. In Calexico, he felt that even if his car broke down, he was close enough to San Felipe that he could hire someone to deliver him and the raft to the Sea of Cortés.

In Mexicali there was a government office where Neutrino could obtain the papers he needed "to float the boat in San Felipe," he said. If they refused permission, he would leave from San Diego or even New Orleans, sail across the gulf to the Yucatán, then travel through the Panama Canal.

"I've closed my circle now," he said one day. "It goes from El Centro, about ten miles north of Calexico, south to Mexicali, with a funnel going down Baja to San Felipe." The challenge of so much isolation still worked on his mind. "When I said to you originally that I wanted to make this trip, I was totally in contact with what it meant to give up relationships, maybe forever in this lifetime, to being alone, and to dealing with whatever there is to deal with," he said. "I know it's going to be lonely, and I am prepared to deal with that loneliness, but it's been very hard, more difficult really than I thought it would be."

Then he brought up the raft. "My vessel is going to be terrific, though," he said. "When the big boats go down, they put you in the small boats, right? So why not start off in the small boat?"

In Calexico he worked each morning on the raft, then rested, then worked again. The labor was fatiguing, especially because he had to muscle around heavy sheets of plywood by himself. The owner of the storage yard didn't like Neutrino's building the raft on his property—if he permitted people to work on cars, every shade-tree mechanic in town would open a garage on the premises—but Neutrino tipped him a few dollars to tolerate it. At the end of the day, he would drive around Calexico looking for Styrofoam and wood. "I'm pacing myself like an athlete," he said.

Chapter 6

From a mexican in calexico, Neutrino heard that here and there along the Sea of Cortés were dangerous rocks. To sail among rocks, Neutrino needed a motor. To buy one he would have to sell his car. "I have to find someone who's willing to buy it when it needs a new water pump," he said on the phone.

I asked how much a water pump costs.

"About two hundred and fifty dollars," he said.

"But the car's worth a few thousand, isn't it?"

"Not the way I've treated it," he said.

If he sold the car, he could live on the raft in the storage yard, but then he would have to do all his errands on foot. Being without a car would also shrink his horizons. He liked to listen in the evenings to the radio.

At night he slept in the parking lot of the Wal-Mart. Four or five other people did, too. The security guards knew them and left them alone. By himself in the car in the darkness, he would imagine being on the ocean aboard the raft. "I talk to the dog at night, the same as I used to talk to Betsy," he said. "I'm alone in a shopping mall, and it's not pleasant, but I have to know that when I'm with the same dog, having the same talks on the water, under the stars in the darkness, I'll be all right."

Chapter 7

Driving back one day from an errand in El Centro, Neutrino met a man at a rest area who saw that Neutrino's car was leaking water and said that in two hours and for fifty dollars he could fix it. Neutrino agreed, and the man began to take the water pump apart. He also began drinking. Before long he started dropping screws and tools, then he was too drunk to continue working. With the pump disassembled, Neutrino couldn't drive his car.

The man left, saying he would be back in the morning. Evening came. Neutrino opened a can of sardines and shared them with his dog. He slept in the rest area. He didn't think the car would be safe if he left it. The next morning the man arrived and began working and drinking again. He mentioned that he had recently been released from the penitentiary. On the third day, he attracted another ex-convict, and they worked and drank together. Other people they seemed to know arrived.

"I was in this grouping of alcoholics and psychopaths, and I thought, I can't even start the car to leave," Neutrino said. "Once he had the engine apart, I was at his mercy." Neutrino happened to have a few more cans of sardines. On the fourth day, the mechanic finished his work and asked Neutrino for a hundred and thirty dollars. Even though the repair would likely have cost a hundred dollars at a garage, Neutrino considered it a fair price to be shed of him.

A friend of Neutrino's in New York said he would advance him the money for a motor. Neutrino would pay him back in monthly installments, using the Social Security money he was spending on the cell phone and the car insurance he would no longer need once he was on the ocean. He bought the motor in San Diego. Then he drove back to Calexico, put the motor in a storage bin, and returned to working on the raft.

Neutrino planned to sail to Peru, so that he could begin his voyage from where Heyerdahl and Willis had begun theirs. "I don't know what this raft is going to look like when I get to Peru," he told me on the phone. "I may tear the entire cabin off once I'm on the water." The raft he would sail down the coast would not be the raft he would take across the ocean. "Because I've crossed the Atlantic in a raft, I pretty much know what she should look like when I cross the Pacific," he said. "Bigger, for one thing. More cabin room, more storage. But to go down the coast of South America, I may have it be even more barren than it is now. I may have to carry more fuel than I think—I don't know if I'm going to do mostly motoring or a combination of the two. With all the things I might have to carry, I might not have the luxury of a cabin, it might just have to be an open deck, like Huck Finn."

"What about the sun?"

"I'll string up a shade, a canopy. My approach is, I get down to the water and see if she will get up and plane. *Plane* means she rises out of the water and bounces along the top of a glassy sea. A planing raft is four to five times as fast as a displacement one. Let's say I have to go two hundred miles between ports. I can only go during the day, because I have to sleep. At five miles an hour on a displacement raft, it's going to take me four days. In these four days you might not have a constant weather window. If I can do twenty-five miles an hour on a planing raft, it's going to take me one long day. When I get to Peru, I build an ocean-going raft so I can carry more food and water and fuel—a displacement raft to move with the current and the wind. When I get across, I'll dismantle it and get it back to where it will plane, so I can go through Asia. But first, I have to survive going down the coast. I've done river rafts, I've done intercoastal, I've done the ocean, but I've never done a twelve-foot raft like this down the coast, so I don't go all out and make an overall design, and say I'm ready now. That would be foolish. If it planes, it also tells me how much weight I can add on to it. If she can't get up and plane, I have to start taking her apart."

When I asked how he was doing, he said, "I've made a break with my family. We've talked and said good-byes."

"It must have been terribly hard."

"Very," he said. He paused. "Where I am physically and mentally," he said next, "I think it is possible to make a circumnavigation on this raft, and I think I'm in shape to do it, but I can't go at the same pace a young man goes. I think I'm also over the fear. Once you start, you don't come back, unless you're a failure. You make it, and you've reentered Rome with a wreath on your head, or you've died in battle. If you come back otherwise, it's in disgrace. Last time, with the Atlantic, I won, and because I did, all kinds of things were possible for me. I'm down as the first scrap raft across the Atlantic. That's mine, it's locked up. No one can duplicate the feat, the century is closed. I'm starting on this new one, and it could be the biggest thing I've ever done. Old man circumnavigates the globe in a twelve-foot scrap raft. So I ask, Are you going to let loneliness conquer you? I'm practicing with the dog in the car for the solitude. It's not going to be much different on the water. I've adjusted my psyche and my attitude to it, and I think I have a high percentage chance to make it. I've never had a raft trip fail. There are things I don't know, and can't know until I'm on the ocean, but if I knew everything already, there wouldn't be any adventure."

By the end of November, Neutrino had collected in his storage bin in Calexico charts for the Sea of Cortés, life jackets, a GPS he had got from someone in San Diego who had just bought a new one, pots and pans and a cooking stove, his motor, and two big watertight suitcases, given to him by National Geographic, in which he kept his video equipment. He still needed a certain kind of foam he called two-part foam, which had to be laid on by hand and would fill cracks and crevices, and some fishing net for his sail. Within a few days he had got hold of the foam but not the fishing net, but he decided that he was ready to go to Mexico and that he could find fishing net there.

One evening around Thanksgiving, in the parking lot of the Wal-Mart, as he was lying down to sleep in his van, his chest constricted, and his arms went numb. He told me it felt as though someone were tightening an iron band around his chest. It seemed about as powerful as his first heart attack, the one that had knocked him out and put him in the hospital for two weeks. For an hour he lay on his bed. He found his phone and called a nurse he knew in Los Angeles. The two of them believe in other means of healing than conventional ones and he said, "She sent me a healing over the phone." Then he said, "I know you don't believe in that."

He didn't mean this contentiously. He knew that I didn't believe in half the things he believed in. Neutrino often says that he is going to live until he is eighty-six, "active to eighty-six anyway." He avoids doctors, partly from a fear that they will discover something wrong with him that needs immediate attention and overnight he will turn into an old man dependent on a walker or a wheelchair. He told me he was going to rest for a few days.

"I've withdrawn from contact with the world, more or less," he said. "I'm going to play some music, drive around a little, move cautiously, then see how I feel about going back to work."

Chapter 8

At the beginning of the second week of December, I flew to San Diego and the next morning drove east across the mountains and through the desert to El Centro, then turned south to Calexico. Pretty much the first thing you come to in town is the Wal-Mart. Neutrino was parked at the far end of the lot. He was wearing a dark shirt and a pair of dark nylon shorts over his dark trousers. I said I had never seen that look before. He said his zipper was broken. Then he asked if I thought it looked strange, and I said I thought it looked fine, and, oddly, on him it did. The day before he had walked into Mexico and gone to a bathhouse, then got a shave and had his shoes shined. He wore a brown canvas trilby that he had cleaned using carpet cleaner he'd bought at the Wal-Mart.

At a family-style restaurant that Neutrino was fond of, we stood in line with a lot of Mexican families. He said that he had found a plastic plumbing pipe, about twelve feet long and three inches across, that he could use as a mast. "I have the money I need, I have most of the equipment, I have seclusion, what will stop me?" he asked. "I have to make sure no one steals the dog or the engine." Out of the same superstitious feeling that prevents baseball players from mentioning a pitcher's no-hitter until the last batter is retired, I did not ask, "What about the heart attack?"

In reading on the plane the notes I had taken of our conversations, I realized I hadn't been sure when certain events in his past had happened. I said that in one case it seemed to me he was in three places at once.

"It's possible I was in three places at once," he said. "In my whirling Sufi dervish days. Definitely a possibility. I certainly tried to be."

One of the episodes I asked about was his first marriage. He had been nineteen, and his wife was eighteen, and the marriage failed quickly. I asked whether he knew if she had remarried and had an okay life. I don't think he saw any point in the question. "An okay life? I'm not even sure what that is," he said testily. "I don't want an okay life. I want 'Wow!' And if I can't have it, I don't even want to be around to have an okay life. I want to make things happen. I don't want to see what happens, I don't want to wait for things to come to me. I don't want, for example, to see what happens when I get on this raft. Only a fool would do that. I want to prepare thoroughly and make it do certain things. I don't like unpleasant surprises, and they come to you if you allow them to, if you live your life without vigilance. I want large and powerful things to happen to me by my own crafty, diligent, and careful design."

In his hands Neutrino held some dollar bills, which he was rolling up in a piece of newspaper, then unrolling and rolling again.

He leaned toward me, as if to confide something. "When I was young, I had tremendous emotional feelings," he said, "but I had no intellectual equipment. Nobody in my family thought. At all. About anything. There were no discussions about ideas. There were very few books. There was a set of encyclopedias, but nobody read them. No poetry. There was only motion and movement. So I didn't know how to express the feelings I'd had once I'd been to North Beach and saw the existence and possibility of them. What they meant and where they could lead you. I had no words for them, but I felt now and then, especially during periods of great pressure and hardship, that it was as if God, or the holy spirit or whatever you want to call it, had entered my body and given me a clarity to appreciate the experience I was undergoing. Crossing a mountain one time in Montana while I was hitchhiking, it was dusk, and no cars had come by for hours, and I hadn't eaten for two days and was hungry and cold and tired, and I thought I wasn't going to make it. I thought I might fall down and die where I was. I wasn't being dramatic, it just seemed a possibility that loomed larger as time passed. No one seemed aware of my existence, no one was out looking for me, I was in some ways at the end of the earth. And then I remember it was just like a switch had been thrown, and my awareness expanded suddenly, as if it leapt right to the horizon and into the sky above me, so that I was part of everything and everything was part of me, and I felt this simple amazement at where I was, and at what I saw—the rolling tops of the mountains, the snow, the clear sky rising to the heavens."

He folded his money in the newspaper.

He sat back. "If I had to do it all over again," he said, "by even more vigilance, I couldn't probably make the good things

happen, but I could stop a lot of the bad things from happening."
Then he shrugged and said that he wanted to rest for a while, and
we left. In the parking lot he realized that his money was still in
the newspaper, which was on the table, and he ran back to get it.

"I roll it up to hide in the car," he said sheepishly when he returned, "and I guess I wasn't paying attention."

I asked if he had other things hidden in his car.

"All over and everywhere," he said.

Chapter 9

THE NEXT MORNING AROUND NINE I drove to the
Wal-Mart and knocked gently on a window of the van. I asked
Neutrino if he was inside.

"I am," he said. "Somewhere between Tolstoy and Dosto-
yevsky. Give me a minute."

We ate breakfast at the family-style place, then parked a few
blocks north of the border and walked across to Mexicali. We
went first to the government office so that Neutrino could obtain a visa for a six-month stay. He showed his passport to a man
wearing a uniform and standing behind a counter. His hair was
not long in the photograph, but he had a beard that went several
buttons down his shirt and was brushed and parted in the middle.
He looked like a Greek Orthodox priest. The Mexican official
performed a suave double take when he saw it, raising only his
eyes from the passport.

After Neutrino got his papers we searched for a pharmacy
that sold the medicine he needed for his prostate. There seemed

to be one on every block, and all of them had it, but in doses so small that it would cost Neutrino more than he was comfortable paying to get the six-month supply he felt he should have in case he couldn't find it as he traveled. By a bus stop we came upon a small blind man sitting on a bench with his arms folded over a guitar. He was looking straight ahead of him, as if waiting to be summoned. Neutrino put a dollar in a cup he held in one hand, and at the slight pressure of the gesture, the man stood. In Spanish, Neutrino asked for a song. The man played "Feliz Navidad." His teeth were brown and ground nearly to stumps. His voice was nasal. Several men sitting nearby snickered at his performance, but he had more elegance than any of them would ever approach. When the chorus arrived, Neutrino leaned toward the man and sang a line of harmony. A little boy who had seen Neutrino give the man money tugged on Neutrino's sleeve and asked if we wanted to buy chewing gum. Neutrino bent over him, as if bowing, and asked how much, but he couldn't understand the boy's answer. He held out his hand with all his change in it. The boy carefully picked up one coin after another until he had all of them, then he said solemnly that we could each have one piece of chewing gum.

On a corner, a man held his hand toward us and asked for money to buy a taco. In his palm he had a small pile of coins. Neutrino gave him paper money and said, "I taught you that," and the man grinned. As we walked on I asked what he had meant. "He was begging the other day by the bathhouse," Neutrino said. "His hand was empty, and I told him, 'People aren't going to give you money if you have none. Show them you have some, and they'll give you more.'"

The dark-haired girls on the sidewalk who appeared to be about sixteen and wore tight, short dresses and were gathered around an older woman as if for protection were not on their way to church, as I had assumed—it was a Sunday—but I didn't know this until we passed a doorway and stairs leading to a landing and saw more of them standing in the shadows and peering out at the street.

Along the flat roofs of the two- and three-story buildings were television antennas like messages written in Chinese characters. People sat on the sidewalk and leaned against the buildings. Over everything lay a powdering of dust, and each time a bus passed I could feel it set an edge on my teeth.

We came to a public square, and Neutrino waved his hand before him. "We lived among these people for years," he said. "Sleeping in doorways, scheming for food. We hopped trains."

"Didn't you regard it as a deprivation?" I asked, and immediately felt I should beg his pardon.

"I did, and it was," he said, "but I always saw it as temporary."

He said that once the Flying Neutrinos were playing in a Mexican park like the one in front of us, and while their attention was elsewhere, someone stole one of their children. The crowd had observed the abduction and saw the kidnapper take the child into a building across the street. The musicians stopped playing, and the crowd surrounded the building and began to search it and found the child. The kidnapper had fled.

We were walking back to the border when Neutrino stopped. "Want to see me sing on the street in Mexico?" he asked. He crossed to the corner and stood beside a department store window that had children's clothes in it, and next to a metal vending box that held newspapers. On top of the box was a paper cup. Neutrino shook out the cup and asked me for some coins, which he put in the cup. "Stop crying, I'll come back to you some sunny day," he sang; lines from "Mexicali Rose." A few feet from him two men were sitting on a bench. They ignored him. Neutrino sang louder. "Every night you know that I'll be pining."

Two women walking with a little girl in a pink dress stopped and listened, but they didn't give him any money. When he finished singing, he took the coins from the cup and threw the cup in a garbage can.

"See, what I need for the street is a box," he said. "No one wants to put the money in a cup. You get a box, and you write, 'One Mexican peso,' on it." We crossed the street. "The Mexicans have a word for people like me," he said, then he pronounced the word. I asked what it meant.

"It means that I have no embarrassment," he said.

Chapter 10

THE NEXT MORNING WE ate a big breakfast at the family-style restaurant, then drove to a storage place on the edge of town where Neutrino had rented a cubicle with a sliding door. We retrieved his power drill and toolbox and some nylon rope, then we drove to the parking lot to work on the raft. The lot enclosed several acres of flat, dusty ground that was as brittle and hard as dry clay. Neutrino had parked the raft in the farthest section of it, past rows of trucks and trailers and cars that seemed abandoned, as if they'd perished where they lay, like the skulls of cattle in western movies. When the owner at the gate said that Neutrino wasn't supposed to be working in the lot, Neutrino raised a finger and said, "One more day."

Since I had last seen the raft, in Buckeye, Neutrino had raked the bow and insulated the cabin walls with Styrofoam. Over the Styrofoam he had nailed pieces of cardboard. The mast, some boards, and a big folding umbrella stuck out of the cabin, and we lay them on the ground. The seams in the cabin where the boards met imperfectly were intentional, he said. "If water gets in, it will go right out immediately, I won't have to bail it," he said. On the cabin roof were three sheets of plywood and beneath them a metal door filled with foam that Neutrino had found thrown out in Calexico and thought he might use for a lee rudder. "You drop it off the back in a storm, and the raft goes downwind," he said. On the back of the cabin it still said ATHA FOR AYOR. Standing on the deck, Neutrino edged the plywood a sheet at a time across the roof until it tipped into my hands. The door was too heavy to handle, so I stood back and he shoved it, and it fell to the ground and raised dust. Every eighteen inches or so we drilled holes in the roof and the sides and threaded rope through the holes and knotted it. This took us about an hour, and then Neutrino placed two folding chairs from the cabin in the shade and we sat. He seemed tired. He held his dog in his lap.

"Fifteen minutes, and I'll be ready for another attack," he said. He leaned over and sang softly to the dog. "There's only one thing in my soul," he said when he finished. "It's attack. Whether it's musical, spiritual, emotional, it's a multileveled attack. If you don't attack, you're just receiving all the blows of life. It's not the attack of a soldier trying to kill a foe, it's a probing, a finding of the door that will open, you hope, into a larger and grander experience."

He thrust his chin quickly at the raft. "I know you see this raft trip as my wandering off to the horizon and maybe into oblivion," he said.

I thought that was possible—an old man with three heart attacks, one of them recent, never mind all the perils of the ocean—but I was embarrassed that I hadn't managed to conceal it. "Well, not really," I said, "I mean—"

"That's all right," he said. "I don't mind." He leaned over and put the dog on the ground, then he sat up. "I see it as having a club in each hand and spikes on my feet and saying, '*Now* you bastards, *now* I'm coming after you.'"

He stood up and said that he was ready. The dog lay down in the shade cast by the raft in the dirt. Neutrino started his car, and reading my hand signals in his side-view mirror, he lined up the tow-bar ball with the trailer. When we tried to lift the trailer onto the ball, we discovered we couldn't move it. Neutrino stepped back and looked at the raft. He took off his hat and scratched his head and resettled his hat. He walked once around the raft. The dog stood up and watched him. Neutrino shook his head.

"Funny thing about weight," he said finally. "When you have an ounce too much, it's too much." He considered knocking down the cabin, then decided it wasn't sensible. "There's nothing in this raft but wood," he said, shaking his head. "If I'm going to get this on and off the beach . . ."

He started walking toward the car. It occurred to me that he might walk away from the raft, as he had done years ago from the bus in the junkyard. He began removing wood and tools and clothes from the van, as if he were searching through a closet. He walked back toward me carrying a jack, then he went into the cabin and came out holding scraps of two-by-fours. Piling the scraps on top of one another, he made a little tower and put the jack on top of it and began to raise the trailer. When the ball arrived at the level of the hitch, he placed one of the folding chairs next to the jack. For a lever he used the plastic pipe that he was intending for the mast, and with the chair as a fulcrum, he tried to raise the trailer off the jack and onto the ball. The pipe bent then it cracked slightly, but it didn't break. He dropped the pipe.

"Well, we tested the mast anyway," he said. "It's fine, it's strong, it won't break."

With his foot, he shoved the mast aside, then he lay down on his back in the dust to inspect the latch inside the trailer hitch. When he stood up all the creases in his dark shirt and dark pants were lined with dust. He tugged up his pants, and a thin cloud rose from him like a vapor.

"Looking good, looking good," he said.

Neutrino planned to move the ball underneath the hitch, then have us shove the trailer so that it fell off the stack of wood and settled on the ball. He needed to raise the trailer a few inches higher and put another block of wood on the tower of blocks. The task required a flat piece of wood. The only piece he had left was rounded. "I wasn't going to use it, but we have to," he said. He shrugged. "Besides, in this, as in all matters, I never do things correctly."

Neutrino turned the jack handle, and I slid the block on top of the pile. The raft tilted slightly. I didn't actually see the trailer fall off the blocks. I heard Neutrino yell, "Out of the way!" The dog ran. The trailer hit the ground hard, but the raft didn't fall off. We stacked the blocks and jacked the trailer again. When we got the hitch on the ball, the latch wouldn't withdraw, so the trailer wouldn't settle. With the head of an ax Neutrino got from the cabin, he struck the hitch, and it fell into place.

Neutrino leaned the ax against the raft and sat on the folding chair. He picked up the dog. "You've got a new blue harness and a red leash," he sang softly to her, "and you're black and white with brown eyes, shall we dance?" Then he drank some water. Then we hoisted the plywood and the metal door back onto the roof and lashed them to the cabin. Heat shimmers rose like dancing figures from the hoods of the wrecked cars around us.

"It's difficult to realize that there's no more having to wait for anything," Neutrino said. "Everything's here." He shrugged. "So there was a little difficulty hooking up the trailer, because of all the emotional turmoil it represented, but now there's no more excuses."

He stood and banged his chair against a fender of the trailer to close it. "The Flying Neutrinos are going to explode on the world's consciousness shortly. Not just in music and dance," he said, "but ideology, philosophy, endeavor, and adventure, and by the time the various authorities move to get hold of me, I'll be out of reach. A stateless citizen. They'll have to go through the UN to get me."

He walked once around the raft, tugging on the ropes. When he finished he said, "I just held on to stay here," meaning in Calexico. "I didn't flourish. Something in me said, 'You're not going to have a good time, because if you do, you'll be captive.' So I stayed free, did what I had to do, but it was hard. Very meager. I can't start from scratch anymore. I just want to think and sail with the wind."

Chapter 11

THE NEXT MORNING from his storage space Neutrino withdrew a mosquito net, a crowbar, a chess and checkers set, gas cans, foam insulation, a guitar, coils of rope, a tin filled with sunglasses he planned to give away as the occasion arose, a Skilsaw, and a painting of the raft on the water that was half completed. He worked without talking, moving things around in the storage space to organize them, and he seemed melancholy.

"God I feared this day," he said finally.

"Why, tedious?"

"Tedious, and it reminds me of how scattered my life is," he said forlornly. He paused. "And what a slob I am, too, I guess."

Three Mexican women loaded boxes from the trunk of their car into a cubicle near Neutrino's. A little girl belonging to one of them kicked at a piece of Styrofoam that had fallen from Neutrino's car until it came apart. In a box Neutrino found a notebook and asked if he could read me something. It was a description in the third person of his meeting Maxine and their taking the motorcycle ride. He asked if I thought it was good, and I said I did, and he said, "Okay. Thank you for listening." He closed the notebook and put it on the dashboard of the van.

"It's important that I have a good time doing this last errand, that I don't get upset or come apart," he said. From a box in the cubicle he took some videotapes and asked me to carry them back to New York and hold on to them for him. Then he leaned into the cubicle, took a final look, and said, "This is it, amigo."

The next morning I left my car at the storage lot. Neutrino covered the front seat of his van for me with his corduroy coat. Towing the raft, we drove around Calexico at about the speed of someone riding a bicycle, looking for a place to buy car insurance for Mexico. By the time we had signed all the papers, it was early in the afternoon. As we drove the few blocks to the border, Neutrino made a last phone call, since his phone wouldn't work in Mexico. "I'm on my way out of the country," he said to whoever answered.

In Mexicali we drove past shacks and hovels behind fences strung with razor wire. At an intersection, women with broad faces and black hair held boxes of candy toward us, and at another, by a sign with an arrow for Tijuana, a man wearing a loincloth and a headdress banged on a skin drum. Beside him stood a man playing a wooden flute. Neutrino drove so slowly that I could look them in the eye. The air smelled of gasoline and the eucalyptus burning in oil drums by the side of the road. Around the drums, men squatted on their haunches and tended the fires.

Neutrino was delighted to be moving. He sang. He told stories about his past. He said that once in Florida he and the Navy had arrived in a town that had a law against sleeping in public. It was the sort of town where it looked as if the people vacuumed their lawns. He didn't have money for rooms. He saw a stairway leading to the roof of the police station, and when the sun went down the Navy tiptoed up the stairs and slept on the roof, because Neutrino felt sure the police would never look for anyone there. They left just before daybreak.

Beyond Mexicali we drove through farmland, then a line of hills rose up on our right and accompanied us into the desert. Neutrino said that he had once tried to walk over them and found that they went on for miles. They were brown when we started, and as the sky grew darker they turned blue. A quarter moon hung above them like a lantern. The road had been laid on a bed raised up from the desert. Every few miles there were shrines to car crashes, and by one of them, a small tin cross with 1975–1992 scratched into it, we stopped to check the ropes on the plywood. Neutrino tightened several of them then we started again.

San Felipe is about 120 miles south of Calexico. After three hours we were still roughly 25 miles short of it. Night had fallen. The desert was so dark and still that it was as if someone had turned out the lights and left. Each time the van climbed the gentlest incline, the transmission slipped and the engine raced briefly. Even before Neutrino said, "What's that?" I knew that the faint bumping that began suddenly in back of us was a tire on the trailer going flat.

Neutrino drove slowly off the road and into the desert. I said he should be careful not to go too far, because the sand was soft.

He said he didn't care about getting stuck, the important thing was to get far enough off the road that a truck didn't hit us. The rim had shredded the tire. Neutrino had no spare. Briefly I entertained the image of his moving the Navy around the country for twenty years, with a difficulty like this probably every three miles. The raft pitched about fifteen degrees from center. When Neutrino turned off the headlights, to save the battery, it seemed as if the darkness rushed right up to the windows. He said, "Let's pray." Then he walked off into the desert and stood awhile thinking. When he came back, he said that we should leave the raft and find a place to stay. From the cabin we removed his tools and the watertight suitcases, lest they be stolen, and put them in the van. Then we put some wood blocks on the ground and jacked up the trailer again. The higher we raised the raft, the more it looked as if it would tip over, but all that happened was the trailer fell suddenly off the jack and settled in the sand. "If the raft had fallen over, I would have cut the cabin off, right down to the deck," Neutrino said. "The important part's the deck and the foam. And the motor transom. That's the beauty thing about a raft. It can take a lot of damage."

As we drove away, I watched the raft, scarlet in the taillights, grow smaller and smaller in the side-view mirror until the darkness enclosed it. I wondered if I would ever see it again. "Stuff like this is going to happen," Neutrino said. "You're going to break an oar, a sail will tear, you'll run aground just as you're entering a harbor, and you have to wait twelve hours for the tide to turn again in your favor. What I found heartening is the control I had over the car, even with only one wheel."

I thought of how many nights in the world darkness had fallen with his still needing to solve a pressing matter.

After ten miles we came to a bar where Neutrino stopped and asked about somewhere to stay. Not too far down the road, it turned out, was a motel, and if we drove around the side of the bar and up a small hill we would find a restaurant. Inside the restaurant were maybe ten tables and six people eating and about eight or ten men and women at a bar. All of them seemed to be Americans and to be acquainted with one another. On the left side of the room was a stage with a microphone. Beside it sat two women at a folding table. On the table were a microphone, a pen, and a sheet of paper: karaoke night. Neutrino headed directly for the women and said that he wanted to sing. He was covered with dust, and there were streaks of mud on his chest where he had wiped his hands. The women leaned back in their chairs. I called to him and pointed to a table, and when the women saw that he had someone with him who looked like an ordinary person, they seemed to exhale. They gave him a catalog of tapes and told him he could pick three songs. He wanted to go on the stage right away.

"We actually have a line of people ahead of you," one of the women said primly.

Neutrino nodded. The other woman asked his name, and he told her. "Okay, we'll call you when it's time, Poppa."

Neutrino spread the catalog on our table and pored over it as if he were a scholar with a fascinating text. On a piece of paper from my notebook he wrote "It Had to Be You" and "Strangers in the Night." Meanwhile the women called a name, and a tall, skinny man in shorts and a T-shirt standing at the bar put down his drink and walked almost bashfully to the stage. He sang "Okie from Muskogee." He was about forty-five, and he had a good bar-band voice. He held the microphone in one hand and the cord in the other, like a crooner. The waitress took our order.

The women called Neutrino to the stage, and he sang "It Had to Be You." He is accustomed to singing by himself and extending phrases or shortening them as he likes, and it took him a while to grasp the tempo firmly, but he sang with a kind of charming and emphatic determination, as if he were trying to win a prize.

"Wow, Poppa, that was lovely," one of the women said when he finished. "We'll be inviting you up again in a few minutes," she said.

Neutrino had a wild look in his eye when he sat down. "I have to perform, or I don't feel right," he said. He rubbed his hands together and picked up the catalog to choose his third song. "It's the one thing I can do without ever getting tired," he said.

After another man from the bar sang "Wake Up, Little Susie," quite badly, the women called Neutrino's name again. "Is it Poppa, or P-a-p-a?" she asked. He stood on the stage while they looked for the tape for "Strangers in the Night." Under the lights he seemed to shimmer. Once again he got tangled up in the tempo, but he recovered and made it to the end with the gravity of a liner coming into a berth.

"Well, now, Poppa, that was won-der-ful. Make sure you sign up again," one of the women said.

"And be sure to come to open mike on Sunday afternoon," the other said.

"Can I bring my guitar?" he asked. "I play the guitar, too."

"Absolutely," one of them said.

Chapter 12

A NOTE ON THE DOOR of the motel office said "I'm in room 314, first door around the corner," and there was an arrow drawn to show which corner. Through the window of the room, I saw a man lying on a bed watching television. The second time I knocked, he said, "Go around to the office, I'll meet you." It was about ten o'clock. He had the flu, he said, and had been resting. When he saw from my license that I was from New York, he said that he was from Boston. Through the glass door of the office he could see Neutrino at the wheel of the van. He asked how many rooms. I said one, and when I said a double bed was fine, he looked hard at me.

When I got up in the morning, I called to Neutrino through the window of the van and got no answer. I called again, then I tapped on the side. A window on the other side of the van stood partway open. Through it I could see a corner of his sleeping bag and the foot of the bed but couldn't tell if he was in there or not. Then it occurred to me to call the dog. When I got no answer from her either, I decided he probably wasn't in there dead. I turned to see where he might have gone and across the desert, about half a mile away, saw the Sea of Cortés. In the night I hadn't realized we were anywhere near it. I followed the print of his sneakers to the road then picked it up on the other side, going down a sand road that led toward the water. After about a hundred yards, he had wandered into the desert and the ground turned hard, and I lost the track. I started walking back to the motel, then it occurred to me that maybe he had had another heart attack. I called his name. A car went by, and the people in it looked at me intently, as if they had heard a gringo was wandering in the desert, and it was worth driving out to see him.

I gave up and walked back to the motel. When Neutrino arrived, there were so many creases in his clothes that he looked like a piece of cubist sculpture. He said that he had followed the road to the beach and found a little settlement where the people had been welcoming. He said that if anything had happened to the raft it had happened during the night, and there was no point rushing back to it. The worst that might have happened, he thought, was that some Mexicans had stripped it for the plywood.

After breakfast we drove toward San Felipe looking for a garage where we could buy a tire. Neutrino said that once, as a young man, when he had been in a bar with Frank Turpin, he and another man had got into an argument. Neutrino put his hand on the man's forehead and banged his head against the wall behind him, and he fell to the floor unconscious. As it happened, the man was a middleweight boxer in town for a title fight. Being knocked out in the bar meant that he couldn't fight, and he missed his payday. He tracked down Neutrino and said that he would meet him that afternoon in a lot near the bar, and they would fight. Neutrino thought, I'm done for now. He showed up with Turpin, hoping that the beating would be over quickly and Turpin could get him to the hospital. As Neutrino and the fighter were facing off, Turpin whispered in the boxer's ear, "Watch out, he's got a knife, and if he starts losing, he's going to cut you." The boxer put up his hands and called off the fight.

In the time it took Neutrino to tell the story, we came to an open-sided structure built from four brick columns about twenty feet high, with enough room within them to park two cars. The columns supported a sheet of tin for the roof, and on the tin was a tire held upright by metal struts. In back of the garage was a low, cinder-block house, with a refrigerator by the front door. A woman and a little boy stood beside the refrigerator, and a man came out the door and walked toward us. Neutrino asked how much he would want to collect the trailer and fix the tire. The man looked off toward the hills, as if expecting the answer to be written there. He named a price, and we accepted it. By Neutrino's odometer, the raft was seventeen miles behind us. To show the man what the raft looked like, Neutrino got from the car a newspaper story written about him in Key West that had a photograph of it.

The man thought it would take two hours to retrieve the raft. We drove into San Felipe. Neutrino wanted to see the harbor. On the way down the two-lane road toward town, he described a trip he had made with the Navy through Mexico years ago, in a school bus. "I had a knack for finding school buses for a hundred dollars that weren't supposed to last six months and ended up running for years," he said. They had been crossing the Sierra Madres and were lost. They were on their way home and had already been through all the parts of the country that they had thought might be dangerous. When they saw a car behind them, they pulled over and asked directions. There were six or seven men in the car, and they drew guns and told everyone to get out of the bus. They seemed drunk. When they boarded the bus and saw the musical instruments, they made the family play them and forced the children to dance. After a while Neutrino was able to sneak back on the bus. He poured gasoline into several Coke bottles and stopped them with rags. While the bandits were passing some liquor around, he got everyone on the bus and started off. The bandits chased them.

"We're at the top of the mountains, on the Devil's Spine," Neutrino said. "You look down one side, and there's clouds below you, and you look down the other side, and there's clouds below you. We're tiptoeing along the ridge, but we have the middle of the road, and they can't pass us." He was nervous about lighting the Molotov cocktails and having one of them spill inside the bus, but he decided that he had to. Before he did, though, they came to a turning and the bandits took it, waving to them as they grew smaller.

San Felipe turned out to be an impoverished little town on

the water, with fishing boats on the beach. Some of the streets were paved and some weren't. Along the main street were several forlorn looking hotels painted in pastel colors and trinket shops and a few restaurants. Neutrino drove slowly through the streets. "Oh, if only I could see Dolores, not Marjorie or Florence," he sang. He drove so slowly that it was as if we were passing things on a river, holding them in view before releasing them. "There's no sign painters in this town," he said. "There's been sign painters through, though." I asked how he could tell. "Too many beat-up signs for there to be one who lives here," he said. At one end of town was a small, muddy boatyard with a ramp. "Here's where we'll put it in the water," he said. The wind blew steadily onshore. "If I had gone to the ocean side, the wind would have been offshore," he said. "One failure of the motor, and you're into open water. Here you're headed across the gulf to the far shore at worst."

We ate lunch in a restaurant by the water where Neutrino could park close enough that he could hear the alarm if anyone opened the door. The restaurant let him bring the dog in, and the waitress made a fuss over her. She kept bringing to our table other waiters and people who worked in the kitchen. Then she would hold the dog's lips back and everyone would laugh at the tiny front teeth. After lunch we drove back to the garage, but the man wasn't there. "Two Mexican hours is five hours American," Neutrino said.

A few miles farther out of town, by a sand road where a man with a can of red paint and a paintbrush was painting stones as a signpost, Neutrino left the paved road for one that led toward the water. About a quarter of a mile down the road was a house trailer with a porch on one side of it. Beside the trailer was a flag-pole flying Mexican, American, and Canadian flags. Strung above the trailer were several lines of triangular pennants flapping in the wind, as if at a gas station. A sign by the parking lot said COUNTRY CLUB. A driving range is what it was. Neutrino had seen it that morning from the road. The porch faced the fairway. We bought two buckets of balls, picked out some clubs, and went out to the porch. The desert rose slightly away from the porch, and in the distance cars went by on the paved road. Beyond the road were the mountains. Neutrino hit one ball after another deep into the desert. Some of them rose so high that they disappeared into the pale sky, and I never saw them land. Others raised sand as they landed, like gunshots. A man and a woman arrived. The man wore cowboy boots and jeans and a white shirt with blue and red stripes on the shoulders and white stars, and the woman had on shorts and a halter top. They each ordered a bottle of beer. Neutrino fell into conversation with them. I hit some more balls, then I went to use the bathroom, which was just on the other side of a thin wall from the porch, and I heard the man say, "You taking this guy with you to Peru?"

Neutrino hit a few more balls, then we drove to the garage. On the way, I asked if he ever felt lonely. He took a moment to answer. "At a certain point when I was young, there was such loneliness that I was almost in despair," he said. "On those Route Sixty-six experiences, I was always looking for prayer meetings, tent meetings, card games, dice tables, practically any gathering to soothe the loneliness. Then suddenly something shifted, and it seemed to me that everyone was the same in some inexplicable and fundamental way, and what became important was a person's capacity for contact. Not who the person was, I mean, not whether I already knew them, not whether they looked interesting or handsome or pretty, but whether they could have an exchange of sufficient intimacy that it satisfied my need, my longing really, for companionship. As I got better at that kind of contact, I realized I could find company anywhere, with a little bit of luck, and I stopped feeling alone."

When we arrived at the garage, there was a truck parked in front of it. On the side of the truck it said JUAN'S AGUA DELIVERY. I said, "I don't see the raft," and Neutrino said, "That must be bad news." We got out of the van. The raft, it turned out, was parked behind the truck. It had just arrived. The man we had dealt with was standing beside it and shaking his head. He said that the jack kept sinking in the sand and that to lift the trailer and keep the raft from falling over had taken "cinco hombres." He had had to return to the garage and collect them, then drive back to the raft, nearly seventy miles altogether. He said he was sorry he had taken the job. He had lost his entire day over it. He wanted more money. Neutrino waved his hand and said, "No más," but then he agreed with me that the job had been larger than the man had reckoned, and that the request was fair. Furthermore, he thought the man might turn out to be helpful.

After we gave the man his money, Neutrino pointed at the raft and said, "I'm looking for a place to leave this."

The man said, "What is it?"

Neutrino said, "It's a boat."

The man began laughing.

Neutrino pointed at his chest and said, "Cruzo Atlantic." He showed him a newspaper clipping about the crossing. "Paree, New York, Irelando, France," he said, waving his arm as if they lay out there in the desert.

The man pointed halfway up the side of the raft and said, "Water aquí?" meaning, How high would the water rise?

Neutrino pointed lower and said, "No, aquí."

The man couldn't stop laughing. He had black hair and dark

skin, and he was wearing blue jeans and a T-shirt that said PEP-
PERDINE UNIVERSITY, PARENTS WEEKEND, 1995.

He said Neutrino could leave the raft in his yard. Neutrino
asked if he knew where he could launch it, and the man nodded.
He said he would help, because he wanted to see if it would
float. Neutrino arranged that we would come back the next
morning at ten-thirty.

On the way into town, Neutrino said that he had modeled
his singing on Edith Piaf's, and I let that pass. We ate lunch at a
restaurant by the beach. The fishing boats were gone. I watched
them arrive in the evening, raise their motors, and drift onto the
sand, and a pickup truck drive onto the beach and collect the
catch, then pull the boats above the reach of the tide. The last
thing the fishermen did before they left was unscrew the pro-
pellers from their motors.

Chapter 13

THE NEXT MORNING when we pulled off the paved
road into the yard of the tire shop, the man was standing by the
raft. He said, "Hola." He seemed uncertain, as if he weren't sure
he should have offered his help, but perhaps he was simply shy.
His name was Aleseo, he said. The trailer was already attached to
his pickup. We slid the plywood and the metal door off the roof
of the cabin and leaned them against a fence. Neutrino got his
power drill from the car. From the deck of the raft he took a
scrap of board about the size of a book and brought it down

sharply against one of the gunwales. It split unevenly. Then he drilled holes through each of the pieces and screwed them into the gunwales. He didn't have all the screws he needed, so he removed a few from the cabin. The screws when he sank them went in at angles, and their heads stuck out unevenly from the plywood. "Raft building," he said. He lay down in the sand and sank several screws in the bottom of the raft. The wind blew ropes of dust across the road and over him.

After a few minutes he looked out from under the raft and said, "What time is it?"

"Almost eleven-thirty," I said.

"All right, we're ready," he said. He stood and dusted himself off. He put his drill back in the car, then he went around the raft with a hammer, banging the screws like nails and breaking the heads off some of them. On the back of his hand there was a small patch of blood, mixed with dust. His hat had fallen off, and he bent over and picked it up and slapped it against his leg. Dust rose from it like smoke. Then he checked to see if his anchor was still in the cabin and was pleased that it was.

A man arrived in a pickup. He was tall and gaunt, with dark skin and a mustache and thin lips. His eyes were small, and their expression was dull. I thought he looked like someone I might see in a bar and sit as far from as I could. His best feature was a set of very white teeth. He asked Neutrino where he was going.

Neutrino said, "Peru."

The man grinned. In a dry, raspy voice, he said, "You want to dead?"

Neutrino, unfolding a finger at a time, said, "Mexico, Honduras, Peru."

"I know where is Peru," the man said. He spit in the dirt and put his hands in his pockets. Neutrino asked Aleseo if he could buy some gas, then he filled a plastic can from a tank in the bed of Aleseo's truck. Two little dark-haired boys came out the door of the house and rolled an old tire around. A dog followed at their heels. The other man seemed to want to say more but not to know what it might be.

We got in the van. Neutrino's dog climbed onto his lap and put her front paws on his shoulder. The man strode up to the window. Pointing at the dog, he said, "Food for the *tiburónes*."

I said, "What's *tiburónes*?"

Neutrino said, "Sharks." He shook his head.

The Mexican jabbed his finger at Neutrino. "You too, old man," he said. "*Más* food for the *tiburónes*." It came out like a curse. Then he spit again and stuck his hands back in his pockets, pleased with himself. He watched us stolidly as we pulled away, following the raft behind Aleseo's truck. Skinny as he was, in the side-view mirror he looked like a nail driven partway into the ground.

Chapter 14

WE FOLLOWED THE RAFT into San Felipe. Neutrino sang the first lines of "Over the Rainbow." The wind blew constantly, making the patterns of dust on the road seem as if they were part of some restless territorial migration, the subtle and relentless movement of the earth from one hemisphere to the other.

Neutrino drove without talking. He seemed to be brooding. I know that he believes in omens and engages in magical thinking, and I wondered whether the man's remarks had disturbed his peace of mind. When he finally said something, it sounded like a reply. "Until I'm stopped finally," he said, "I'm unstoppable."

Aleseo took us through town then south a few miles, to the port, where the big shrimp boats were moored inside a breakwater. The water within the jetty was a greenish blue and scuffed with whitecaps. By a dock was a row of fishing skiffs that rose and fell together on the waves like a chorus line. On the ramp were fishermen taking a boat called the *Punta Estrella XII* from the water. When they arrived at the top of the ramp, Neutrino spoke to them and learned that they thought the wind was too strong for them to fish. He came back toward us. He shook his head. He said he couldn't launch the raft. "We can't have a disaster," he said. "If I had the motor on it, and the power to move easily, maybe I could make a judgment, but not the first time. If I knock into someone's boat, and the captain of the port comes down, and he thinks I'm a jerk with no command of myself, and he says, 'Call yourself a sailor?' I'm in big trouble, you follow?"

Aleseo maneuvered the trailer to the curb and out of the way of any of the fishermen using the ramp. Neutrino and I collected flat stones and piled them under the trailer hitch. Aleseo said he would come back the next morning at ten-thirty and help us try again, then he left. Neutrino set up a folding chair. "Ten minutes, and I'm ready for another attack," he said. The wind whipped his clothes against his body. He looked like he was made out of sticks and padding. From his pocket he took a cracker he had saved from dinner the night before. He asked if I would bring him some water from the car. When he rose from the chair a few minutes later, he retrieved his power drill. He laid two pieces of wood across the seam of the cabin door and sank screws through them. "Just to slow anyone down," he said. "If they're really intent, they'll get in there anyway." In the van, he had a box of shoes he had picked up at a Goodwill store in Calexico. He had thought he might use them in a trade, but he left them now on the deck, hoping that they would satisfy any thieves.

Chapter 15

I WOKE AROUND FOUR the next morning and listened in the darkness for the wind, and didn't hear it. By nine, when Neutrino and I went to breakfast, it had risen a little, but the boats had gone out. I had decided to leave the next day. When I made my plans to meet Neutrino, it was with the expectation that we would drive to Mexico, and he would launch the raft and leave. Clearly he wasn't going soon. He hadn't even got the mast put up. I wondered if I had understood how forbidding an adventure this was. My view of it was romantic. I saw as heroic his leaving the world behind, the old man undaunted by the forces of nature, by the imminence of death, and so on, but I hadn't ever been alone on the ocean in a boat I had built, wishing to hear the sound of another human voice, and I hadn't ever had a heart attack, let alone three. The remarks by the witless man at the tire shop seemed to have cast a pall over him.

It occurred to me that perhaps he wasn't ever going to leave, that he was waiting for something to come up, someone to contact him and say they needed something done that only he could do, a summons. In my mind's eye I saw the raft, years from now, among the skiffs on the beach in San Felipe, worked by a fisherman who had been destitute before Neutrino had given

him a means of making a living, then had left for Arizona or
New Orleans.

Chapter 16

A FTER BREAKFAST WE DROVE to the marina. The
shoes were where Neutrino had left them. The wind had risen.
By the top of the ramp, four fishermen were standing beside
three pickups and the *Claudia Vanessa* on a trailer. The tide was
low. Neutrino thought they might be waiting for higher water.
He said, "Más agua?" The fishermen said, No, too much wind.
They leaned on the hoods of their trucks in the attitude of men
leaning against a bar.

Aleseo didn't arrive. Neutrino thought that we might find
sufficient shelter from the wind by the ramp at the far end of
town, which stood in the lee of some hills. We hooked up the
raft and drove slowly away from the water. On the main street of
San Felipe, we saw an American man we had spoken to briefly at
dinner the night before. He had been on his way out the door
when he passed our table and stopped. His name was Stan, he
said, and he was from California and had lived in San Felipe for
five years. He was talking now to a woman selling shrimp from a
basket on the tailgate of a car. Neutrino stopped beside him and
said, "Stan." The man looked startled. "We met last night," Neutrino said. "You're Stan, aren't you? Listen, where can we put in
our boat?"

Stan said, "What have you got?" Apparently he hadn't identified the raft as a boat.

"I've got a little flat-bottomed skiff, about fifteen feet," Neutrino said.

"A little what?"

"I've got a little, I've got a raft," Neutrino said.

"Can you lift it?"

Neutrino said, Thanks, never mind. Half a block farther was another American man with a crew cut and a blurry tattoo on his forearm. Neutrino stopped the van beside him and asked if he knew a place to launch, and the man said, "I don't know, maybe ask the fishermen." He held a pamphlet toward Neutrino. "Let me give you some literature," he said. "Be sure to read it." He passed the pamphlet through the window. He was a Jehovah's Witness. Every other Tuesday, he said, they preached in San Felipe.

We drove to the ramp by the hills, and Neutrino held his finger out the window and said of the wind, "It's died a little," but it hadn't really. We went to lunch. A man playing guitar came into the restaurant. When he stopped at our table, Neutrino spoke to him in Spanish, then gave him ten dollars. The man sang three Mexican songs for us. He had asked for three dollars a song. When he finished, he showed Neutrino the chords to a song that Neutrino liked to sing but hadn't known how to play. Then Neutrino borrowed the man's guitar. He stood and put one foot on his chair and held the guitar and sang. The waiter did not ask us to leave, but he did not come to our table for a long time either.

After lunch we drove back to the marina. Neutrino wanted to put the trailer in the water up to its wheels, to see how the raft would float. Some fishermen at the bottom of the ramp were loading their skiff, and we waited for them to leave. Then Neutrino gave me his video camera, so that I could record his backing slowly down the ramp. When the water reached the hull, the raft lifted off the trailer and drifted a few feet to one side. Neutrino stopped the car. If the raft got too much water under it, it might float off the trailer and we would have to fight the wind to get it settled again.

Neutrino got out of the car. "Like a cork," he said. "She really wants to sit right up on top of the waves." He asked me to point the camera at him, with the raft in the background, and he made some remarks about the occasion. He walked out of the frame and said, "Did you get it?" Then he rubbed his hands together and said, "She's going to be fast. I want her to be able to make a hundred miles a day." His car, with the transmission slipping, barely managed to drag the raft from the water and up the ramp.

Neutrino hadn't wanted to part with his car. He felt that if something went wrong on the crossing and he had to turn back, he was homeless without it. He had in the last ten months climbed back from being destitute to being just barely not destitute, and he didn't want ever to do it again. We had planned that, after he left San Felipe, I would drive the car to Calexico and leave it in the storage lot, and Neutrino would cover the dollar-a-day charge with his Social Security check.

Instead Neutrino left me at the bus station as night was falling. He said, "You have everything?" I said I did. He got back in the car. "Saying good-bye is really difficult for me," he said, without looking at me. I watched him back out of the dirt parking lot, turn onto the street, and drive slowly away. The taillights of the trailer disappeared behind a building, as if it had gone into the wings of a stage. I had briefly the childlike sensation of feeling that he and the raft, in disappearing, had been effaced. I tried to sustain a picture of them passing through the town, but I could do it for only a moment. Then it was as if a thread had broken, and I went into the station and bought a ticket to Mexicali.

PART FOUR

IN DECEMBER, TERRELL TOLD Neutrino that she was coming to see him. He was very excited. Shortly before the new year, she changed her mind. If she came to San Felipe, she felt that there was a good chance that she might end up sailing with Neutrino, and she wanted to get her degree. He told her that they might not ever see each other again, but she didn't relent.

When Neutrino told me on the phone that she wasn't coming, his voice was flat, and he almost whispered. A few days later he drove to Arizona to see Frank Turpin, who was gravely ill with cancer. They talked about the adventures they had had with each other, so many years ago. Turpin said, "We had a great time, didn't we?" Neutrino agreed that they had. Then he took a deep breath and said, "Frank, if you just visualize what you want in front of you, you can turn this sickness around." Turpin said irritably, "There you go telling me what to do." The conversation ended badly. "It was a terrible way to conclude fifty-five years of friendship," Neutrino said.

Neutrino felt sick at heart. He spent a few days at a campground in the desert in California, then he drove back to San Felipe and fell into a depression. "Two weeks of total blackness," he said. "I just slept and walked the dog and crawled back into the car and tried to nurse myself from one moment to the next. I started to wonder if I still had the fight in me. I didn't know anymore. All I could think was that, once I'm on the ocean, I have the fight to get to shore."

He began to feel that the impediment to his leaving was the car. If he sold it, he would have to move onto the raft, which he thought would help him recover his momentum. He began asking people in San Felipe if they knew anyone who might want to buy it.

Walking his dog on the beach one evening toward the end of January, Neutrino met a woman in late middle age who was also walking a dog. The intent expression on her face made him think that her sight was somehow afflicted. He told her he was building a raft to travel down the Sea of Cortés and on to Peru, then across the Pacific. He asked if she wanted to have dinner. They met at a rice-and-beans restaurant by the beach. Neutrino brought his guitar and sang for her. He also brought clippings describing his other trips. Her name was Nancy Braun. She told him that she lived in a camper at the RV park on the beach. She had six children and had been married twice, the second time to a man she said was the love of her life. Around the time they were married, he retired, and they bought a farmhouse in the Middle West. For months he was despondent over having nothing to do. To engage him, she began raising exotic animals—miniature donkeys, cockatiels, cockatoos, peacocks, potbellied pigs, and llamas—which they sold for pets. He had died a few years earlier. Eventually the farm became too difficult to manage. One by one the animals left with new owners. When all of them were gone, she sold the house and the barns and the fields and bought a camper. She had spent the summer traveling in Canada and had been working her way south. A month earlier she had happened upon San Felipe.

Then she said that she had a kayak, and she asked if she could follow Neutrino down the Sea of Cortés. They decided this was impractical, and she asked if she could go with him on the raft. He asked if she understood what living on a raft would be like. She said that she was slowly going blind. Her children wanted to put her in a home, and she wanted to have as many adventures as she could before that became necessary. They decided that she would tow the raft behind her camper down Baja to Cabo San Lucas, where they could take a ferry to the mainland and continue to South America. Then Neutrino would put the raft in the water in Peru.

A few days later, Neutrino met a couple from California who had the same model car that he did. When he said he had one for sale, they said that they had always wanted another. They asked if he would take a check, and he said he wouldn't. They agreed to have him deliver the car to Calexico for cash.

Braun had throughout her life suffered troubles with her teeth. In San Felipe she had found a dentist to cap them. She was lying in the dentist's chair when Neutrino appeared and told her that he had sold the car and was driving it to the border. He said he would be back in a few days. She said that as soon as the dentist had finished working, she would drive to Mexicali and pick him up. Since Neutrino had no idea how long his business would take, they arranged to meet by the crossing at six, seven, eight, or nine.

That evening, Neutrino walked back over the border with fifteen hundred-dollar bills in his pocket and found Braun blocking traffic by the crossing and peering through her windshield. She had engaged several small boys who were running back and forth looking for him. He was impressed by her determination. When they returned to San Felipe, he moved his few possessions into her camper and began occupying the guest bed.

O<small>N</small> JANUARY 31, 2005, Neutrino sent me an e-mail
saying that he was waiting for a check that would arrive within a
few days. With the money he was going to pay for the permit
necessary to travel in Mexican waters and to shelter on any
beach. He was also intending to buy

> two hydraulic jacks, some pipe, a come-along to power
> the raft up on the beach when the sand is too soft to sup-
> port the weight of the raft. Everything must be done here
> to insure the success of the project. There is no place
> south of here to get what I may need. I am playing chess
> with events and funds and raft parts. I am fully committed
> to crossing the Pacific. I have no plans to return to the
> United States until after the trip. I have everything I need
> to succeed, except how to spell these damn words, and I
> don't need that particular talent to pull this off. [I have
> corrected the mistakes.] I am in prime position and it
> will never come again for me. On the fourth or fifth of
> February I will put the raft in the water, immediately move
> onto the raft, proceed to accomplish going on the beach
> and off the beach. After that is accomplished I will leave
> the harbor either on my own or by tow south. The story
> is in me of crossing the Pacific on a scrap raft and practi-
> cally no money. My random mind will find a way to ac-
> complish the task.

The next day I flew to San Diego, then drove through Tijuana to Ensenada, then east over the mountains and south to San Felipe. I passed the place where the tire on the trailer had gone flat, the motel where I had spent the night, the karaoke place, the driving range, and the tire shop, and arrived in town in the middle of the day. It took me a while to find Neutrino. I had the right campground but the wrong description of Braun's camper. I drove slowly among the rows of campers and house trailers looking for him. The driver in the pickup truck who pulled up beside me as I was about to ask some people at a picnic table if they had seen Neutrino turned out to be the campground's owner. His name was Victor—it was Victor's Campground. He said that if I thought I could just come in and look around his campground at my leisure, I was mistaken. I apologized and said I was looking for an old man with a little black-and-white dog. He pursed his lips and shook his head. I said he was staying at the campground, and Victor said he wasn't. I insisted. He insisted, and there was nothing to do but leave. I drove out of town to the beach Neutrino had walked to the morning after the tire had gone flat. On the phone he had told me that he'd found a place out there to work on the raft. In the dusty yard of a flat-roofed house I saw the raft on its trailer, so I knew at least that he hadn't left San Felipe. An old man opened a sliding glass door. The barking dog beside him would not let me out of the car. I asked if he knew where I could find Neutrino, and he said, "At Victor's Campground."

On the main street of San Felipe, I found Neutrino walking his dog. He was wearing sweatpants and a corduroy coat and a festive straw boater with a black band. The brim of the boater had been chewed by his dog. We drove back to Braun's camper. She was at the dentist. Sitting at the table, Neutrino said that he had got his papers and that he also had his radio and his GPS. He said that he needed to shorten the outriggers. I asked how he knew. "Faulty mathematics, faulty intuition, and faulty experience," he said. "You hope the three wrongs come together and make it right." He said that lately he had also felt lonely. He had sung karaoke and gone to pool tournaments and played chess in order to meet people, but he hadn't crossed paths with anyone with whom he could talk intimately or who believed in the same things that he did. His relationship with Braun, he said, was "strictly platonic."

There was a knock on the door of the camper, and a woman called out, "Hello," then the door opened and Braun climbed the steps and sat down. She was a tall, slim woman with blue eyes and blond hair cut short. She had a cute little high-strung mutt dog the size of a Chihuahua. She said that she was glad to meet me and have someone confirm that Neutrino was actually who he said that he was.

Neutrino wanted to put the raft in the water that afternoon, so we left Braun and drove back to the tire shop and arranged for Aleseo to come by in two hours and tow the raft. Then we drove to the property where the raft was. Jesús was the name of the old man who owned the place. The dog barked at us, but he recognized Neutrino. Nevertheless, he lay down between us and the house and if we walked toward him he stood up. Neutrino said that the dog would tolerate him in the yard but wouldn't let him approach the house. "I wish I had that dog on the boat," he said. "I could leave it and know that everything would be there when I got back."

From around the raft and underneath it, we picked up scraps of wood that Neutrino had discarded as he worked. He tore up a red T-shirt and with his power drill screwed parts of the shirt onto the ends of the outriggers, as warning flags. Then we lashed to the outriggers the mast, some metal pipes Neutrino had collected because he thought they might eventually be useful, and some wood stakes he had picked up in San Diego to use as batons in the sail. Neutrino talked to himself while he worked. "What do I do? Do I put a piece of wood on the tip? That's what I do. That's very clever." I noticed that the cabin seemed to block the view from the helm.

"How do you see?" I asked.

"You don't," he said. "It's a bit of a problem. Once I get on it and start to work, I'll find out what the trials and tribulations are."

It was a cloudy day. Jesús had six or seven parakeets in a cage by his terrace, and they chirped and quarreled with one another. Neutrino sat on a box and used rope to braid a chain to his anchor. "If I had the money, I would have bought the proper metal pieces, like a conventional yachtsman," he said, "but this will do." When Aleseo didn't show on time, I suggested that we might wait another day, since it was growing late. "The reason I want to go today," Neutrino said, "is that for twenty dollars to Aleseo I can get the raft in the water and see what all the problems are. I don't want to go tomorrow and not know what I have." We drove over to Aleseo's. He was just loading his wife and two children aboard his truck.

At Jesús's, with Neutrino saying, "Little bit more, little more, that's it, hold it, *stop*," Aleseo backed the truck up to the trailer. The four of us lifted the trailer hitch onto the ball, and Aleseo banged it with a hammer to settle it. Neutrino gave Jesús a hundred dollars, and from the way that he quickly raised his eyes from the palm of his hand, I judged that he was pleased.

We followed Aleseo's truck out of the driveway, up the dirt road, and onto the highway. He drove just fast enough that the breeze lifted the tails of the red T-shirt. The trailer bed was canted inward to accommodate a boat keel. To support the flat-bottomed raft, Neutrino had put blocks of wood underneath it. The first pothole Aleseo hit knocked two of the blocks loose, and they fell onto the road in front of us. Neutrino was concerned that Aleseo might clip one of the outriggers against a car or a light pole, which would involve the Mexican police. "If he has an accident," Neutrino said, "we just keep going. We don't take any part of it. It's his problem."

At the marina Aleseo backed the trailer to the head of the ramp. A woman driving a white van stopped and rolled down her window and asked Aleseo what the raft was. There were three or four other women in the van. When Aleseo said it was a boat, they laughed so hard that the woman's foot must have slipped off the brake pedal, because the van began inching forward. Then she began driving slowly, toward an intersection, and I could hear them laughing wildly almost until she turned the corner.

Eight or nine fishermen were standing around the ramp with their hands in their pockets and some of them with the hoods of their sweatshirts drawn, and one of them stepped forward, as if delegated, and asked Neutrino where he was going. "Panama, Peru, *un año*," he said. The fisherman returned to the others, and from their conversation and the way they shook their heads gravely and raised their eyebrows, I gathered that none of them thought that the raft would float. When Aleseo began backing down the ramp, one of them waved his hand and shouted, "Vamanos," and they fell in beside the raft and walked it to the water. A funeral procession is what it looked like, with the raft as the cheap plywood casket. Other fishermen stood in a line along the pier and the edge of the parking lot, under a beer advertisement, and looked down on us as if we were in a theater. When the wheels of the trailer hit the water, Aleseo braked, then drove slowly backward until the hull rested in the water. Neutrino stepped from one of the outriggers onto the deck and lowered the motor.

The raft drifted free of the trailer. Neutrino waved to Aleseo to withdraw, then he started the motor. The raft didn't move. He turned the motor hard to the right, and the raft wheeled slowly, like a skittish horse. "Are all the lines clear?" he yelled. "I'm stuck, she won't move." The lines were clear. The fishermen snickered and clapped and whistled. One of them pointed a finger at his temple and asked me, "He is all right in the head?" While Neutrino peered over the stern, the raft drifted onto some rocks. A fisherman wearing white rubber knee boots detached himself from the others, stepped into the water, and pushed the raft back to sea. Neutrino gunned the motor, and suddenly two logs the size of small railroad ties appeared like corks on the surface in a swarm of bubbles and the raft lurched ahead. The fishermen applauded and yelled, then ran up the ramp and got in their trucks and drove along the breakwater, following Neutrino. The raft sat high in the water and moved slowly against the wind. Standing on the rocks and in the beds of their trucks like sentinels, the fishermen watched until it was apparent that the outcome they hoped for wasn't likely to occur.

Neutrino's plan was to beach the raft by the campground, where he could watch it easily. I drove along the hills above the Sea of Cortés, keeping him in view. He was several hundred yards offshore, traveling coastwise, and because the engine couldn't run at more than idle speed until it was broken in, hardly moving at all. I could see only the cabin, a small square like a screen, honey-colored in the late afternoon light, and utterly discordant with the usual geometry of the water, the vertical masts and triangular sails and sleek hulls.

It took half an hour for him to reach the campground. By the time I had parked the car, he was standing in his socks and shoes in water to his knees and was holding the raft by a rope. He was very excited. "It couldn't have gone better," he shouted as I came toward him. "She's a little bow heavy, but she really took the waves. I need to shift the weight, but that's all."

I knocked on the door of Braun's camper and told her that Neutrino was on the beach with the raft, and she said, "He's what? Where? Right now?" and came running out. We found him at the center of a circle of people. He had anchored. Looking down the beach toward town, he saw a pickup truck approaching. "Here comes a guy going to give me a tow up on the beach for twenty dollars," he said, but by the time the truck arrived, Neutrino had decided that the raft was so heavy that the truck would probably pull the front of it off. To drag it safely, he would have to drill a hole in the bow for a tow rope. He walked up the beach to admire the raft. A small red-haired woman with an Irish accent came up to him. "What's that?" she asked.

"What's it look like?" he said.

"A box with a motor," she said. She apparently didn't realize it was his. "I've been sitting here at the hotel bar drinking," she said, "and he's been a long time coming this way."

Neutrino said, "Where you from?"

"Dublin," she said.

"I landed in Ireland once," he said. He began walking toward the raft. The woman pursued him. "Where did you come into Ireland?" I heard her ask.

Every few minutes, as the tide rose, Neutrino picked up the anchor and walked the raft a little farther onshore. He was waiting for the tide to turn so that he could remove the motor. I asked why he was bothering. He had a lock on it, and all the fishermen left their motors on.

"That's them, not me," he said.

By the time the tide began to ebb, night had fallen. The people had left. Neutrino and Braun stood in the waves and hoisted the motor off the stern, and the three of us carried it up the beach to my car. Neutrino grew winded about every twenty feet, and we had to put the motor down in the sand and let him rest. Braun had agreed to let him keep it in her camper. He had run a tape measure over it and had concluded that it would fit underneath the kitchen table. Once we got the motor in my car, Braun left us and walked back to the camper.

"If I lose this motor, I'll be dependent on Nancy, and her psychology will pick up on it," Neutrino said. "This is all I have in the world. If I lost it, I'd be the world's biggest idiot."

Braun opened the camper door to us, and they found a better place for the motor between the front seats and the beds. She said that the smell it gave off made her ill, so they covered it with trash bags, then we went to dinner. Afterward Neutrino and I arranged to meet for breakfast around nine-thirty, and I left them on the beach. There was just enough light from the windows of the cabins behind me that the sky and the water were the same deep black—that is, the view was foreshortened, as if there were a wall at the tide line. Each wave lifted the raft slightly. Neutrino sat in the sand, and Braun sat in a folding camp chair. As I walked away, I heard Braun's voice in the darkness.

"I must go down to the sea again," she said.

"To the lonely sea and the sky," Neutrino said. "John Mase-field."

THE NEXT MORNING, AROUND eight-thirty, Neutrino woke me by knocking on the door of my room. The dog was with him, and he had on the shirt and sweatpants he had been dressed in when I left him. He was wearing white socks but no shoes. He had ruined his shoes by walking in the water, he said. He sat on the couch. "You ready?" he asked. I got dressed and started to shave. The next day was the start of a carnival celebrating the anniversary of San Felipe, and I told Neutrino that I had almost lost my room because of it.

"Yeah, well, I lost mine," he said.

"What do you mean?"

"Nancy threw me out."

"I don't understand."

"Just now," he said. "What happened is, around one in the morning there was a big banging on the door. I was asleep. She jumped up and yelled, 'What's going on?' and started running around, and she kicked my dog right across the room, like a football. Didn't know she was there, I guess. It was just like a dropkick." He shook his head. "Anyway, it was the police," he said. "She just panicked. I answered the door, and Victor who owns the campground was with them, and he was real apologetic, said, 'I'm sorry to wake you up.' Meanwhile she's running around behind me yelling, 'Would somebody tell me what's going on?' because of course she can't really see anything. Victor said the police wanted to know about the raft. So I got dressed and went down to the beach and showed them the papers. It was just a routine matter. They wanted to be sure it wasn't a refugee landed in their town. I came back and went to sleep. When I woke up about forty-five minutes ago, she was sitting there, and she said, 'I think it's time for you to collect your things and leave.' "

He shrugged. "Well, don't look at me like that," he said. "It's not like I planned it. Anyway, I need you to drive over there with me, and we'll pick up my stuff, and the motor, and take it to a storage space I have rented up by Jesús's place, and tonight I'll move onto the raft."

I finished shaving. As we started out the door, I said that Braun had impressed me as very determined and capable—she had, after all, run a farm on her own—but perhaps she had got more excitement in dealing with him than she had planned on.

Neutrino stopped and looked at me closely. "Everybody I ever took with me anywhere got more than they bargained for," he said.

Chapter 4

A T BREAKFAST, NEUTRINO TALKED only about the raft. She hadn't planed as well as he had hoped she would, but he still thought she would be fast. He said that he was going to sink an anchor through the center of the hull. If a thief raised the forward anchor, the raft still wouldn't move, and he wouldn't know why. No one would think there was an anchor underneath her, because in a boat there couldn't be. He said he had also figured out how to latch the cabin door securely. He would fasten a line to the door, then run it across the cabin, through a hole in the forward wall, and attach the line to a cleat on the bow. It would look like part of the rigging, and a vandal probably wouldn't realize that it was what was preventing him from opening the cabin door. He said that he loved the way the raft had climbed the beach and worked her way up it on the tide. Braun figured in the conversation only when he began to worry that now he would be lonely.

"I'll have to create a new society around me," he said. "It doesn't have to be a big one, but it has to have chess, and it has to have classical music, and it has to have books."

After breakfast I let Neutrino drive my rental car to Braun's so that he could pack his things. When I got to the beach, there was a line in the sand about sixty feet long that the anchor had made as the raft, receding on the tide, had dragged it. Braun was standing by the anchor, but the raft was so heavy that she hadn't been able to stop it. The three of us pulled the raft back up out of the water. Braun's manner was reserved but not awkward or impolite. The only indication on Neutrino's part of the strife between them was that he seemed a little reserved.

On the way to the storage space, we stopped at an auto parts store, then at a flea market to buy Neutrino a jack. He wanted to be able to arrive on a beach at high tide, plant blocks of wood in the sand, and jack the raft above the waves. The auto parts store had a jack that was too expensive and too powerful; it would lift twenty tons. The one he turned up at the flea market was too old. From a table of secondhand sneakers he selected a blue-and-white pair, which he thought went smartly with his blue-and-white shirt and blue pants.

That afternoon the tide carried the raft far enough from shore that the anchor line grew taut. The anchor line was about sixty feet long. The beach sloped away from the anchor, and the line was elevated about two feet above the sand. A young man and woman on one of those four-wheeled motorcycles came along, and their front wheels hit the line, and it flipped them in the air. They appeared to believe it was their fault. After that, Neutrino took pains to see that there was slack in the line, and that the anchor was buried.

Braun kept watch periodically from a folding chair on the seawall, and that evening we asked if she wanted to have dinner with us, but she shook her head and said she didn't. She wasn't unfriendly about it. She seemed to feel that it wouldn't be proper.

After dinner Neutrino wanted to pull the raft above the tide line. If he could, he would have twelve hours of not having to worry about its wandering. He thought the tide would turn around nine-thirty. He kept shining a flashlight on the hull to see if it had settled on the sand. With the anchor in my hands, I leaned back on my heels. Each time a wave lifted the raft, I pulled as hard as I could. On every third or fourth wave, I gained about an inch. Around ten-thirty a man walking along the seawall shone a bright light on us. He came toward us staggering, as if struggling against the movement of the earth. He was tall and thin, with a mustache, and he turned out to be the hotel's night watchman. He appeared to be drunk. He stood unsteadily, moving his feet, so that they made a pattern on the beach like dance steps. He walked down to the edge of the water and swept his light over the sea, which was black as oil, then he told us the tide would turn at twelve-thirty and he left.

Neutrino tried to settle the hull in the sand by standing on one of the outriggers. When he stepped back on the beach, the water lifted it slightly. "She's almost settled," he said a number of times. When he decided that she finally had, it was around one in the morning. He asked if he could sleep on the couch in my room. I asked if he snored, and he said he didn't, so far as he knew, but he wished I hadn't asked him that, because it made him self-conscious. I said I was sorry. We went back to the room with the dog and his sleeping bag.

The couple next door came in around two and turned on their television set so loud that I didn't identify the sound as coming from the next room. I thought that, as part of the carnival, someone was showing a movie against the wall of a building. In the morning Neutrino said that he had slept soundly and felt much better for it. Actually, he had wheezed and gasped and snored with such vehemence that I found myself listening to him as if I were keeping a vigil. Each time there was a pause in his breathing my attention was deepened. Throughout my awareness as I slept fitfully was threaded the dreamlike impression that I was a traveling performer, possibly in nineteenth-century Russia, who worked with a bear and had grown so attached to it that we slept in the same room. Around eight Neutrino rolled up his sleeping bag and left. I said I would see him later at the raft.

When I got to the beach, Neutrino and Braun were standing beside the raft. The lines and chains of footprints leading up and down the beach all converged around them, like a knot made in a necklace. There was also a set of tire tracks. The Mexican document that Neutrino carried in his breast pocket allowed him to travel in Mexican waters and to shelter on the beach, but it wasn't clear whether someone—Victor, for example—could object to his living aboard the raft on the beach in front of his hotel. Neutrino had arranged with a man who owned a restaurant in town to park his raft in front of the restaurant, among the fishing skiffs, and to display a sign for the restaurant on the cabin. In exchange, the man agreed to give Neutrino tortillas and rice and beans. Neutrino gave up the idea when the tire tracks led him to conduct a check of the raft and he discovered that the metal poles we had lashed to the outriggers were gone. He thought the raft would be picked apart a piece at a time in town.

Neutrino and I ate breakfast, then we walked down onto the beach and looked among the fishermen for someone who might tow the raft above the high-water line. Neutrino asked one of them what he would charge. The man shrugged and said, "I don't know, me go look." Neutrino put his hand on the man's shoulder and turned him toward the raft and pointed to it, a little square about a quarter of a mile down the beach. It took a moment for his eyes to find it, then he said, "Oh, yeah," in a way that suggested that everyone in San Felipe was aware of the peculiar vessel.

"What's the maximum?" Neutrino asked.

The man looked off at the horizon. "Fifty dollars," he said.

Neutrino leaned close to him. He said, "No, no."

The man shrugged and said, "Twenty-five?"

"*Veinte,*" Neutrino said, twenty. The man asked if he had a rope, and Neutrino said he did. The man said he would meet us at the raft in an hour. We walked back to the car through the carnival and a parade in which a brass band of schoolchildren in blue-and-gold uniforms played "Louie Louie."

I left Neutrino at the raft so that I could buy some drinking water. When I returned, he and Braun were sitting side by side on the seawall. They were leaning toward each other, in the posture of conspirators. Braun was writing on a piece of paper. They had made a new plan, they told me. They were going to put the raft on the trailer, leave San Felipe, and drive over the mountains to Guerrero Negro, on the Pacific coast, where they were going to build a raft for Braun. It would be the same size as Neutrino's raft and attach to his by means of a six-foot deck where the dogs could run. Guerrero Negro occupies a beach alongside a lagoon in which they would be able to take small trips so that Braun could practice her seamanship. Her raft could be built in a couple of days, and Neutrino figured they would be ready to leave in a few months. Instead of sailing coastwise to Peru, they would cross from Guerrero Negro. Braun was writing down the things she would have to buy to build her raft. Neutrino said they would likely leave in May. "My mind was on Peru," he said. "Now it's on the Pacific."

I went to retrieve something from my hotel room. When I got back, Neutrino was sitting on the seawall, singing to himself. He had drilled a hole in the bow and threaded a long rope through it, and he was holding the rope in his hand, like a leash, and looking down the beach for the fisherman's truck.

"Someone tried to get into the cabin last night," he said. "They screwed one screw loose on the door." By and by we saw the truck heading slowly toward us. The fisherman had a dark-haired boy in the cab when he arrived. He attached Neutrino's rope to his bumper, and it stretched and creaked as the truck moved slowly forward. I expected it to snap, but it didn't. "If it breaks, you just knot it and try again," Neutrino said. As the raft climbed the slope of the beach, it left a smooth, flat path behind it, as if trying to erase its tracks. It took five or six minutes for the fisherman's truck to pull it to the level ground on top of the beach. Neutrino gave the fisherman twenty dollars and tipped him ten. Then he sat on the seawall.

"I have a home," he said.

Chapter 5

THE TRUCK TIRES HAD dug deep holes in the sand, and Braun was concerned that someone might step into them and turn an ankle, so I got a shovel from her camper and filled them in. She and Neutrino sat on the seawall, studying a map of Baja. When I finished I sat with them, and he said, "I don't have to worry about the tides anymore." He seemed tired. "I'm going to fight a battle in my head of every scenario," he said. "What's the worst? We've gone upside down, and we can't right it? These vessels float upside down. I can check that off."

A few hundred feet down the beach, a fisherman was sitting in his boat, about twenty yards offshore. Pelicans had gathered around him. Now and then one of them would lift itself from the water and perch solemnly on one of the gunwales. Eventually three of them sat with him in the boat. It looked as if he were telling them a story. Braun walked over to see what accounted for their interest. "I have to rest a bit," Neutrino said when she had gone. "I need to get my bearings for the next move."

He sat on the sand and leaned against the seawall, with one foot underneath him and the other pointing toward the water. For a while, each time his chin settled on his chest, he lifted it abruptly then the intervals of rest grew longer.

Without opening his eyes he said, "Do me a favor, will you? Go on the raft and get the anchor, so no one will steal it while I'm asleep." I set the anchor beside him, and with one hand on it he slept deeply. Two little girls separated themselves from their fathers and ran over to the raft. They were wearing shorts over their bathing suits, and their hair had been braided in cornrows. One of them put her hand on the hull. Then she shook her head. "This isn't much of a boat, when you look at it," she said. Her friend, rubbing her foot in the sand, exhaled slowly and said no. The first little girl, looking down the beach at their fathers' approaching, yelled, "They're coming," and they ran.

The shadows of gulls passed swiftly over the beach, like

thoughts. A Mexican man and his wife and child came out the door of one of the hotel cabins behind us and spread a towel on the beach. Neutrino woke. The man walked over to us. "What about the boat?" the man said. "You make it?"

Neutrino nodded.

He pointed at the lettering and the sheet of wood that was painted yellow. "Something that means something to you, or just from regular plywood?" he asked.

"Stuff I found, here and there," Neutrino said. He asked the man where he was from, and the man said Mexicali. He said that his parents had brought him as a child to San Felipe, and that he liked now to come as often as he could. Then he asked if Neutrino was going to break a record on his voyage, and Neutrino said no, he was just going to sail.

The man walked back to his wife and child. They sat on the towel, and he stood beside them, looking out at the water, like a sentry. Neutrino said, "I'm releasing all the tension. It took seven months to get to this point, all through Arizona and California and here." He sat down and fell asleep again.

When he woke, he said, "I can fight my battles now." He sank a screw through each end of the piece of wood spanning the cabin door, and we went and ate lunch.

That afternoon Neutrino moved his foam and his sleeping bag onto the raft and arranged the cabin. I met him at Braun's camper for dinner. When I arrived, she was at the campground shower. Neutrino was sitting at the table, and around him were drawings for the raft. "I'm going to build a masterpiece raft," he said. "Twenty feet long and twenty feet wide." Braun came back wearing a robe and asked us to leave so that she could dress.

The restaurant we went to had candles on the table. Neutrino and Braun talked about their trip. Braun ordered a Manhattan.

She said, "You don't want to go down the Sea of Cortés?"

Neutrino said, "Yeah," but it wasn't clear if he meant it to affirm that he did or he didn't.

Braun said, "You're the boss."

"But we need to find a place where there are materials to build the raft," Neutrino said. "You want to do the Sea of Cortés?"

"I'd like to discuss it," she said.

"But that's what you'd like to do, the Sea of Cortés?"

"Well, what if we did?"

Neutrino thought for a moment. "Here's what you do," he said. "Leave my boat where it is on the beach. We drive up to Calexico, buy all the foam and the wood we need, bring it back on the trailer, and build your raft in San Felipe. We'll build it right beside mine on the beach in front of Victor's. Then we leave from the harbor, down the Sea of Cortés, scrap Guerrero Negro, and it's a good place to store the trailer."

"I think that's a good idea," she said. "Would you mind doing that?"

"I brought it up."

"Victor would probably store the camper."

Neutrino nodded. "You could leave the camper at Victor's, have the night watchman watch it," he said.

"That's good."

"We get the materials in the next few days," he said.

"Where do we get them?"

"Calexico," he said.

"What about San Diego?" she said. "Don't they have all kinds of nautical supplies in San Diego?"

"Calexico won't cost as much as San Diego, it's closer, and it's easier to get across the border at Mexicali than Tijuana," he said. "But you're going to have to hire people down here to build the raft, you follow? I'm too tired for that task. There's carpenters here cheap."

"That's all right."

Neutrino called the waiter over. "Amigo, coca light, no ice, por favor." Braun asked for another Manhattan.

"So we hook up the trailer, shop in Calexico, bring all the wood and the foam back to town," Neutrino said. "That's the thing to do."

Braun stared into her drink. "You should read the book about the Sea of Cortés," she said, "with the snakes at night at the door of the tent and all that."

Neutrino waved her remark aside. "By the time we get down to the bottom of Baja, you'll be a seasoned sailor, ready for the crossing," he said.

"And I hope we don't have to spend too many nights on the beach," she said. "He writes about those sand roaches, they sound terrible." She shuddered. "I'd rather anchor off the shore."

"By Cabo San Lucas you'll know all about the boat."

Braun gave up trying to get a response. "I think that's a good plan," she said finally. "And I'll tell my kids I'm just going down to Cabo. They don't have to know I'm going down on a boat, a handmade boat. In the meantime, we can stay right here in San Felipe, which I think is the most beautiful place I've ever been."

The waiter put Neutrino's Coke and Braun's fresh drink on the table. He bowed and withdrew. "Now I'm excited," Neutrino said. He leaned back from the table and widened his eyes.

"Do you suppose they'll just let us build our raft on the beach here?" Braun asked.

Neutrino shrugged. "My raft's got to be here," he said, "because we have only one trailer."

Braun raised her glass. "I feel so much better about this than going down to South America, and we don't know where we're going to put my motor home."

Neutrino nodded. "Bandits," he said. "There's bandits all over South America. It's a totally different arrangement."

"I'll just pay another month's rent on the camping space," she said. "We'll sit down and make a list."

Neutrino spread his hands on the table. "We need two-by-twelves, twenty feet long," he said.

"Two-by-twelves, those are expensive," she said glumly.

"Twenty bucks apiece," he said. "Not that bad. We won't need any of the equipment for the crossing until we get to Cabo, though. We won't even order it. That'll save us money right there. The main thing we need for the crossing is a really powerful radio." He held the palm of one hand in front of his mouth and pretended to be talking into a radio receiver. "That way we can go, 'Help us.'"

"SOS."

"You know what SOS means?" I asked.

"Save our ship," Neutrino said.

"No," said Braun, and she gave the correct answer. "It means save our souls."

Chapter 6

THE NEXT MORNING NEUTRINO was standing beside a pickup truck, talking to the driver, Victor. When I joined them, he was telling Victor that he had crossed the Atlantic Ocean in a raft and was describing the new one he wanted to build.

To me Victor said, "He want to build something bigger than that shoesbox there." Then he drove off, and Neutrino and I went to the camper. "I've been awake half the night thinking about the design," he said. Braun answered his knock. They discussed the new raft briefly. "We want to build it so that you can take your motor home and leave if it doesn't work out between us," he said. "I'm thinking we'll do it front to back, instead of side to side. It'll be thirty-two feet. By running you ahead of me, we need only one anchor. There's so much stuff we won't need."

Braun nodded, and then she left to walk her dog.

Their new alliance was short-lived. That evening, when I met them at the camper for dinner, they were sitting at the table listing on a piece of paper the things they needed to buy. We went to the restaurant we'd been to the night before. Braun ordered a Manhattan and Neutrino had another Coke, and we read the menu. She said that her teeth had bothered her all day, and she didn't feel much like eating. Neutrino said he had eaten too much. Braun leaned toward me and over the top of her menu said in a stage whisper, "We're going to have to put him on a diet when the trip gets started." The waiter came over and took our order.

Neutrino seemed to be thinking about something. He held the menu to his chest. Then he turned to Braun and said, "Did you just say you were going to put me on a diet?"

"Yes," she said. "You need to."

Neutrino's eyes narrowed. "How dare you?" he said. "You have no right to say that. We're not married."

Braun lowered her head. She stirred her drink with her finger. Neutrino began telling stories about his past, about being broke in Mexico, about starting the band, about taking it to New Orleans and New York City. He described the first weekend the family made a thousand dollars playing on the street. The waiter laid our plates in front of us.

Braun said timidly, "Do you still want to go to Calexico tomorrow?"

"I was ready to go yesterday," he said.

"Well, I need to be back in two days for my teeth. They're ready then. We could go tomorrow and come back the next day. I don't want to stay more than two days, do you?"

Neutrino said two days was fine. He called the waiter over and said, "Más tortillas," and handed him the basket they had come in. He said mildly, "Thank you, thank you very much." He leaned back in his chair and nodded, as if to indicate that he wanted our attention. "We're going on this trip," he began, "and it's going to be beautiful and peaceful, and we'll have great respect for each other, and positive feelings, and each of us will honor the god within the other."

With her head lowered, Braun said quietly, "That'll never happen."

Neutrino narrowed his eyes again. He told her that if that was how she felt, she shouldn't go, and she said that was fine with her. Then she thanked me for dinner and left.

After dinner, I drove Neutrino back to the raft and said good night. "Hold on," he said. "I need my screwdriver to get into the raft, or I'll have to sleep with you tonight." The screwdriver was in Braun's camper. I watched Neutrino, in the light from the windows, knock on the door, and Braun answer in her nightgown. She bent down to hold back her dog. She closed the door. In a moment the door opened again, and Neutrino began walking back toward me. She watched him briefly. He stopped and turned and said to her something I didn't hear. In his hand he had the screwdriver.

Then he walked down the beach to the raft. What drew them to each other then made it so difficult for them to get along I didn't understand at all.

THE NEXT MORNING WAS my last in San Felipe. I found Neutrino walking his dog on the beach. He asked if I would help him move the motor and what he had left at Braun's to his storage space before I departed, and we decided to do it before breakfast.

Braun had been sitting at the table, drinking coffee and writing in a book, when we arrived. Part of the page was obscured by her cup. I read only the last line, "Good riddance."

Neutrino carried the motor out to the concrete patio beside the camper. He filled a plastic bucket with water from a hose, then we stood the motor in it, and I held the motor upright while Neutrino started it, and we ran it for several minutes to cleanse it of salt water and use up what gas was still in it. Then we lay it on a tarp in the back of my car. Braun opened a small door in the side of the camper that concealed a storage space. She pulled out the shovel I had used to fill the tire tracks and said, "Do you want the shovel? You paid for it." She also handed him the ball for the trailer hitch and said, "Here, you can use this, too, if you need it."

We drove to Neutrino's storage space, about four miles out of town, just past Aleseo's. Neutrino was intrigued by Braun's having given him the trailer hitch. "She's not out of it yet," he said. "Giving that trailer hitch was like, what do you call it, a palm leaf?"

"An olive branch."

"Right. She's still on the fence."

Separate from the row of metal stalls at the storage space were two tall wooden crates. Neutrino had rented one of them, because it was cheaper. Before delivering his car to Calexico, he had emptied it of everything it held—his clothes, books, tools, blankets, cameras, videotapes, files of clippings, cans of food, dog food, his guitar, his chess and checkers set, the folding chairs—and put the contents haphazardly into the storage space. A lot of things were in plastic trash bags, and he began going through them. A dog appeared and barked at us. "Hello, sweetheart," Neutrino said. He spread some food for her on the ground. "Think about what you need here," he said to himself. "You need your cart." He put his folding luggage cart in the car. He found medicine he needed. He put his cameras into the waterproof suitcases, and then he put the cases in the car. He moved everything else aside to make room for the motor, and we carried it over to the bin and laid it on a tarp, and he locked the door.

We ate breakfast by the beach at a café run by a woman from California. "All the Americans like to eat here," he said, "because it's clean." The dog sat in his lap. Neutrino said he still hoped Braun would come around. "It'll be good for me to be living on the beach in preparation, though," he said. "I'll be able to imagine landing, I'll be able to imagine storms. I'll see what it's like to come up with the tide."

When we'd finished, he walked me to my car. We stood for a moment without speaking. "Remember, this isn't the old man who rides into the sea and that's the end of it," he said. "This is just the link to the legend."

We embraced. "Until I'm stopped permanently," he said, "I'm unstoppable."

For the next few days Braun and Neutrino avoided each other. Then Braun sought him out one morning in early February while he was working on the raft and said that she wanted to accompany him to Cabo San Lucas, although not on the crossing. She had concluded that she would never again have the opportunity for such an adventure. Their differences she would work to overcome. Neutrino resolved to behave in as gallant a manner as he could, and they fell in happily again with each other.

Neutrino returned to thinking about how to convert his raft into one that would be large enough for two people, each of whom needed a cabin. Meanwhile, Victor asked him to move the raft about a hundred yards up the beach, so that the building of it would serve as an amusement to the people sitting around his swimming pool. Neutrino was pleased by the invitation, by the offer of an audience, but finally declined, because he thought it would be too distracting for him.

Neutrino first thought that he would build Braun's cabin beside his own. The raft would be nearly square. It would also be very slow. Then he had the idea to build one cabin in front of the other, with a deck on the bow and another in the stern and a door between the cabins. The new raft would be thirty-two feet long. He would turn his own raft around so that its stern extended six feet beneath Braun's cabin to form part of the new hull. Her cabin would be larger than his. To accommodate its width he would build outriggers. A self-righting multihull is how he described his design, "the first in the world, so far as I know," he said.

Having arrived at his design, he and Braun bought wood at a lumberyard near the harbor in San Felipe. With a jack, he raised his raft two feet off the beach and put cement blocks underneath it so that he could extend the hull, and built buttresses to help bear the weight. He had intended to hire carpenters and instruct them—he felt too old for so much work and he worried about his heart—but having the plans for the raft mostly in his head, he decided it would be more difficult to explain the plan to someone else than to build it himself.

At the end of February a man from California named Andy Johns arrived in San Felipe. He was thirty-six years old and out of work and was intending to paddle a kayak to Cabo San Lucas. His brother had driven him to San Felipe and left him with the kayak. Facing the Sea of Cortés, Johns had had second thoughts. He put the kayak up for sale. Walking the beach, he came across Neutrino working on the raft, and they hadn't talked for long before Neutrino had invited Johns to follow the raft in his kayak. In exchange, Johns would help Neutrino finish the raft. With Johns's help, Neutrino completed in two weeks work that might have taken him months. In the meantime, he and Braun drove in her camper to San Diego to buy the last things they needed. On her birthday, Neutrino took her to dinner at the café on the terrace by the bookstore and hired a guitar player to sing for her.

Neutrino sent me an e-mail message saying that he and Braun were getting along fine. He said that she was "as happy as a teenager." Even so, they had several confrontations. The worst one took place at night in the campground. Braun had bought a bed with a futon for her cabin and wanted Neutrino to tell Johns to assemble the frame. Neutrino said that Johns was not an employee, and that she should set it up herself. The exchange that followed was conducted at sufficient volume that it became public. It ended when Braun announced that the raft was leaving San Felipe, but she wasn't.

As Neutrino was in his cabin preparing for bed, he heard Braun calling his name. Her manner was penitent. "I know what's bothering me, I saw the cause of my behavior," she said. "I'm terrified."

Early in March, Neutrino sent me another message, saying that he was putting the raft in the water on March 21 and leaving San Felipe on the twenty-third, so I went back. He hoped that once he was launched he would continue to Cabo, he said, but how far he sailed depended on how the raft performed and whether he felt he had to pull into a harbor somewhere and do more work. I arrived on the twentieth. The night before, Braun had moved aboard the raft. The next morning she carried pots and pans and cans of food from her camper to her cabin. Neutrino had the sail up when I got there. He had sewn the sail from burlap he found in Calexico. It was rigged with yellow nylon rope secured to the sail by duct tape. The rigging seemed complicated, and I asked how he had thought of it. "It's an abortion of a system I saw in a picture of a Chinese junk," he said.

The raft itself was strange and arresting but beautiful. For the wild specificity of it, the simple there-is-nothing-else-like-this-in-the-entire-world quality, it put me in mind of the Watts Towers in Los Angeles, made from bottles and cement and pieces of glass that the artist picked up around the city. The raft's prow was raked. Behind it was a small deck with a mast, then Braun's cabin, which was wider than it was long, and then Neutrino's cabin lengthwise behind it, as if it had been plugged into it, and a larger deck on the stern with a transom at the end for the motor. The whole craft was made of unpainted plywood. It didn't look any more like it would float than the first one did. From Victor,

Neutrino had bought a catamaran, which he lashed to the raft, like a sidecar, to carry gas and water. Also, from a prosperous boat owner named Larry Boyd, a retired contractor from Utah who had taken an interest in him, Neutrino had bought an inflatable rubber dinghy, called a Zodiac. It was shaped like an oval, with two points on each side of the bow, and it had a small outboard. Should anything cause him and Braun to abandon their raft, they could make it to shore in the Zodiac at almost thirty miles an hour.

I thought I should make myself useful, so following Neutrino's commands, I lashed to the raft four steel pipes that he had bought in order to roll the raft up and down the beach. Each time I finished a line, Neutrino would tie it off. Observing the raft had become a part of many people's day. Typically, women came to talk to Braun and men to Neutrino. Braun would have her arms full of cookware, as if she were saving what she could from a flood, and the women would take her aside and, with their eyes widened, ask her quietly if she was really still going, as if the evidence in her arms weren't enough. The men tended to stand beside Neutrino and wait until he acknowledged them and then say, "How's it going?"

"Either it'll be slick, or it's a disaster," he told one of them.

After we finished lashing the pipes, he paused. "I'm in the dark about how to proceed," he said.

"With the trip?"

"With the next step," he said. "What's the next step? That's my style—to get involved then see what the next move is."

Neutrino was wearing blue jeans and a white, short-sleeved shirt that had sailboats on it and lighthouses that were striped like barber poles. He still had the sneakers he'd bought at the flea market the last time I'd seen him. Through the top of one of them his big toe had worn a hole. He was wearing a straw hat, but not the one that his dog had chewed. The next thing, he decided, was to raise the storm sail.

"It's for when you're in heavy weather, and you still need running power," he said, "but you don't want your mast to crack or your sail to tear up." On two-by-fours that Andy Johns had screwed into the side of Neutrino's cabin as footholds, Neutrino climbed carefully onto the roof of his cabin, then he stepped across Braun's cabin and raised a small patch of burlap sewed onto a square piece of net. The wind filled it immediately. Neutrino nodded, then he lowered the sail and climbed back to the deck.

Braun arrived. She had planned to go in her camper to buy some lumber, she said, but had hit a car in the campground parking lot so had decided that she would wait and try again the following day.

Victor had offered to launch the raft with his tractor, and he and Neutrino arranged that they would do it the following morning at ten-thirty.

Chapter 9

I GOT UP EARLY and had breakfast by myself the next morning at the café where the Americans went, in the center of town. Two of the tables were occupied by older couples. With his back to them, a man sat by himself at a third table, working a crossword puzzle. I didn't want to have to listen to other people's conversations, so I took a table at some remove from all of them. Even so, I couldn't help overhearing parts of their exchange. One of the women had a brassy laugh, a bar laugh, the laugh of someone who responds too antically to things that aren't really funny. She appeared to think something was very funny.

"Well, I guess it's time to break out the champagne," one of the men said. The woman laughed.

"It's this morning, right?" asked the man.

"That's what I heard," said the second woman. "Ten-thirty."

The man doing the crossword puzzle raised his head and over his shoulder said, "I heard she's not going."

The third man nodded his head. "That's right," he said. "They had a falling out."

"Another one?" the first man said. He smoothed the napkin in his lap.

"He wouldn't put her futon together," the second woman said. The other woman laughed.

"The futon," the man doing the puzzle said. "That's in her stateroom, right?" The woman laughing bent forward as if she were going to lay her head on the table, then she sat up and clapped her hands.

"No, they're back together," one of the men said. "They made it up. I heard that this morning."

The man doing the puzzle sat back in his chair and shook his head. "She's back on? See, I hadn't heard that."

The second woman said, "They're hard to keep up with."

The woman who was laughing had calmed down sufficiently to narrow her eyes and say cannily, "I bet she doesn't go."

A truck going past obscured their remarks. The next thing I heard was one of the men say, "He's how old?"

"Seventy-six," said the other man.

"*Jeepers*," said the woman with the laugh.

"This will be *his* last sail," one of the men said. That caused all of them to laugh and one of the men to bring his hands down hard on the table, making the silverware rattle.

The rest of what they said I couldn't hear. Either the wind blew too loudly or another truck went by. It seemed to me that they had gone on to other matters, but every now and then the conversation would lapse and one of them would say, "I built this boat with my own bare hands," and their shoulders would heave.

When I got to the beach, Neutrino was sitting on a deck chair under one of the palm umbrellas that Victor had put up for his guests, and he was reading the instructions for his motor. It was about nine o'clock. The day was cloudless, with the sea spread out like a tablecloth and hardly a fold in it anywhere. He laid the instructions in his lap.

"The last seven months have been a period of such labor and effort," he said. "I didn't falter. I didn't give up." He looked out at the water, then back at me. "Nancy woke up this morning and said, 'I'm absolutely terrified.'" Then he stood up and hitched his pants and walked around the side of the raft, and I heard the clangy sound of tools being moved around. He appeared holding a crowbar, as if to show me what it was. I thought he was going to say more about Braun, but he didn't. "In sailing, it's always the next thing," he said. "It never ends, the boat thing never ends. It only changes if you have to jump over one task to another, because you can't get the first one done at the moment."

Braun arrived, and she and Neutrino discussed the need for one of them to get water, then they decided there would be time to do it on the following day. "Next thing is working the anchor," Neutrino said. "Then putting the prop on the motor, then taking the motor off the transom."

I asked why he was taking the motor off, if he was putting the boat into the water.

"Because with the angle the raft's going into the water, the stern will be underwater before it can lift up," he said. "Half of the hull will have to be in the water before there's enough buoyancy to lift the stern. If the motor went under, I'd have to strip it apart and flush the salt water."

I asked Braun how she was.

"I'm okay," she said.

"A little nervous?"

"I'm scared to death."

"That something might happen?"

"I don't know what," she said. "Who knows what? Everything."

Neutrino came over and, gently, as if he were talking to a favored but excitable child, said, "Nancy, dear, have you got a sharp knife?" She walked up the beach to her camper to get one. A man named Ed Meders, who with his wife, Catalina, runs the San Felipe Bookstore, arrived. The Meders had become friends with Neutrino and Braun, and they had come to help with the launching. Meders began threading the anchor line through the bow, and Braun came back with a knife, and Neutrino cut the rope. I became aware that people were gathering around the raft, like a flock of birds settling. Some of them unfolded beach chairs. Some had cameras. Others stood in groups of three and four, with their arms folded across their chests, as if paying close attention in case they might be called on later to testify.

Victor came around the corner of the campground riding his tractor, tipping from side to side in the sand like a man on an elephant. Andy Johns arrived and began removing the screws on the buttresses supporting the raft. Braun took photographs, and Neutrino taped her and Johns with his video camera. Larry Boyd arrived with his wife, Eva.

Victor drove down to the water, then backed his tractor up to the stern. Neutrino called out, "Everybody clear the raft," and the circle around it widened. Neutrino laid the steel pipes under the hull. Several men stood by the bow. "We're going to tilt the raft," Neutrino yelled to them. "And when we do, we need you to pull the cement blocks from under the bow." Two men separated themselves from the others and lined up on each side of the raft, to grab the blocks. Boyd and Eva and three other men pushed down on the stern. Eva, who is small and lean, raised herself off the sand like an acrobat and pressed down with all her force. Neutrino stood back to tape them. The raft didn't move. Neutrino walked toward them waving his arms. "Bad idea, bad idea," he said.

Boyd called out, "Where's your jack, Captain?"

"I'm getting it right now," Neutrino said.

Kneeling under the bow, Neutrino placed some two-by-fours on the sand and the jack on top of them, then raised the raft sufficiently that the men could pull the blocks out. Then he stood back and tried to figure out how to remove the jack. Boyd got down on his knees and dug out the sand beneath it until it tipped over. "That's what a college education will do for you," Neutrino said.

He turned his video camera on the people who had gathered behind the fence at the campground. When he said, "Say something," several of them raised their arms over their heads and waved them slowly, like figures in a water ballet, and one of them said, "Bon voyage." Neutrino put down the camera and unscrewed the rudder. Braun watched him. She had on jeans, a white short-sleeved top with a pattern of flowers, dark glasses with thick lenses, and a little canvas porkpie hat, which had a drawstring that she had fastened under her chin. To a woman standing next to her, she said, "I'm not ready." She pressed her lips, as if collecting herself. She shook her head. "I'm scared," she said, "but I'm going." The woman nodded. Braun put her hands in her pockets. "It's going to be the adventure of a lifetime," she went on. "People keep telling me that anyway."

One of the men laid a two-by-six between two hooks on the back of Victor's tractor, to make a platform for lifting the raft. Victor lowered the platform and backed up and raised it until it met the hull. His tractor was at an angle to the raft. He lifted the hull. There was a sharp crack, but no one could tell if it was from the raft or the two-by-six. Victor got off his tractor to inspect the platform. Men looked under the raft. Victor shrugged and climbed back aboard the tractor and began again lifting the raft. It moved ponderously. One side appeared to rise slightly higher than the other. Then the raft seemed to tilt. Then it slid off the platform. It happened so quickly that no one could form any words. There was simply a rush of voices and people running in case the raft tipped over on them. It settled so heavily that it cracked two cement blocks it landed on. Neutrino put down his camera.

"You've ruined my raft," he yelled. "You've ruined my raft," but he was grinning. "That's what I love about rafts," he said. "Bang it up, drop it, throw it around, just drag it any way you can down the beach, and it's still fine."

Victor placed the platform under the raft once more, and Boyd ran a rope through the stern then fitted it through a hole in the frame of the tractor and tied a knot. Victor raised the raft several feet. He began moving slowly forward. The raft had gained about a foot of ground when the rope snapped. A man announced that he had a nylon tow rope in his car, and he ran across the sand to get it. The wind rose sufficiently that some pennants by the hotel began to stir. The back cabin door swung open, and as if enacting a scene from a surrealist drama, Neutrino picked up a golf club lying on the deck and smacked the door shut, then dropped the club. When the man delivered the tow rope, Neutrino deliberated about where to fasten it, for fear that it might pull the stern off. Boyd found a way to wrap it so that the stress was spread broadly, and he attached the other end to Victor's tractor.

By now about thirty-five people had gathered to watch. A tall old man so gaunt he looked like a wading bird, walking with a cane and holding a cardboard box under his arm, approached Braun. "I told him I'd give him a lantern," he said to her. He handed her the box. "It's got a handle, and you just use regular gas," he went on. "Straight gas, not boat gas that's treated. Remember that. Straight gas." Braun nodded and said, "Straight gas." Victor dragged the raft over the pipes. When he had hauled it most of the way down the beach, he uncoupled his tractor from it and drove back up the beach to the bow to push it. As the raft slid into the water, the stern went completely beneath the waves as Neutrino had said it would. Water poured over the deck and into the cabin. Half of the hull was in the water before it settled on the surface of the sea. Then it turned sideways to the shore and rose and fell gently on the waves.

"I wonder if my futon got soaked," Braun said. Two fishing boats—*Veronica* and *La Pamita III*—came along the shore, and Neutrino hailed them. He threw one of them a line, then said, "Momento, momento," while he tied it to his bow. The fishing boat turned and headed out to sea. Neutrino stood with his back against the cabin and his arms spread to brace himself against the line's growing suddenly taut. After the fisherman had towed the raft about a hundred feet offshore, Neutrino dropped his anchor. The people on the beach began clapping. Neutrino knelt on his deck, as if in prayer, to untie the line from the fishing boat. Larry and Eva Boyd launched the Zodiac to bring him back to shore. Boyd couldn't start the engine, though, so he and Eva paddled out to Neutrino. "He sold us the motor," Braun said, "so if it's going to break, it's good it did it now."

Neutrino stepped carefully into the Zodiac, and when he

reached the shore he seemed tired. "I have to rest awhile," he said. "I got a little amped."

"I'm sure you did," Boyd said. "At least it's in the water and the anchor works. So far, anyway."

Neutrino walked up the beach, toward the hotel, and sat on the seawall. Behind him, from the parking lot, a man approached. He was quite short, only slightly larger than a child, and fat, and he was wearing a clean white T-shirt and white shorts and white sneakers. His hair was cut in a brush cut. Under one arm, like a purse, he carried a plastic drink cooler.

"Well, well, well," he said. "They got it in the water without breaking it in half. That surprises the hell out of me. I thought they would break it in half." He stood on the seawall beside Neutrino and bent one knee and cautiously lowered his other foot to the beach, like a man stepping into a rowboat, then grunted with the effort of settling his backside on the wall. He opened his cooler and with two fingers almost delicately hoisted a can of beer. He seemed to take Neutrino for an observer.

"Yes, sir, yes, sir," he said. He took a sip from his beer. He shook his head. "Never did think that thing would get off the beach," he said. He had a nasal, high-pitched laugh that sounded like he-he-he. "Sure to sink now," he said and laughed.

Neutrino turned and looked at him. He seemed almost too tired to speak. Then he said, "We need some skeptics."

"Well, hell," the man said. "I'm a skeptic." His tone suggested surprise at Neutrino's not recognizing it.

Neutrino said, "Good. Go get a bunch of your friends and bring them back and put a curse on me."

The man seemed now to be aware of Neutrino's identity. Somewhat contritely he said, "So when you taking off?"

"Tomorrow," Neutrino said.

The man sipped his beer. He nodded.

"Did you drag it down and launch it nose first, or backwards?" he asked.

Neutrino said backwards.

The man nodded again.

"Now you get to sit here and watch all that unlaminated plywood separate," he said. "He-he-he."

Neutrino studied him. "Somebody must have sent you," he said finally. Then he stood up, and to me he said, "Let's move over here."

Neutrino settled himself about fifteen feet down the wall, with his hands on his knees, and watched the raft. "Let me give you an honest appraisal," he said. "Stability wise, she's exceptional. I could feel when I pushed her with my hand when she was on the beach how responsive she is. She moved under even the slightest pressure. Only problem I see is, she's a little heavy in the bow. See the waves swamping the bow? I didn't think that would happen. Might be all those provisions Nancy has in her cabin. She sits about two inches lower than I thought she would." He took some crackers from his pocket and ate them. "Because it's a raft, though, I can make corrections and trim it until she's absolutely perfect."

Chapter 10

THAT AFTERNOON BRAUN and Andy Johns took to the lumberyard some drawings Neutrino had made of wood he wanted cut so that he could build a splash guard across the bow.

Ed Meders stayed to watch the raft, and Neutrino and I went into town for lunch. When we came back, the raft was clearly sitting higher. The bow was riding over the waves. "Probably what happened is so much water got into it while we were launching and didn't immediately get out that it weighed it down," Neutrino said. "She looks much better now." To his list of chores he added cutting larger scuppers.

I had things to do that afternoon, and I got back to the raft at dusk. Ed and Catalina Meders had brought tuna fish salad and chicken salad and things to drink and set up a table under one of the palm umbrellas. Ed was with Johns and Neutrino on the raft. It took past nightfall for them to finish building the splash guard, which was about two feet high and enclosed the front deck. Braun and Catalina Meders and I sat on the seawall and watched the raft turn colors under the deepening sky. The men seemed to fade gradually into the air around them. Finally they were simply dark figures, as if at work underground. The stars came out. The Big Dipper hung above them like a kite. I could hear their tools knocking against one another as they were loaded into the Zodiac. Then the Zodiac itself emerged from the darkness as they paddled—the motor still wouldn't start.

Neutrino walked up the beach. His feet were bare and covered with sand, and his pants were wet to the knee. Above the knees I could see other lines of dry salt, like rings of growth in a tree. He sat heavily in a chair. The rest of us sat around him in a kind of half circle. "I'm so tired," he said. "We did all this work, and tomorrow we start again. Tomorrow's another attack." While we ate, Braun talked about the dangerous wildlife of Baja and the Sea of Cortés. She appeared to believe that the entire toxic population of the territory would be lined up to meet them whenever they put in to shore. "There's all kind of insects," she said. "Beach roaches, I think I already mentioned them. Apparently some places the beach gets so thick with them you can't even stand."

"Plus scorpions," Johns said. "You have to shake out your clothes and your sleeping bag before you get into it."

Braun nodded. "The most poisonous snake in the world is in Baja, too," she said. "The yellow-bellied something or other. It's in a book I read."

"Does the book have stingrays?" Johns asked. "They're big down here. Seventeen feet wingspan. They can rise to the surface and flip your boat."

"So the snake can get you," Braun said. "It's a sea snake. I'll go find the book." She rose and walked across the sand, into the shadows and toward her camper. She came back leafing through the pages as she walked, but she couldn't find the entries concerning poisonous creatures.

Neutrino had no interest in the subject. He ate while they talked. He began describing the career of a sailor he revered named Tristan Jones, an Englishman who had had adventures all over the world, many involving starvation and danger and almost none of them known except to other adventurers. Toward the end of his life he was penniless. He walked into the Explorers Club in New York, hoping to find someone who would help him, Neutrino said, and was greeted by a man who said, "Ah, Mr. Jones, we've been waiting for you." Listening to Neutrino, I remembered that a man named John Lorette, who had sailed on a raft with Thor Heyerdahl and had served as the president of the Explorers Club, had told me that he had tried to get Neutrino to join the club. "I had already spoken to someone about seconding him," Lorette told me, "and I gave him the application, but he never filled it out." Neutrino was pleased by the acknowledgment of his deeds, and he understood the honor involved in the invitation, but he felt he was too busy having adventures to sit around a fire in a club and discuss them. (Later, however, he changed his mind and was voted a member.)

With his hands on his knees, Neutrino recited a poem he had written about Jones. "Tristan Jones lived off his bones, while sailing to the west," he said. "A sailor's day, without no pay, is what he did the best."

By the time we were finished eating, the tide had receded and cut little rivers into the flats. The raft was aground. We carried the food to the car, and I retrieved for Neutrino his screw gun from Braun's camper, so that he could open the door of his cabin. I handed it to him on the beach.

"I'll see you at ten in the morning," he said. "We can get some breakfast."

I said I could arrive earlier if he liked.

"No, no, I need to rest as long as I can," he said. "This was a long day for me."

I said it had been a day of accomplishment. All those months of loneliness and work.

He said, "Thank you."

"You're a great man to do all this," I said. I hadn't planned to say it. Often I say things I regret; it's nearly a habit with me. In case something happened to him, though, I wanted him to know how I felt. "Against all the odds and the obstacles," I added.

"Thank you," he said shyly. "I *am* a great man. But you and I are the only ones who know it."

"I THOUGHT OF A NEW TRIAD last night," Neutrino told me in the morning. "Love, hate, ambivalence." He was sitting on the seawall with a tall, thin man named Chuck, who drew a pension check from one of the services. Chuck had white hair that he combed straight back, and he was wearing cutoff jeans and a sleeveless white shirt. He and Neutrino had been discussing Ireland when I arrived.

"I can still go anyplace in the world Uncle Sam goes, space A," Chuck said. "I better hurry up and get that on my want list as a mini-goal, Ireland."

The Zodiac sat on the beach a few feet above the tide line, and the raft floated about a hundred feet offshore. "Boy, does she move fast," Neutrino said. "I pulled on the anchor last night, and she just stepped across the water." He was wearing a life vest that said on the back PROPERTY OF POPPA NEUTRINO.

"Did your lady friend sleep on the boat last night?" Chuck asked, a trifle avidly, I thought.

"In the front cabin," Neutrino said. "I slept in the back."

"Oh," Chuck said, and he seemed disappointed.

Andy Johns had slept in Braun's camper, and now he walked through the gate from the campground. He asked Neutrino how the raft had ridden during the night.

"Beautiful," Neutrino said, "except the Zodiac kept bumping against the side, until I got up and made a temporary stanchion."

Neutrino planned to move the raft that afternoon to the harbor, so that he would be protected by the breakwater if the wind should rise. He said he wanted to leave around one. "I want plenty of daylight," he said. Johns was carrying a backpack that had tide charts in it, and he took them out.

"You ever watch trotters?" Neutrino asked. I said not really. "They have to keep their pace," he said. "It's a rule. If they go faster, if they break it, there's a penalty. They have to move to the back of the pack. Right now I can feel I'm on my pace, but I can also feel the urge to break it." He deliberated for a moment. "The warrior can't fail at this point. Absolutely must not," he said. "If something were to happen that could have been avoided, and I lost the trip, I've gone from being a great man to being a fool. And my aim is to be a great man, not a fool."

He thought for a moment more. "The smart thing," he said, "would be to pay someone to watch the boat. Keep the thieves off it—they'll strip it in a quarter of an hour—and do what I need to. First, though, I have to get the boat moored safely. I have to figure out what among my possessions is coming with me, what's staying, what has to be put away. I think I can do that in two hours. Let's get breakfast, then I'll work, and I think I can be ready to move the boat by two."

I was going to crew for Neutrino on what he was calling the maiden voyage, so after breakfast Larry Boyd and I drove our cars to the marina, and I left mine in order that Neutrino and I would have a means of returning. When Boyd and I reached the hotel, I saw Braun walking her dog in the parking lot. She had a stricken look on her face, as if she were searching for someone sympathetic and finding no one. I asked Boyd to let me out, and I went to talk to her. She and Neutrino had argued again. Neutrino, wanting to move the Zodiac up the beach, had taken hold of the rope attached to its bow. He asked Braun to help him pull. Instead of grabbing the same rope that he had, she took hold of one along a side. Neutrino said, "Nancy, we're old, we have to

pull together," and she said, "This is the way we did it on the
farm." When Neutrino said that he didn't care how they did it
on the farm, Braun dropped the rope and lowered her head and
said, "I'll just do whatever you tell me to, and I won't open my
mouth." Whether she had intended the remark ironically or not,
Neutrino took it that way.

Their relationship was none of my business, but that didn't
stop me from trying to repair it. Naturally, I only made matters
worse. I said that I thought her being so apprehensive about the
trip had made her more sensitive than perhaps it was practical to
be. "You have to be careful not to let your fear of the trip over-
take your reason," I said.

"I'm not afraid at all," she said. Her tone was vehement. She
shook her head. "I have no fear of this trip at all," she said. "I
never did."

I had no wish to contradict her, but I couldn't think of anything else to say either.

I saw that I should have stayed out of it. I asked if there was
anything I could do for her, and she said no, so I got back in
Boyd's truck.

We found Neutrino sitting on the beach. He felt contrite, but
he also didn't see how the exchange could have been avoided. He
stood and said he still hoped to be headed for the harbor by the
early afternoon, so he went back to work. The wind began to
pick up. Above the horizon were long, thin clouds that looked
like brushstrokes.

"The prevailing winds are from the north," Boyd said. "Let's
go out and see if your vessel can get a footing, Captain, and pull
the anchor up."

On the way to the marina, we would be heading into the
wind. "This will be a good test," Boyd said to me. "I estimate the
wind is fifteen to eighteen knots. We'll see if you two can go into

this and still maintain a heading. If you can, he should be all right later on his own."

We went down to the water. Boyd was going to follow us in the Zodiac. Neutrino climbed into it and sat in the bow. "Let's go get wet," he said. I held the Zodiac into the waves while Boyd tried to start the motor, which yet again wouldn't turn over. Neutrino and Boyd picked up paddles.

Once Neutrino and I were aboard the raft, Neutrino sent me to the bow to raise the anchor. Boyd sat in the Zodiac about twenty feet off the bow, between the raft and the beach. I was pulling line as fast as I could. Some of it fell overboard, and Boyd yelled to me to gather it so that it didn't foul the prop. When the line became vertical, I let the rise and fall of the bow work the anchor off the bottom then lifted it aboard.

Neutrino's motor still wasn't broken in, so we traveled slowly against the wind. After a few minutes he called to me to sit on top of the cabin. He had rigged lines from the tiller to the roof so that he could steer from up there, where he could see everything, and he had me try using them. The waves were about three feet tall, and the distance between them was such that every third or fourth wave would lower the bow and raise the stern and the prop lifted out of the water and the engine raced, but that was the only problem we encountered.

Neutrino was very pleased. He had, after all, imagined this craft, drawn it on napkins then built it by hand, and even as homely as it was, he was now seeing that it held its place in the waves and against the wind and cut a straight path and didn't roll or pitch too strenuously. When the wind lifted Neutrino's straw hat and sent it spinning through the air, Boyd turned the Zodiac around and retrieved it. Several times, when we seemed to turn too far from the shore, and the opening of the marina, Boyd yelled, "Starboard, Captain, starboard."

The trip took about forty-five minutes. On the rocks at the mouth of the jetty, there was a flock of pelicans, waiting like dignitaries. A few of them flapped their wings as we passed. Others raised their beaks as if clearing their throats before speaking. Boyd led us to a corner of the harbor where there were no other boats. Neutrino yelled to me to drop the anchor, but I didn't hear him. When he came forward and saw me coiling the line, so that I wouldn't catch my foot in it when I threw the anchor over, he yelled, "I told you to drop the anchor," then raced back to the stern and reversed the raft. I started to say I hadn't heard him, then realized that wasn't the point.

Boyd took us ashore in the Zodiac. "I feel better now that I've seen it ride," he said. Then he said, "Make sure you go see the captain of the port. He's God almighty around here."

We pulled the Zodiac up the beach, then Boyd and I left Neutrino to watch the raft and walked toward the car. Neutrino called to me. I turned and he said, "I'm sorry I yelled at you." He waved. I said it was fine.

It took me about half an hour to drive Boyd to the hotel where he had left his truck, then drive to my hotel and change into dry clothes. Meanwhile, Ed Meders delivered to the raft a Mexican man named Alejandro, whom he had engaged as a watchman. Alejandro brought his son, Victor, who was twelve. Neutrino was asleep on the beach when I returned. I said his name. He came to slowly. He sat up. "Let's go see the captain of the port," he said. "Actually, let me put my shoes on first, or he'll be insulted."

The captain of the port turned out to be a small, trim man in a beige uniform. He was leaving his office as we arrived. From a corner of the sand yard in front of it, we could see the white plastic plumbing pipe that served as mast and a part of the raft's main cabin. He pointed his finger at it and said something in

Spanish, and I said I didn't understand. He pointed again, then pointed to his eye, and eventually I realized he was asking if someone was watching it. I nodded. "Twenty-four hours," he said, meaning that as soon as it was unattended it would be broken into. He put his hands in front of him with the palms down and raised one of them and tilted them. Then he brushed one hand in front of him. I figured out that he was saying that the tide was ebbing and he wanted to know if the raft would tip over on the flats. I said it had a flat bottom. "No keel?" he asked. I shook my head. He said that we should be fine then.

In the car Neutrino was subdued. His clothes were wet. "I need to go someplace warm," he said. "I'm cold and tired and depressed." The exchange with Braun was preying on his mind.

"If she came and said she wanted to try it again, out of respect for her generosity, I would say, 'Let's try it again,'" he said. "If she doesn't, I'll be so relieved. Because I would have a better boat without the struggle. I have to admit it, two old people haven't got the strength for the work. We'd be constantly in each other's way. Plus, having Nancy around weakens me. In addition to having to explain everything and losing time when I should be working, I have to be sweet, and I can't be the forceful person I need to be to protect the boat and have it travel without mishap. On a boat, if you're not vigilant, you spend all day on the rocks trying to get free and keep from sinking, all because you failed to do one simple, necessary thing, then you're exhausted for all the other things you have to do and don't have the strength for."

He sat quietly looking out the window at the water. He slumped. "Still," he said, "Nancy's put a lot of hope into it, a lot of effort, and it doesn't seem right. We get along so well otherwise. I don't mean to be fierce, and maybe she could take orders from someone else who went about it differently, but when the pressure's on I don't know another way to do it. I'm so used after all those years of leading the group and being responsible for everyone's safety, of being in charge, that I'm like a sheep dog or a wolf—I bite you to bring you into line, but I don't mean it personally, it's a call to vigilance, and I have to be sure we're safe. I'm old, and I can't recover like I used to—I don't have the balance or the strength or the reflexes—and I get tired more easily, and that means I have to be even more careful about preventing risks from appearing unexpectedly. In my life I want adventure, but once the adventure is under way you have to protect yourself and the people around you, and you do it by an almost ferocious and furious kind of attention. The ocean is not a bully, but it can turn into one if you allow it to."

His dog had got tangled in her leash, and he said, "Come here, honey," and he unfastened it. "If Nancy backs out for certain," he said, "I know who I'm going to ask."

"Someone you met here?" I asked.

He nodded. "Her name's Felicia."

"Mexican or American?"

"A little of both," he said.

"What does she do?"

"Prostitute," he said. "Built like a man, a great worker." Then he said that unfortunately he probably wouldn't see her before he left.

Chapter 12

WE HAD LUNCH at the café on the terrace by the bookstore. Ed and Catalina Meders said they had watched the raft from the terrace. "How'd it look?" Neutrino asked. They said it looked very stable in the waves, and Neutrino's spirits seemed to rise.

"She handled those waves beautifully," he said. "Steered into the wind, and I don't even have a daggerboard yet, or a fingerboard or a keel. That's like getting an arrow to fly straight without feathers."

Neutrino ordered a tuna fish sandwich. "I feel so confident now," he said. "When she has daggerboards, and I build some scuppers to drain the bow, she'll go even faster." His dog stood on her hind legs and put her paws in his lap, and he bent over and picked her up.

The waitress placed Neutrino's sandwich in front of him, and he pointed at it and said, "Uno más, por favor," because it was so small. Then he talked about Braun again.

"Maybe there's really something wrong with me that I think I can take people where they haven't been and they'll enjoy it, grow into it, increase themselves," he said. "And maybe they can't do it, and the real problem is I can't see that. Everyone looks ripe to me."

"The answer is always somewhere in the middle," I said.

"*Your* answer's in the middle," he said. "My answer is always to the extreme—what if I take the extreme and expand it past the frontier, and add these two complications, and these three factors, and seven considerations, and go one more step beyond where any other person would have stopped, and turn it upside down and backwards, and read it by candlelight in a mirror with a magnifying glass."

The rest of the meal we ate in silence.

After lunch we drove to Braun's campsite to collect gas cans and water jugs and rope that Neutrino wanted. Braun's camper was gone. It turned out that she had driven to the harbor. She was climbing the beach with a yellow nylon duffel bag over one shoulder when we arrived. Neutrino spoke to her. Then he came back to the car. "She was nice," he said. "She was resigned. She said, 'You can have everything that's aboard the raft.'"

We unloaded Neutrino's belongings from the trunk of my car, and Alejandro and his son helped carry them. Neutrino and Braun occupied opposite sides of the beach while they worked. That evening I saw Catalina and Ed. Alejandro had told them that all afternoon the lady with the hat took things off the raft, then the old man put things back on in the night.

Chapter 13

The next day was Wednesday, March 23, 2005, the day Neutrino had planned to leave San Felipe, before he had decided that he should have a day of rest. I picked up Alejandro and his son at their house around eleven. The tide was in, and the raft was floating at anchor about two hundred feet off the beach. I called to Neutrino. He appeared from the cabin and spread his fingers like two fans and yelled, "Ten minutes." He went back in the cabin, and when he appeared again he had the dog in his arms. He placed her carefully in the Zodiac. He paddled and drifted to shore, with the gravity of a gondolier.

He said that while the raft had sat aground on the flats during the night, he had heard voices outside the cabin and a pack of dogs that had started his own dog barking. Then he said that Andy Johns had been by and had said that he wasn't going to make the trip. "If it wasn't for having to get the rest of my stuff from Nancy's," he said, "I'd be ready to go." He put his dog on her leash, and the four of us dragged the Zodiac up the beach. Alejandro and Victor, his son, sat beside it and spread towels over their heads like desert tribesmen. Victor picked up handfuls of sand and threw them at the flies, which were so thick along the tide line that I had taken them for seaweed. They rose like a dark mist.

"My mind is in a thousand pieces," Neutrino said. "I still feel worried about Nancy." He sat on the edge of the Zodiac. "I have to rest," he said. "My energy's low."

I remembered how happy he had seemed on the raft and said maybe he would feel better once he was under way.

"If I can find beaches like this, I'll be fine," he said. The dog chased the flies. "She's a great sailor," Neutrino said. "She just sits there patiently, not too close to the edge, and watches what I'm doing." He asked if I had seen Catalina and Ed Meders, and whether they had mentioned Braun.

"Not much."

"What'd they say?"

"Just that they'd heard you weren't together on the trip any longer."

He nodded. "Andy arrives a few hours ago," he said, "and he presents me the picture of total defeat. I tried to get him to sit in his kayak on the beach and visualize himself in the water, with everything going well. 'Look at the water, you have to be patient. You can handle it,' I said, but he didn't want any part of it. He gave me his tide charts, though, and that's a big help." He shrugged. He thrust his chin toward the raft. "The next thing she needs is scuppers," he said. "The water comes in and goes out. Just like a surfboard. A surfboard only has to be a little bit above the water."

Before we had breakfast at the café, we stopped by the bookstore. Neutrino began to tell Ed and Catalina what had taken place between him and Braun, and Ed said, "It isn't necessary," but Neutrino told him anyway. Then we had breakfast. "I feel good," Neutrino said, "but I need someone to sherpa for me today. I can't do anything. I have no vitality, and if I press matters, I'll lose everything I've gained."

I said that I would carry his tools and supplies from Braun's camper to the beach and that, with Alejandro's help, I'd get them aboard the raft. I left Neutrino sitting in a chair outside the bookstore, talking to Ed and Catalina. When he felt he could, he said, he would walk back to Braun's campsite and meet me. Braun's camper was gone from her spot; she had left town early in the morning, I later learned. I loaded as many of Neutrino's belongings as I could into my car and drove to the raft. I called to Alejandro, and he and Victor climbed the beach to help me. I pointed to the water jugs and gas cans and jacks and bolts of canvas, and then I pointed at the raft. Alejandro didn't seem happy, but he smiled when I said, "Más dinero."

Everything left at the campsite fit into my car. Getting it all onto the raft took another hour. Neutrino was sitting at a picnic table beside Braun's empty parking space and reading charts of the Sea of Cortés. I drove him back to the raft, and until nightfall we moved boxes and tools and arranged them in the cabin so that they left a clear passage between the bow and the stern. Neutrino thought that towing the Zodiac would slow him down too much, so we stood it on one of the outriggers and lashed it to the front cabin. The full moon hung above us like a coin. I asked Neutrino what time he planned to leave. First light if he could, he said. He was planning to reach Puertocietas, about fifty miles down the coast, which he expected would take ten hours, and he wanted to get there before dark.

THE NEXT MORNING I opened my eyes and saw a line of red above the horizon, like a vein in a stone. It was five-fifteen. When I arrived at the harbor, just before daylight, the tide was out, and the raft wasn't where it had been the night before. I thought Neutrino had already left. Then I found it in deeper water, out by the big shrimpers, which loomed above it like judges. I ran down the rocks of the breakwater, nearly to the end, before I was even with where the raft was, about a hundred feet off the jetty. The points of the Zodiac stuck above the roof like horns. All over the harbor I could hear gulls barking, disputing territory—it's mine; no, it's mine. I watched the raft change color in the rising light, as if, having blushed, it were composing itself. Then I heard the power drill removing the screws from the door. The hinges creaked. Neutrino stepped out on the deck and picked up something, like a man retrieving the paper from his doormat. Each time he moved, I had the strange feeling of knowing beforehand what would happen. Next he will start the engine and leave, I thought, but it didn't happen that way.

Neutrino clapped three times to get my attention. He was all one color in the shadow of the cabin. We waved to each other. The raft turned slowly on its mooring, as if preparing to say something, and then, having thought better of it, swung slowly away. Below me a fisherman appeared on the deck of a small boat. He opened a book, and I heard him turning the pages, as if searching for a place. The sun climbed the sky and sat briefly on some long, thin clouds on the horizon, like a bird on a wire.

Neutrino shouted, "Fifteen minutes," then he went back into the cabin. The fisherman began singing softly. It occurred to me that the book was the Bible.

When Neutrino appeared again, he asked if I was cold, and I said I wasn't. I asked how he had slept, and he said, "Beautiful." As the light increased, the gulls fell silent, as if sulking—court had closed; a whole day and night would have to pass before they could address their claims again. The sun was high enough now to illuminate textures and shapes, and for a moment, with the colors so rich, I felt as if everything were being tuned to one enormous chord. The wind rose slightly, stirring the water around the raft so that it looked like gravel. The raft parked in the storage lot at Calexico was what it made me think of. At the other end of the breakwater, I saw two figures making their way toward me, stepping carefully over the rocks. The man with the coffee cup in his hand, wearing shorts and a sweatshirt, and with binoculars around his neck turned out to be Larry Boyd. Eva, he said, was behind him. She was sitting down now and then to cross gaps in the rocks. "She's a pretty good rock hopper," he said. "She'll be here in a minute." While we were talking, Neutrino appeared again on the deck. He was wearing his corduroy coat. He climbed to the roof of the cabin. Boyd yelled, "Good morning, Captain."

Neutrino waved, then he said, "Larry, how do you start your motor?"

"Push the choke out, pull it hard a few times, then pull the little red switch."

"Up or down?"

"It's got to go up."

Neutrino looked around him. "Where's the choke?" he said.

"Right in front," Boyd said. "Black knob on the left-hand

side." Then to me he said, "It needs new spark plugs is what it needs."

Neutrino stood in place.

"It ain't going to start standing there," Boyd said. To Neutrino he yelled, "You need to get the boat out of here right now, Captain, while the seas are calm." And again to me, "That motor's been sitting in my shed, and I should have put in new spark plugs. Probably got a bit of bad gas in there, too, but I would have thought I'd have run that out the other day following you." He sipped his coffee. "He needs to get going," he said. "He's got to trust me. I tried to tell him that this was a mean piece of water. There's a storm coming down from California, and every time they get a strong Santa Ana wind, we get a norther."

Here and there fat, silvery fish about the size of my hand jumped like stones being skipped. I asked if Boyd knew what they were.

"Mullets," he said. "They just seem to like the air."

Boyd raised his binoculars to his eyes. "He needs to get around that point before the wind kicks up," he said. Neutrino had climbed down to the rear deck. He seemed to be examining something over the stern. "Looks like he's going to try and start that motor," Boyd said. "I'm wondering if that old boy can pull that motor hard enough to start it," he said. Then, "We're wasting good time here, Captain."

Eva arrived and asked, "Is he up?"

"No, the anchor's still down," Larry said. She was wearing shorts and a green sweatshirt like her husband's. On the front was written HALEIVA, the name of their boat. His sweatshirt said CAPTAIN LARRY, and hers said ADMIRAL EVA.

Neutrino got both motors started. "He's got to get that anchor up and slide out of here," Boyd said. Eva nodded. He lowered the binoculars. "He could probably get ten knots out of that thing with both motors going," he went on, "and if he waits any longer, he's probably going to need ten knots." Neutrino disappeared into the cabin, then appeared on the bow. "He's up-ping anchor now," Boyd said. Eva knelt and took a video camera from her bag. It was six-thirty. Neutrino went back into the front cabin. In a moment he appeared on the stern and pointed a video camera at us.

"You haven't got time for pictures," Boyd yelled.

"Don't rush me," Neutrino said.

He drove the raft in a small circle then cut the motors and drifted. He went around the hull checking his lines and tied some new knots on the catamaran.

"He gets out of here now," Boyd said, "he saves two or three gallons of fuel not having to fight the wind."

"He's doing it the Mexican way," Eva said.

Two more figures approached, walking carefully along the rocks—Ed and Catalina Meders. Through Boyd's binoculars I saw Neutrino bend over, then stand and give the thumbs-up sign. He started the motor and wheeled the boat around so that it pointed toward the opening in the breakwater and made his way slowly toward it.

"Fair winds, calm seas," Eva yelled.

Catalina and Meders shouted, "Adiós."

"Punch it," Boyd yelled. "I know the road."

It happened to be Semana Santa, Holy Week. Someone lit a firework on the beach. It rose above the water and made a shiny mark on the sky, like a light turned on in a daylit room. At the detonation that followed, flocks of waterbirds lifted themselves from the rocks and the riggings of the shrimpers and took to the air shrieking.

Once Neutrino had made it through the breakwater, we climbed down the rocks to the beach and walked back to our cars. "If he'd gone out at four o'clock," Boyd said, "he'd have made it around that point before he got a breath of wind."

We arranged to meet at the café for breakfast. While the others drove north, into town, I drove south to follow Neutrino. I parked at the top of a hill. For a while the raft looked like a cup and saucer on the water, or an ornament on the hood of a car. When the sun caught its wake, it sent little silver flashes of light, like code. By slow degrees it grew smaller. For a time it seemed to travel like a snail along the horizontal line made by the wings of a telephone pole. Or, it occurred to me, like an absurdly slow-moving target in a shooting gallery. The sand-colored hull made me think of the reed boats in Egyptian mythology that carry the dead across the river to the afterlife, and I realized that I might never see him again.

When I lost him in the bright light on the water, I walked back to my car and drove into town.

I wondered how far he would go. It took two years and three attempts to get the Atlantic crossing under way. William Willis needed two years and three tries to get his Atlantic trip started, and he interrupted his Pacific crossing for eight months while he went to New York. It would be unreasonable to expect that Neutrino had built a vessel that would behave perfectly in all conditions. He might have to stop somewhere and exchange one version of the prow for another, or a following sea might make more trouble than it had on the trip to the harbor. Cabo San Lucas lay about eight hundred miles ahead. Neutrino was sure to take months to arrive. If he put in at some flyspeck harbor to sit out the Mexican summer and the storms that it brings and in the meantime took up another adventure—if he decided to walk to

Asia across the Bering Strait, for example—I wouldn't have been surprised. His life was governed more by circles and wheels within wheels than by any linear design.

Larry and Eva and Ed and Catalina were standing on a terrace outside the bookstore when I arrived. From there, it turned out, they could still see the raft. Five or six miles away, not yet at the point, Neutrino seemed to drift toward the shore and the hills behind it, then he recovered and headed toward the point. We sat down at a table on the terrace. My seat faced the water. Between me and the raft was a sign for a business on the street, but if I raised myself in my chair, I could still see the raft, a barely discernible notation of color on the water. In the harsh morning light it was nearly black, as if its own shadow.

The waitress poured us coffee. I began telling stories about Neutrino. About having his front teeth knocked out and putting them back in wrong. About his mother showing up in his classroom to collect him so the family could go to Reno. About moving Frank Turpin into the bed beside his in the army barracks. About the shotgun that no one wanted to fire. The Salvation Navy and the Atlantic crossing. The family band and the heart attacks. Eileen, Maxine, and Betsy. Triads and the three deepest desires. His near-ceaseless efforts to free himself from material bonds, so that he could leave the world peacefully and unencumbered. His having said, "I don't know the truth of life, but I know how to make the fire," and asking people, "Do you want to live as you're living, with no fire, or a fire that's gone out, or with half a fire, or a fire that only works sometimes, or do you want to live like me, in the fire all the time?" A philosophy formed, embraced, suffered for, and never given up is what it was. A life of undeviating purpose, the spine beneath the serpent made of fabulous gestures. Who else could have stood it, I wondered. He had never faltered, never grown discontent. His poverty had exposed him again and again to the harshest torments, and yet he behaved as if no one could be as fortunate as he was to wake up with the whole long day to invent. Moreover, he had been as much an adventurer as anyone else in his century. He had crossed the ocean in a vessel he made from things that other people had thrown away. He had taken wood from the streets of New York City and "set it in motion." And even though elderly, he was still attacking, still the warrior, with a club in each hand and spikes on his feet, facing the horizon and saying, "*Now*, you bastards, *now* I'm coming after you." William Maxwell, the writer used for comfort to say, "Nothing bad can happen, because it can't," a superstition, he knew, but serviceable nonetheless. The Neutrino corollary, I thought, would be "Nothing bad can happen unless you let it." I had viewed him initially as an outcast—as a specimen, a vagabond, and a florid eccentric—and I had come to feel that in his capacity to bear suffering, in his kindly heart, in his persistence to improve himself, in his humility, his courage, and his unshakable sense of his soul's own merit he embodied attributes that were admirable and rare.

A woman in a doorway shook out a red tablecloth. A little girl came and stood beside her. Suddenly it was borne in on me to look at the water. I raised myself in my chair and realized that while I had been trying to evoke Neutrino—to conjure and praise and memorialize him even—he had sailed round the point and was gone.

Before long he fell quite sick. Fortunately, Nancy Braun drove down the coast to see how he was doing and found him. From San Felipe she brought him medicine. By the time he recovered, the Mexican summer, with its heat and storms, had arrived. He moored the raft in an inlet with a deep tidal draft, so that much of the time it sat on dry land, and then he left Mexico. For a few weeks he walked in Yosemite. He rode a bus east and for a while he slept on a couch in the apartment of a friend in Brooklyn—the two of them discussed having a street act in which they would dress in leather jackets and perform songs from *West Side Story* for people leaving the Broadway shows. In August he went to Provincetown and lived on the beach in a boat that someone lent him. Betsy came to visit him, and throughout the late summer and fall the two of them made a leisurely tour by car of the middle and southwestern states, then he went back to Mexico. He had found a man to sail with him. They had known each other for years, but apparently not as well as Neutrino had thought. Almost as soon as they sailed, Neutrino felt uncomfortable, and they came to a stop. Neutrino wanted to ask the man to leave but, having invited him, didn't feel that he could. He kept hoping the man would leave on his own. The man liked living on the raft. He was reluctant to work and spent most of his time in his cabin reading. He appeared to believe that he was on a cruise. Their difficulties took months to settle. Neutrino left Mexico and spent the hurricane season in

New Orleans, building rafts for people to escape the flood if the levees broke again.

Meanwhile, he resolved that when he returned to Mexico he would sail alone.

Chapter 16

WHENEVER I WANTED to make Neutrino smile lavishly, to see him beam with the bashful pleasure of a child, and so broadly that he would raise to his mouth the back of one hand to hide his loopy, jack-o'-lantern grin, whenever I wished to provoke this artless effect, full of deep and unaffected happiness and charm, I had only to call him the Father of Modern Football. He fell for it every time.

After I left San Felipe, I spoke to Mike Canales, at the University of Arizona. He said that he had worked on the play but hadn't been able to solve two problems. The first was how to hold up attackers long enough so that the play could unfold efficiently, and the second was how to alert the team that the play had been called, so that everyone could act in harmony. His team had won three games and lost eight, and had so many problems, he said, that there hadn't been much time for innovation.

Pita Olomua at Red Mesa, however, told me that he planned to work the Neutrino Clock Offense vigorously. The Navajo boys really liked the play's novelty, and he hoped that one day it would enable the sign by their field to say RED MESA REDSKINS, ARIZONA STATE CHAMPIONS.

ACKNOWLEDGMENTS

In addition to the people whose names appear in the text, I am grateful to Francisco J. Castillo, who years ago clipped an article about Neutrino from a newspaper and gave it to me, saying, "You should write about him." Also to Will Dana and Charles McGrath for reading early versions of the manuscript. To Ann Goldstein for help with matters of style. To Louisa Thomas for vigilantly checking the facts. To Daniel Menaker for suggesting what further work was necessary, and to Tom Perry for the title. Also to Jin Auh at the Wylie Office, and to Andrew Wylie himself.

Above all I am grateful to David Remnick, whose work, advice, and example have inspired and broadened me, and to Dana Goodyear. No one encouraged me or helped me more with this book than she did. A gift from life is what she has been, and I would imagine the other writers who work with her feel the same.

ABOUT THE AUTHOR

ALEC WILKINSON has been
a writer at *The New Yorker*
since 1980. Before that he was
a policeman, in Wellfleet,
Massachusetts, and before that
he was a rock and roll musician.
He lives with his wife and son
in New York City.

This book was set in Garamond, a typeface originally designed by the Parisian type cutter Claude Garamond (1480–1561). This version of Garamond was modeled on a 1592 specimen sheet from the Egenolff-Berner foundry, which was produced from types assumed to have been brought to Frankfurt by the punch cutter Jacques Sabon (d. 1580).

Claude Garamond's distinguished romans and italics first appeared in *Opera Ciceronis* in 1543–44. The Garamond types are clear, open, and elegant.